William Shakespeare's
King Lear

William Shakespeare's *King Lear* (1606) continues to enthrall audiences and readers around the world.

Taking the form of a sourcebook, this guide offers:

- extensive introductory comment on the contexts, critical history and production of the play, from early performances to the present
- annotated extracts from key contextual documents, reviews, critical works and the text itself
- cross-references between documents and sections of the guide, in order to suggest links between texts, contexts and criticism
- suggestions for further reading.

Part of the *Routledge Guides to Literature* series, this volume is essential reading for all those beginning detailed study of *King Lear* and seeking not only a guide to the play, but a way through the wealth of contextual and critical material that surrounds Shakespeare's text.

Grace Ioppolo is the author of *Revising Shakespeare* and the editor of plays by Shakespeare and Middleton. She is currently based at the University of Reading, having also taught at the Shakespeare Institute, Stratford, and in the United States.

Routledge Guides to Literature*

Editorial Advisory Board: Richard Bradford (University of Ulster at Coleraine), Jan Jedrzejewski (University of Ulster at Coleraine), Duncan Wu (St. Catherine's College, University of Oxford)

Routledge Guides to Literature offer clear introductions to the most widely studied authors and literary texts.

Each book engages with texts, contexts and criticism, highlighting the range of critical views and contextual factors that need to be taken into consideration in advanced studies of literary works. The series encourages informed but independent readings of texts by ranging as widely as possible across the contextual and critical issues relevant to the works examined and highlighting areas of debate as well as those of critical consensus. Alongside general guides to texts and authors, the series includes "sourcebooks", which allow access to reprinted contextual and critical materials as well as annotated extracts of primary text.

Available in this series:

Geoffrey Chaucer by Gillian Rudd
Ben Jonson by James Loxley
William Shakespeare's The Merchant of Venice: A Sourcebook edited by S. P. Cerasano
William Shakespeare's King Lear: A Sourcebook edited by Grace Ioppolo
William Shakespeare's Othello: A Sourcebook edited by Andrew Hadfield
John Milton by Richard Bradford
Alexander Pope by Paul Baines
Mary Wollstonecraft's A Vindication of the Rights of Woman: A Sourcebook edited by Adriana Craciun
Jane Austen's Emma: A Sourcebook edited by Paula Byrne
Mary Shelley's Frankenstein: A Sourcebook edited by Timothy Morton
The Poems of John Keats: A Sourcebook edited by John Strachan
Charles Dickens's David Copperfield: A Sourcebook edited by Richard J. Dunn
Charles Dickens's Bleak House: A Sourcebook edited by Janice M. Allan
Herman Melville's Moby-Dick: A Sourcebook edited by Michael J. Davey
Harriet Beecher Stowe's Uncle Tom's Cabin: A Sourcebook edited by Debra J. Rosenthal
Walt Whitman's A Song of Myself: A Sourcebook and Critical Edition edited by Ezra Greenspan
Robert Browning by Stefan Hawlin
Henrik Ibsen's Hedda Gabler: A Sourcebook edited by Christopher Innes
Thomas Hardy by Geoffrey Harvey

* Some books in this series were originally published in the Routledge Literary Sourcebooks series, edited by Duncan Wu, or the Complete Critical Guide to English Literature series, edited by Richard Bradford and Jan Jedrzejewski.

William Shakespeare's
King Lear
A Sourcebook

Edited by Grace Ioppolo

 Routledge
Taylor & Francis Group

LONDON AND NEW YORK

First published 2003 by Routledge
2 Park Square, Milton Park, Abingdon, Oxon, OX14 4RN

Simultaneously published in the USA and Canada
by Routledge
270 Madison Ave, New York NY 10016

Routledge is an imprint of the Taylor & Francis Group

Transferred to Digital Printing 2005

This volume first published as *A Routledge Literary Sourcebook on William Shakespeare's King Lear*

Typeset in Sabon and Gill Sans by RefineCatch Limited, Bungay, Suffolk

British Library Cataloguing in Publication Data
A catalogue record for this book is available from the British Library

Library of Congress Cataloging in Publication Data
Ioppolo, Grace, 1956–
A Routledge literary sourcebook on William Shakespeare's
King Lear / edited by Grace Ioppolo
      p. cm.—(Routledge literary sourcebooks)
Includes bibliographical references and index.
1. Shakespeare, William, 1564–1616. King Lear.   2. King Lear.
3. Lear, King (Legendary character), in literature.   4. Tragedy.
I. Title.   II. Series.
PR2819.I58 2003
822.3′3—dc21   2002153225

ISBN 0–415–23471–9 (hbk)
ISBN 0–415–23472–7 (pbk)

Printed and bound by Antony Rowe Ltd, Eastbourne

Contents

2: Interpretations

3: Key Passages

4: Further Reading

Illustrations

Annotation and Footnotes

Annotation is a key feature of this series. Both the original notes from reprinted texts and new annotations by the editor appear at the bottom of the relevant page. The reprinted notes are prefaced by the author's name in square brackets, e.g. [Robinson's note].

Acknowledgements

I wish to thank Duncan Wu, Rosie Waters, the wonderful Liz O'Donnell, Neil Dowden and Liz Thompson and the rest of the staff of Routledge for their support in the completion of this book. I would also like to thank the staff of the British Library, the London Theatre Museum, the Kobal Collection, the BBC and the Shakespeare Centre Library for making their archives available to me. I am grateful to R. A. Foakes, Ronald Knowles and my husband, Peter Beal, for their advice and generosity. I especially thank S. P. Cerasano, Jay Halio and Liz Thompson for their scrupulous reading, excellent criticism and thoughtful correction of this book in manuscript form.

The following publishers, institutions and individuals have kindly given permission to reprint materials:

ANTHONY SHER, for *Beside Myself: An Autobiography*, London: Hutchinson 2001.

THE BRITISH BROADCASTING CORPORATION, for the photograph from the 1998 television production of *King Lear*.

THE BRITISH LIBRARY, for illustrations from their copies of Holinshed's *Chronicles* (1577), *King Leir* (1605), *King Lear* (1608), *A Souvenir of Shakespeare's King Lear* (1892). Reprinted by permission of the British Library.

CAMBRIDGE UNIVERSITY PRESS AND R. A. FOAKES, for R. A. Foakes, *Hamlet versus Lear: Cultural Politics and Shakespeare's Art*, Cambridge University Press, 1993.

HARCOURT EDUCATION LTD, for Grigori Kozintsev, *King Lear: The Space of Tragedy*, trans. Mary Mackintosh, London: Heinemann, 1977.

JOHNS HOPKINS UNIVERSITY PRESS, for Dennis Kennedy, '*King Lear* and the Theatre', in *Educational Theatre Journal*, 28 (1976), 35–44. © Dennis Kennedy. Reprinted with permission of Johns Hopkins University Press.

KOBAL COLLECTION, for the photographs from the 1970 Kozintsev and 1971 Brook films of *King Lear*.

MACMILLAN, for *John Gielgud, An Actor and His Time*, London: Macmillan, 1981.

MANCHESTER UNIVERSITY PRESS, for Kathleen McLuskie, 'The Patriarchal Bard', in *Political Shakespeare: Essays in Cultural Materialism*, ed. Jonathan Dollimore and Alan Sinfield, 2nd edition, Manchester University Press, 1994, 88–108.

MICHAEL WARREN, for Michael Warren, 'General Introduction', *William Shakespeare: The Complete King Lear 1608–1623*, University of California Press, 1989.

NORTHCOTE HOUSE EDUCATIONAL PUBLISHERS, for Terence Hawkes, *William Shakespeare: King Lear*, Northcote House, 1995.

THE RANDOM HOUSE GROUP LIMITED, for Antony Sher, *Beside Myself: An Autobiography*, Hutchinson, 2001. (Used in Europe and the British Commonwealth by permission of The Random House Group Limited.)

THE SHAKESPEARE CENTRE LIBRARY and THE TRUSTEES OF THE ROYAL SHAKESPEARE COMPANY, for photographs from the 1950, 1962 and 1982 RSC productions and the 1962 promptbook of *King Lear*.

UNIVERSITY OF CHICAGO PRESS, for Coppélia Kahn, 'The Absent Mother in King Lear', in *Rewriting the Renaissance: The Discourses of Sexual Difference in Early Modern Europe*, ed. Margaret W. Ferguson, Maureen Quilligan and Nancy J. Vickers, University of Chicago Press, 1986, pp. 33–45.

Every effort has been made to contact the publishers or copyright holders of reprinted material. The publisher would be pleased to hear from any further copyright holders and to rectify omissions in future reprints.

Introduction

Since its composition in 1606, Shakespeare's *King Lear* has 'distressed', 'shocked' and 'horrified' its theatrical and literary audiences. Termed 'unbearable' in the eighteenth century, 'unactable' in the nineteenth century, and 'dangerous', 'misogynistic' and 'unstable' in the twentieth century, the play has nevertheless drawn admiration from critics, scholars, directors and actors as Shakespeare's 'greatest' play and most important 'achievement'. No other Shakespearean play has had such strong condemnation and such awe-inspiring praise simultaneously heaped on it. It was not until Peter Brook's revolutionary production of the play in 1962 in Stratford-upon-Avon, Shakespeare's birthplace, that these seemingly irreconcilable views of *King Lear* as both horrible and brilliant were portrayed as intrinsically compatible and absolutely necessary. Ever since 1962, the play has taken its rightful place as the finest of Shakespeare's plays and the most representative of his genius as a poet and a playwright. Although Shakespeare expertly made this provocative play adaptable for any period of time and any playing space, we need to place it in particular contexts and particular places to understand it fully. To begin with, we must recognise its unique place in Shakespeare's canon and trace the journey it has taken on the page and on the stage for the last 400 years.

By the time he came to write *King Lear*, Shakespeare had been working as an actor and a playwright for at least sixteen years. He may have begun his theatrical career as an apprentice writer or an actor or in some other way in the late 1580s. However, his earliest plays, including *The Two Gentlemen of Verona*, date from about 1590, when he began writing festive comedies set on the Continent and chronicle history plays illustrating the struggles of various English monarchs. Early in his career he also wrote formulaic revenge tragedies, the type of tragedy favoured by the classical Roman playwright Seneca and adopted by Elizabethan playwrights, producing, for example, *Titus Andronicus* and *Romeo and Juliet*. Each of Shakespeare's plays from this early period ends with a clear sense of resolution and closure and with at least some hope that tragic or comic misdeeds can be redeemed, especially in reuniting warring families.

With the turn of the seventeenth century, Shakespeare seemed to have become bored with, or frustrated by, traditional genres inherited from earlier classical or

English writers. His disaffection may have been due in part to the change in monarch from Queen Elizabeth I, who died in 1603 after a long series of illnesses, to King James I, formerly James VI of Scotland. Elizabeth, a patron of poets and a close observer of the emerging power of theatre, was a strong matriarchal figure. Her reign had begun in 1558, and brought stability, order and the firm entrenchment of Protestantism to England by the time Shakespeare began his career. She had defiantly protected her kingdom from foreign invasion by Catholic powers such as Spain, as well as banishing English Catholics determined to start a civil war. She had also provided support to her Protestant allies, including The Netherlands, and sanctioned the occupation of other territories, including Ireland. Yet her successor, the reclusive James, often seemed ill at ease in his new role and country, and had problems establishing control of his privy council (cabinet) and parliament. At least two extremist religious factions, the Puritans and the Catholics, attempted to jostle for their share of religious control. James also befriended Elizabeth's old Catholic enemies, including Philip III of Spain, spreading fears of foreign invasion or civil unrest in the kingdom. Before 1603, James had published several political treatises outlining a monarch's duties and responsibilities in theory, yet in practice his ineptitude created instability and financial crises throughout the country, nowhere more so than in London, his seat of power.

Those in London's professional theatre took notice, and playwrights such as Shakespeare, Ben Jonson, John Marston and George Chapman began to explore or exploit this transitional period from 1600 to 1606 between the Elizabethan and Jacobean ages. It is not surprising then that from 1600 Shakespeare began to experiment with more complex and irresolvable types of drama. He had by this time grown tired of writing the great cycles of English history plays, and had moved on to other genres to write his later works, including the 'problem' or 'dark' comedies, *Measure for Measure, All's Well That Ends Well* and *Troilus and Cressida*, and the first two of his great tragedies, *Hamlet* and *Othello*, built on Aristotle's concept in his *Poetics* of the tragic flaw which caused the fall of a great man. Shakespeare completed all these plays by 1606, and it was at this point that he began *King Lear*. Clearly he was not yet finished with his experimentations with genre. In *The True Chronicle Historie of King Leir and his three daughters* (1605) (see **pp. 25–32**), an anonymous history play and the primary source for Shakespeare's play, Leir and Cordella finally defeat Gonorill and Ragan, and pardon them for their usurpation. Shakespeare altered the tragicomic material of his source to tragedy alone.

From about 1605, Shakespeare also seemed to have been especially determined to investigate the tragic or tragicomic relationship of fathers (whether absent or present) and daughters. In earlier plays such as *The Merchant of Venice, Much Ado about Nothing* and *All's Well That Ends Well*, Shakespeare comically used marriage to reconcile a father's control and a daughter's free will. However, in such later plays as *Hamlet, Othello, Pericles, The Winter's Tale, The Tempest* and, especially, *King Lear*, Shakespeare seemed to see little that was comical in the nature of this relationship. Instead he suggested that the bond between father and daughter often bordered on incest or tragedy, threatening the foundations not just of the family but of society itself. According to Shakespeare, the potential marriage of a father's daughter could provoke his unconscious anger and jealousy. Rather than seeing marriage as the conclusion of the estrangement between warring fathers and daughters, thus removing the possibility of incest, as he did in his early comedies, in *King Lear* Shakespeare recognises marriage as the real source of such estrangement. Lear's anger at Cordelia in Act 1, Scene 1 (**pp. 105–9**) may have less to do with her response of 'nothing' as her measure of love than with his imminent surrender of her to a husband and rival. Before he wrote this play, Shakespeare was apparently satisfied in the early comedies with showing one or two daughters, at the most, testing a father's power, but after this play he reverted to the single father–daughter relationships of the late romances. *King Lear* is the only one of his plays in which the father–daughter relationship is multiplied three times over, giving his audience varied but increasingly painful accounts of the way in which familial love works. He then mirrors this plot with the subplot of the Gloucester family, in which the patriarch is so stingy with his love that he encourages one son to pit himself against the other. By this point in his career, Shakespeare intended his plays to be both complex and complicated.

Shakespeare composed *King Lear* a few years after James's accession, most likely between late 1605 and late 1606, if we are to take Edmund's references to 'these late eclipses' in Act 1, Scene 2 to mean those that occurred in England in the autumn of 1605. Shakespeare seems not only to recall recent strife during Elizabeth's reign but also eerily to predict the consequences of a civil war in Britain that was to come almost forty years later, yet he probably presented his own period in a way that his audiences would have recognised as perfunctory. It may be that the play was not as shocking, distressing or repulsive as later audiences have come to view it, largely because the world has become a more cruel place in which to live. Or perhaps the reverse is true, for Shakespeare's audience may have accepted cruelty as inherent rather than an aberration in normal life, while later audiences expected a more refined presentation of ideal, rather than normal, life. Whatever the case, for Shakespeare and audience members such as King James, who saw the play at court during the Christmas holidays in 1606, *King Lear* may have been intended as an allegorical, artificial tragedy rather than as the literal, realistic series of events that audiences have since considered it. James had recently become the patron of Shakespeare's acting company and was rewarded here with an exemplar of rulership seemingly based on James's own writings in his books *The True Law of Free Monarchies* (1598) and *Basilikon Doron* (1599) (see **pp. 40–1** and **41–2**). Above all, during Shakespeare's time the play fitted within a controlled sense of monarchy and hierarchy and of institutionalised Christianity which ensured that loyalty and spirituality would be rewarded with support and comfort, either in this world or in the next. This may explain why *King Lear* was deemed appropriate entertainment for Christmas, as Lear's self-sacrifice recalls the possibility of salvation as promised by the birth of the Christ-child who would sacrifice himself to redeem sin.

The play's apparently authorised publication in 1608, so soon after its composition in 1606, suggests that *King Lear* was popular enough to draw reading audiences while not compromising the interest of future theatrical audiences. The play probably continued in performance in the King's Men's repertory until the

Puritan-controlled government closed the theatres in 1642. Although James I managed to prevent the dissolution of his power and his kingdom, his son Charles I could not and was eventually executed in 1649 during the civil war that temporarily threatened the structure and unity of Britain. All that Shakespeare may have been attempting to represent about the nature of civil war, treason and family division in *King Lear* was too fresh and real for audiences after the 'Restoration' in 1660 of the monarch Charles II (son of Charles I), when the professional theatres were allowed to reopen. Audiences had had enough tragedy in real life, and in the theatre they wanted comedy instead. The psychological and emotional complexities of the play for both actors and audiences kept *King Lear* off the professional London stage beginning in 1681, when it was replaced by Nahum Tate's sentimentalised, tragicomic adaptation, in which Lear survives and betroths his daughter Cordelia to Edgar at the play's conclusion. Shakespeare's version of the play remained off the stage for 150 years. During this long period of oblivion, literary critics attempted to justify Shakespeare's methods and the seemingly excessive cruelty in them, but they saw his *King Lear* through the prism of the bloody English civil war and the cultural values of the subsequent Restoration and Enlightenment.

The English actor William Macready bravely returned Shakespeare's play to the London stage in 1834. But the response to it also became fixed from this time. Literary and theatrical critics saw *King Lear* primarily as a cautionary tale about the dangers of royal rule when the confirmed and legitimate monarch abdicates his responsibilities and plunges his kingdom and its subjects into chaos. This monarch plays out the classical Aristotelian concept of a great man's fall through his own actions and faults, thereby taking the audience through a necessary 'catharsis' or purgation of emotion. Lear also frames his actions within the medieval *de casibus* notion of tragedy (taken from Boccaccio's *De Casibus Virorum Illustrium*, or *The Falls of Famous Men*), claiming that he does not act but is acted on by outside forces, and is a man 'more sinned against than sinning'. Such influential critics as Samuel Johnson, Charles Lamb, William Hazlitt, Samuel Taylor Coleridge and A. C. Bradley each debated Shakespeare's success in reconciling the contradictory concepts of tragedy while exploring the demands of kingship upon 'passionate' human nature. Meanwhile theatre directors such as Henry Irving and Harley Granville-Barker attempted to stage the play in its traditional, historical setting while trying to shield their audiences from its disturbing emotional power.

However, the rise of brutal totalitarian regimes, the consequences of two horrific world wars and the spread of nuclear weapons in the twentieth century irrevocably changed the ways in which readers and theatre audiences could approach *King Lear*. For audiences numbed by such global terror, the play was no longer even a realistic series of events but yet another irredeemable example of the depravity of human nature. The recent advent of 'theory', which advocates re-examinations of literary or theatrical texts through the application of a modern, selective set of concerns, such as politics or gender, for example, also forced *King Lear* to take on a wider range of interpretation – or 'hermeneutics', to use a fashionable term. *King Lear* is now seen as the most postmodern of Shakespeare's plays. This has been due largely to the collaboration in the 1960s of two men, the Polish critic Jan Kott and the English theatre director Peter Brook, who radicalised and reinterpreted the play on the page and on the stage. Ever since, *King Lear* has been at the forefront of teaching us how to read *all* literature and how to stage *all* drama.

The modern critics and theatre directors who have followed Kott and Brook have questioned whether Shakespeare is exposing, exploiting or institutionalising the devastating effects of such issues as hierarchy on class divisions, patriarchy on the family structure and misogyny on gender relationships. Such theoretical revisions of the play may not tell us any more about Shakespeare's aims or methods than the more traditional vision of the play as a tragedy, for *King Lear* may remain as ambiguously inscrutable and indefinable for modern playgoers as it probably was for its first audience. However, for Shakespeare, the play may not have been so harsh or grim. Written after *Othello* and before *Macbeth*, *King Lear* is *an* experiment in the nature of drama and tragedy, not the final word on the loss of all hope for the redemption of mankind. For Shakespeare, and for us, the play should stand as *one*, and not the *only*, representation of the power of theatre and literature to question our places within our families, our communities and our cultures. Shakespeare revised this play some time after its composition, and he also continued to return to and rework the play's themes and issues in later plays, most notably in offering the successful reconciliation of fathers and daughters in *Pericles*, *The Winter's Tale* and *The Tempest*. This suggests that he wanted to offer a comforting alternative to the despair in *King Lear* and that he saw this play not as fixed or irrefutable but as infinitely transformable in itself and in relation to his other plays. It is for this reason and many others that critics consider *King Lear* to be his greatest achievement.

Shakespeare may have been inspired to write *King Lear* after watching or reading *The True Chronicle Historie of King Leir and his three daughters*, perhaps because he wanted to experiment with, or even radicalise, the genre of tragedy. Or he may have wanted to hand James a warning about the disastrous consequences of dividing a kingdom. Or, as the father of two living daughters and a deceased son, Shakespeare may have been moved by the idea of expressing dutiful love between father and child. For any or all of these and other reasons, he produced a play that could serve as a myriad of texts, including a perfectly conceived tragedy, a royal handbook, and a poetic testament to the power of familial love. This Sourcebook presents essential sets of materials that allow readers to explore all these reasons for its composition and all these possibilities for its interpretation. These materials can help place this extraordinary and heartbreaking play into historical and modern perspective, both as a drama designed to be performed in front of a communal audience and as a piece of literature to be read and discussed. The first section of the Sourcebook, 'Contexts', presents a discussion of the play's original composition, performance and publication history, as well as a chronology of the author and his times. It offers a broad selection of extracts from the source material, including the plays, poems, histories and political treatises on which Shakespeare based his play. The second section, 'Interpretations', offers selections of early and later critical responses from the most important and influential critics of the play, as well as material on *King Lear* in performance on stage and on screen from actors, directors and critics. The third section, 'Key Passages', offers the most important passages of the play with annotations and glosses designed to enhance critical and theatrical analysis. The Sourcebook concludes with recommendations for further reading and study. Readers are invited to cross-reference, compare and contrast these sections so that *King Lear* can be seen as a play that always has invited and always will invite the devastatingly strong emotional and intellectual response from audiences that Shakespeare so expertly wrote into it.

1

Contexts

Contextual Overview

Although it may be difficult for modern audiences to accept, Shakespeare's audience would have recognised King Lear as a real person and legendary monarch who was central to their own contemporary history. During the pre-Christian Celtic age in which the real Lear's reign took place, Britain enjoyed some sense of union and empire – or, at least, medieval and Renaissance historians insist this had been the case. But since that age, various foreign invading hordes had divided Britain into the three separate, and often warring, countries of England, Scotland and Wales. Beginning in 1606, James attempted to reunite Scotland and England, but by 1607 he succeeded only in extending English citizenship to the people of his Scottish homeland. At the same time, James was pursuing an alliance with England's most feared enemy, Spain. Perhaps Shakespeare was paying attention to James's attempts and grew concerned, as English lawmakers had, that unification would ultimately mean division of the kingdoms and leave England vulnerable to foreign invasion by old enemies. The fact that Lear himself, rather than some foreign army, could divide the kingdom, giving it over to the most scheming and cruel of his children, served as a powerful reminder to Shakespeare's audience that Britain's most feared enemies have often resided inside, rather than outside, the kingdom. But to create such a reminder, Shakespeare had to draw on an unusually large set of source materials.

The title page of the first printed text of the play, Quarto 1 (1608), and its registration in the Stationer's Register in late 1607 proudly note that the play had been performed in front of King James I on St Stephen's night, 26 December 1606 (see **p. 101**). Shakespeare's play shows borrowings from a number of texts printed between 1603 and 1606, so we can assume that it was completed no earlier than 1603 and no later than, and probably closer to, late 1606. The private performance before the monarch may not have been its first performance, as Shakespeare's company, the King's Men, often moved the same play between public playhouses like the Globe and private spaces like palaces and aristocratic houses. If the play began its life at the Globe in the summer of 1606, Shakespeare may have had to do little to it to prepare it for private performance for James later that year. After the royal Whitehall performance, *King Lear* almost certainly entered or returned to the repertory at the Globe and later probably at Blackfriars, a private theatre used by Shakespeare and his company from 1609. The play's 1608 publication in a quarto-sized edition (the equivalent of a modern, cheap paperback) so soon after its composition attests to its probable popularity at that time. In an age without royalties or copyright, once a play appeared in print, any acting company was free to perform it, often to the financial detriment of the company that had initially purchased it from the playwright. The fact that the printers used Shakespeare's original draft or 'foul papers' to set the text suggests that the King's Men (of which Shakespeare was a 'sharer' or stockholder) probably authorised this publication. They may have done so in order to capitalise on the play's popularity or notoriety, or even to distinguish Shakespeare's play from the anonymous *King Leir* play, already in print.

The Quarto 1 text and the text printed later in the 1623 First Folio of Shakespeare's works show significant variants when compared to each other (see 'Note on the Text' **p. 95**). Each text represents a coherent acting version and derives some authority from the author and the acting company that performed it. The Quarto 2 text, an unauthorised reprint of Quarto 1 by the printer Thomas Pavier in 1619 and falsely dated 1608, introduced a number of errors and corruptions into the text. Although Quarto 2 may have been used in part for the printing of the Folio text, it does not appear to represent the text as Shakespeare and the King's Men knew it, and thus this text has been largely discounted by scholars. Shakespeare probably revised *King Lear* some time after its original set of performances. The 1623 text represents a later version of the play, but perhaps not its final form. Playwrights attached to particular acting companies, as Shakespeare was, often revised their plays to suit changing performance venues or acting companies, or even to suit their own artistic interests. In altering his original text to the later one, Shakespeare reduced the force and power of supporting characters such as Cordelia, Kent, Edgar and Edmund, largely by cutting and reshaping many of their lines. In the process, he intensified the centrality of Lear's suffering, adding lines in his speeches and those of others that focus on his character. Shakespeare also shifted the Quarto's emphasis on foreign invasion by France's forces to a civil war between factions within the kingdom.

The sources for *King Lear* show that Shakespeare had a varied and diverse reading list that ranged from comprehensive history books to epic poetry to prose romance to popular pamphlets. The main source from which Shakespeare drew his plot, setting, characters and dialogue was the anonymous play *The True Chronicle Historie of King Leir and his three daughters* (**pp. 25–32**). This play was published in 1605, but it was almost certainly in performance by 1594 and acted by the Queen's and Sussex's Men, a company to which Shakespeare may have had some connection. He may thus have seen *King Leir* in performance, and from 1605 he would have had a printed text available to study. If Shakespeare's play was already in performance by early 1605, the printers of *King Leir* may have put their text into print, and an acting company may have staged a revival of the play, to capitalise on favourable response to Shakespeare's play. But it is more likely that Shakespeare began his play after *King Leir* was printed.

King Leir itself draws on a number of chronicle histories of England, all of which derive in some way from earlier histories, beginning with that written by

Geoffrey of Monmouth. In his *Historia Regum Britanniae* (*History of the Kings of Britain, c.*1135) (**pp. 19–22**), Geoffrey appears to have invented the story of Lear's test of his three daughters' love, his division of the kingdom, and the civil and foreign wars they engendered. Geoffrey may have borrowed the story from traditional folk tales of ungrateful children, or even from the biblical story of the prodigal son who finally redeems his father's good opinion. But Geoffrey's version of Lear's story soon began to be incorporated into succeeding history books as a real event and a cautionary tale. These history books include at least these eight texts:

1   an English translation of a French prose history of *Brut* (fourteenth century), about the line of early Celtic kings, of which Leir is the tenth after King Brut;
2   Robert Fabyan's *New Chronicles* (1516);
3   Polydore Vergil's *Anglicae Historiae* (*English History*, 1534);
4   John Stow's *Summarie of Englyshe Chronicles* (1563);
5   Raphael Holinshed's *Chronicles* (1577 and 1587);
6   William Harrison's *Description of England* (printed in Holinshed);
7   John Stow's *Annales* (1592);
8   William Camden's *Remaines Concerning Britaine* (1606).

Medieval and Renaissance historians since Geoffrey had built upon predecessors to present a slightly different story of Leir's love-test with his daughter Cordella, their estrangement and Cordella's eventual rescue of him from his cruel daughters Gonorill and Ragan. In *King Leir*, as in the history sources, Cordella is triumphant in battle over her sisters and returns her father to the throne. Although the *King Leir* play ends at this point, Geoffrey and his succeeding historians present her further story: after her father's death, she rules England for five uneventful years until her two evil nephews overthrow her in a bloody *coup d'état*. Despondent at the chaos she knows these two will bring to her beloved kingdom, she commits suicide in prison. If Shakespeare's audience members knew this version of the story, they may have anticipated that his play would end with Cordelia's enforced suicide or murder in prison.

The author of *The True Chronicle Historie of King Leir* seems to have been most indebted to the historical material found in John Higgins's *The Mirror for Magistrates* (1574) (**pp. 32–6**) and Spenser's *The Fairie Queene* (1590) (**pp. 36–8**). Although Shakespeare may have relied solely on *King Leir* as the source for his play, he may have read any or all of the primary or secondary source material in whatever text or edition was available to him. As he frequently consulted Holinshed's *Chronicles* (**pp. 23–5**) in writing many of his histories and tragedies, he almost certainly read that rendering of the Lear story. However, he also incorporated material that had not appeared in or been filtered through *King Leir*, including fantastical descriptions of devils in Samuel Harsnett's *A Declaration of Egregious Popish Impostures* (1603) (**p. 40**). The parallel story of the Gloucester family, including the father who places his care and his trust in his lying, hateful illegitimate son and rejects his truthful, loving legitimate son, and who is eventually blinded for his folly, does not appear in any of these sources.

Instead Shakespeare borrowed the material for his subplot from Sidney's *The Countess of Pembroke's Arcadia* (1590) (**pp. 38–40**), written in the newly fashionable genre of the prose romance. Lastly, Shakespeare may have intended his play to celebrate the works of his patron James I himself, most notably in his earlier treatises on kingship *The True Law of Free Monarchies* (1598) and *Basilikon Doron* (*The King's Gift*, 1599) (**pp. 40–1** and **41–2**), in which James acknowledged that a king is a country's most important actor. *King Lear* appears to resonate with echoes of James's advice in these two texts against 'dividing the kingdoms' and keeping watch on 'monstrous and unnatural' children. If so, James may not have recognised Shakespeare's subtle warning in this play that, as king of England, James had not followed the very advice he had dispensed a few years before as King of Scotland.

Shakespeare may also have taken his story from a variety of other texts or actual events. As noted by Geoffrey Bullough in *Narrative and Dramatic Sources of Shakespeare's Plays*,[1] Shakespeare may have known about a contemporary case of father–daughter conflict. In 1603, Cordell Annesley, the daughter of the aristocrat Bryan Annesley, petitioned the government to protect her 'poor aged and daily dying father' from the cruelty of Grace, the elder of her two sisters, and place him in her care instead. After her father's death in 1604 she erected a monument to testify to her 'dutifull love unto her father and mother'. In addition, in the Introduction to his 1997 Arden edition of the play, R. A. Foakes[2] suggests that the failed 1604–5 lawsuit of the 'bastard' son of Robert Dudley, Earl of Leicester, to be named legitimate may also have influenced Shakespeare's presentation of Edmund.

However, *The True Chronicle Historie of King Leir* appears to have served as Shakespeare's main source, even though he departed from several of its key points. To begin with, Shakespeare's play makes no mention of the absent wife of Lear and mother of the three daughters, whose death Leir is still mourning. Lear's love-test of his daughters also seems motiveless and particularly cruel, especially as the two eldest are already married and are not here, as in the source play, being prepared to accept their father's choice of suitor. Cordelia's marriage arrangements are made with coldness and brevity in Shakespeare's play, without the apparent concern of Leir in the source play that his daughter marry for love. The eldest two daughters in Shakespeare's play are free of the early conspiratorial plotting of the two in *King Leir*, who go so far as to rehearse their responses to the love-test. Kent's confrontation with Lear results in his banishment; Leir's with Perillus causes no such parallel event as the banishment of Cordella (and Cordelia in *Lear*).

The far more compassionate author of *Leir* also intercuts the court scenes of Leir's impatient treatment of Cordella and Perillus with the pilgrim journey of the Gallian king, whom the audience comes to trust as loving and noble enough for Cordella when they meet him before she does. Shakespeare instead introduces

---

1   Geoffrey Bullough (ed.) *The Narrative and Dramatic Sources of Shakespeare's Plays*, vol. 7. London: Routledge & Kegan Paul, 1973, pp. 269–308.
2   *King Lear*, ed. R. A. Foakes. Walton-on-Thames: Thomas Nelson, 1997, p. 92.

Cordelia and the audience to her future husband, the King of France, at the same time giving him a brief but powerful speech which defines love negatively: 'Love's not love/When it is mingled with regards that stands/Aloof from th'entire point.' His quick appraisal of her 'rich' worth seems genuine enough in Shakespeare's play, but we see her immediately turned over to a man whom we have not had sufficient time to come to trust. Thus Shakespeare's compression of several scenes from the source play into the first scene in *King Leir* intensifies the anxious, impatient and reckless nature of the plot and of Lear's character.

Lear's angry confrontations with his two eldest daughters for failing to offer him unlimited hospitality follow closely from the same events in *King Leir*, yet the author of the source play shows the daughters actively plotting their father's murder. Shakespeare again seemed reluctant to portray these two daughters as evil from the beginning of the play, with little alteration or development of their already corrupted characters. Instead he offers his audience some justification for the growing anger and impatience of Goneril and Regan. At the same time, Shakespeare has removed the comforting, continuing presence of Cordelia in juxtaposition with these scenes as provided by the *King Leir* author, who also intercuts the growing love of Cordella and her husband with the growing hate of her two sisters for their father. Leir's great recognition in *King Leir*'s climax is that he can rationally outwit, out-talk and subdue his contracted murderer. Lear's great recognition in *King Lear*'s climax is that he can contain his own murderous impulses in attempting to understand basic, flawed human nature, the knowledge of which drives him mad. Leir benefits from accident and coincidence in becoming reconciled to Cordella; Lear's reconciliation with Cordelia occurs due to her active pursuit of him. She seems to have so little strength left to do battle with her sisters that she is quickly defeated. The other Cordella, however, as in the historical source material, helps her father overcome their foes in battle. The future of Leir, of Cordella (as the next queen) and of the kingdom is safe and assured; there is no future for Lear or Cordelia, and their kingdom is left in despair.

In comparison with most of his other plays, Shakespeare drew on an unusually large number of sources in writing *King Lear*, perhaps because he was not completely satisfied with his command of the play during its composition. Instead he continued to add to its shape and meanings by reading and incorporating the material of such influential poets as Higgins, Sidney and Spenser and such important historians as Holinshed. Shakespeare's consultation of the works of Spenser and Sidney, who established the type of literature that we now term 'English Renaissance', especially suggests that he wanted to take his place within this new tradition as a 'poet', the contemporary term for a playwright as well as a writer of verse. Like *The Mirour for Magistrates* and *The Arcadia*, *The Fairie Queene* was written, as Spenser put it in the prefatory letter to his work, to 'fashion a gentleman or noble person', particularly a ruler, 'in vertuous and gentle discipline'. Such instruction manuals were typical of the age: Niccolò Machiavelli's *The Prince* (*c.*1513) and Baldassare Castiglione's *The Book of the Courtier* (1528) were both translated into English in Shakespeare's age. In a politically contentious age, Shakespeare turned to the advice given by Higgins, Sidney and Spenser to present his own guide to rulership, perhaps in the hope that James and his courtiers and advisers would learn by Lear's poor example, and James's own instruction manuals on kingship, how to unify and not divide a kingdom.

In order to supply extracts from as many of them as possible, this section concentrates only on the specific sources of the play itself. When possible, these extracts have been taken from the original text as available to Shakespeare; thus their original spelling has been preserved. There is a very large variety of other contextual materials from this period that may have indirectly influenced Shakespeare or the sources he used and which cannot be presented here owing to lack of space. These include records of James I's political strategies, such as his attempts to bind Scotland and Wales and to pursue an alliance with Spain, as well as increasingly Puritanical pamphlets by men and, later, women on women's duties as mothers, wives and daughters. In addition, other plays of the period, including Shakespeare's analogous stories of father–daughter conflict and rulership, provide a broader set of contexts in which to place *King Lear*. Readers can consult the section on further reading for general guides to such contextual materials in this period.

General Note

Before Samuel Johnson produced the first standard English dictionary in 1755, English words were often spelled phonetically (for example, *doatingly* for *dotingly*), and the same word could often be spelled in a variety of ways, so that spellings, as well as meanings, were not usually consistent or standardised. In order to preserve the linguistic sense and the opportunities for multiple meanings of words as available to Shakespeare, the original spelling of the texts in Sections 1, 2 and 3 has been preserved with three sets of exceptions. Before about 1700, three letters were often used differently: *v* replaced *u* when it appeared in primary position in a word (that is, when it appears at the beginning of a word, for example: *vnto* instead of *unto*); *u* replaced *v* in the medial position in a word (that is, when it does not appear at the beginning of the word, for example: *liue* for *live*); *i* replaced *j* in primary or medial position (for example *ioyes* not *joyes*, and *enioes* not *enjoyes*). These differences cause a great deal of strain and confusion for modern readers, and thus, in these three sets of circumstances only, the letters have been modernised.

Chronology

Bullet points are used to denote events in Shakespeare's life, and asterisks to denote historical and literary events.

1558
* Coronation of Queen Elizabeth I (15 January)

1564
• Shakespeare is born on 23? April (baptised 26 April) in Stratford-upon-Avon

1574
* Publication of Higgins's *The Mirror for Magistrates*

1577
* First publication of Holinshed's *Chronicles*

1582
• Shakespeare marries Anne Hathaway in early December in Warwickshire

1583
• Shakespeare's daughter Susanna is born (baptised 26 May) in Stratford-upon-Avon

1585
• Shakespeare's twins, Hamnet and Judith, are born (baptised 2 February) in Stratford-upon-Avon

1587
* Elizabeth I executes Mary, Queen of Scots, mother of James VI of Scotland

1588
* English navy defeats the Spanish Armada

1590

* First publication of Spenser's *The Fairie Queene* and Sidney's *The Countesse of Pembroke's Arcadia*

1594

• First record of Shakespeare as a sharer in the Lord Chamberlain's (later the King's) Men acting company; first publication of a Shakespeare play (*Titus Andronicus*)
* First recorded performance of a play called 'kinge leare' (6 April) by the Queen's and Sussex's Men

1596

• Shakespeare's son Hamnet dies and is buried in Stratford-upon-Avon (11 August)
* Increased hostilities between England and Spain: Spain seizes the French port of Calais, threatening England's borders; the Earl of Essex and Sir Walter Ralegh lead a successful English raid on the Spanish city of Cadiz

1598

• First publication of Shakespeare's plays with his name on the title page: *Love's Labour's Lost* (Quarto 1), *Richard II* (Quarto 2), *Richard III* (Quarto 2); Francis Meres praises Shakespeare in his book *Palladis Tamia* as 'the most excellent' among the English playwrights for his comedies, including *The Two Gentlemen of Verona*, *The Comedy of Errors*, *Love's Labour's Lost*, *Love's Labour's Won* (now lost), *A Midsummer Night's Dream* and *The Merchant of Venice*, and his tragedies, including *Richard II*, *Richard III*, *Henry IV* (probably Part I), *King John*, *Titus Andronicus* and *Romeo and Juliet*.
* King James VI of Scotland (later James I of England) publishes *The True Law of Free Monarchies* (reprinted 1603)

1599

• Shakespeare becomes a sharer in the Globe Theatre, built on the Thames's south bank, London
* King James VI of Scotland (later James I of England) publishes *Basilikon Doron* (reprinted 1603); the Earl of Essex fails to crush Hugh O'Neill's rebellion in Ireland

1601

* Execution of the Earl of Essex (25 February)

1603

* Death of Queen Elizabeth I and accession of King James I, formerly James VI of Scotland (24 March); coronation of James (25 July)
• James I becomes the patron of Shakespeare's acting company, the King's

(formerly the Lord Chamberlain's) Men; unauthorised? publication of Quarto 1 *Hamlet*

* James I suspends hostilities with Spain; temporary closure of London theatres due to the plague; publication of Harsnett's *A Declaration of Egregious Popish Impostures*; Cordell Annesley petitions to remove her father, Bryan Annesley, from her sister's care

1604

• Authorised? publication of Quarto 2 *Hamlet*

* James signs a peace treaty with Philip III of Spain; he also invites Puritan clergy to Hampton Court for a conference on religious unity (14 January); Robert, illegitimate son of Robert Dudley, Earl of Leicester, begins lawsuit to be named legitimate

1605

* Publication of the anonymous play *King Leir*; series of spectacular eclipses visible in England; 'Gunpowder Plot' of Catholic rebels, led by Guy Fawkes, to blow up Parliament and kill James I foiled (5 November); lawsuit of Robert, son of the Earl of Leicester, to be named legitimate fails

1606

• First recorded performance of Shakespeare's *King Lear* (26 December) at Whitehall Palace before King James I

* James attempts to unify Scotland and England; he also levies new 'impositions' (taxes) on merchants who import or export goods

1607

• *King Lear* entered in the Stationers' Register (26 November), signalling its forthcoming publication

* Attempt to bind the union between England and Scotland wrecked by the House of Commons

1608

• Authorised? publication of Quarto 1 *King Lear*, completed by the middle of January; lease of Blackfriars hall by a syndicate of King's Men actors, including Shakespeare

1611

* James dissolves his first parliament

1614

* James dissolves his second parliament and pursues an alliance with Spain

1616

• Shakespeare dies (23 April) in Stratford-upon-Avon and is buried in Holy Trinity Church

1619
- (Unauthorised?) publication of Quarto 2 *King Lear* (falsely dated '1608')

1623
- Publication of the first collected edition of Shakespeare's works, including *King Lear*, in the First Folio

Sources of *King Lear*

Primary Sources

From **Geoffrey of Monmouth** (also called Galfridus Monumetensis), ***Historia Regum Britanniae*** (*History of the Kings of Britain*), Book II, c.1135. Reprinted from Aaron Thompson's later English translation, *The British History, translated into English from the Latin of Jeffrey of Monmouth* (London, 1718), pp. 50–9

> In Shakespeare's time, this text existed only in a Latin manuscript. It is possible that he consulted it, but more likely he made use of other source texts, including later histories and literary and dramatic works, which had incorporated it. Geoffrey apparently presents King Lear's story for the first time. See Shakespeare's presentation of Lear's test of his three daughters, his confrontations with Goneril and Regan, and his breakdown on the heath in Key Passages on **pp. 102–9, 126–9 and 135–43**.

Chapter XI

Leir, the Son of Bladud, having no Son, divides his Kingdom among his Daughters.

[. . .] He was without Male Issue, but had three Daughters whose Names were *Gonorilla*, *Regan*, and *Cordeilla*, of whom he was doatingly fond, but especially of his youngest *Cordeilla*. When he began to grow old, he had Thoughts of dividing his Kingdom among them, and of bestowing them on such Husbands, as were fit to be advanced to the Government with them. But to make Tryal who was the worthiest of the best Part of his Kingdom, he went to each of them to ask, which of them loved him most. The Question being proposed, *Gonorilla* the Eldest made Answer, 'That she called Heaven to Witness, she loved him more than her own Soul.' The Father reply'd, 'Since you have preferred my declining Age before your own Life, I will marry you, my dearest Daughter, to whomsoever you shall make Choice of, and give with you the third Part of my Kingdom.' Then

Regan, the second Daughter, willing after the Example of her Sister, to prevail upon her Fathers good Nature, answered with an Oath, 'That she could not otherwise express her Thoughts, but that she loved him above all Creatures.' The credulous Father upon this made her the same Promise that he did to her elder Sister, that is, the Choice of a Husband, with the third Part of his Kingdom. But *Cordeilla* the youngest, understanding how easily he was satisfied with the flattering Expressions of her Sisters, was desirous to make Tryal of his Affection after a different Manner. 'My Father,' said she, 'Is there any Daughter that can love her Father more than Duty requires? In my Opinion, whoever pretends to it, must disguise her real Sentiments under the Veil of Flattery. I have always loved you as a Father, nor do I yet depart from my purposed Duty; and if you insist to have something more extorted from me, hear now the Greatness of my Affection, which I always bear you, and take this for a short Answer to all your Questions; Look how much you have, so much is your Value, and so much I love you.' The Father supposing that she spoke this out of the Abundance of her Heart, was highly provoked, and immediately reply'd; 'Since you have so far despised my Old-age, as not to think me worthy the Love that your Sisters express for me, you shall have from me the like Regard, and shall be excluded from any Share with your Sisters in my Kingdom. Notwithstanding I do not say but that since you are my Daughter, I will marry you to some Foreigner, if Fortune offers you any such Husband; but will never, I do assure you, make it my Business to procure so honourable a Match for you as for your Sisters; because though I have hitherto loved you more than them, you have in Requital thought me less worthy your Affection than they.' And without farther Delay, after Consultation with his Nobility, he bestowed his two other Daughters upon the Dukes of *Cornwal* and *Albania*, with half the Island at present, but after his Death, the Inheritance of the whole Monarchy of *Britain*.

Hearing of her goodness, Aganippus, King of the Franks, 'forthwith sent his Ambassadors to the King to desire *Cordeilla* in Marriage', insisting that he loved her and would take her without a dowry, and '*Cordeilla* was sent to *Gaul*, and married to *Aganippus*'.

Chapter XII

Leir finding the Ingratitude of his two eldest Daughters, betakes himself to his youngest Cordeilla in Gaul.

A long time after this, when *Leir* came to be infirm through Old-age, the two Dukes, upon whom he had bestowed *Britain* with his two Daughters, made an Insurrection against him, and deprived him of his Kingdom, and of all Regal Authority which he had hitherto exercised with great Power and Glory. But at last they came to an Agreement, and *Maglaunus* Duke of *Albania*, one of his Sons-in-law, was to allow him and sixty Soldiers, who were to be kept for State, a

Subsistence at his own House. After two Years Stay with his Son-in-Law, his Daughter *Gonorilla* grudged at the Number of his Men, who began to upbraid the Ministers of the Court with their scanty Allowance; and having spoke to her Husband about it, gave Orders that the Number of her Fathers Attendants be reduced to thirty, and the rest discharged. The Father resenting this Treatment, left *Maglaunus*, and went to *Henuinus*, Duke of *Cornwal*, to whom he had married his Daughter *Regan*. Here he met with an honourable Reception, but before the Year was at an End, a Quarrel happened between the two Families, which raised *Regan's* Indignation; so that she commanded her Father to discharge all his Attendants but five, and to be contented with their Service. This second Affliction was unsupportable to him, and made him return again to his former Daughter, with Hopes that the Misery of his Condition might move in her some Sentiments of Filial Piety, and that he with his Family might find a Subsistence from her. But she not forgetting her Resentments, swore by the Gods, He should not stay with her, unless he would dismiss his Retinue, and be contented with the Attendance of one Man; and with bitter Reproaches, told him how ill his Desire of vain-glorious Pomp suited with his Old-age and Poverty. When he found that she was by no Means to be prevailed upon, he was at last forced to comply, and dismissing the Rest, to take up with one Man. But by this Time he began to reflect more sensibly with himself upon the Grandeur from which he had fallen, and the miserable State he was now reduced to, and to enter upon Thoughts of going beyond Sea to his youngest Daughter. Yet he doubted whether he should be able to move her Commiseration, whom [. . .] he had treated so unworthily. [Leir then sails for Gaul and] with deep Sighs and Tears, he burst forth into the following Complaint.

'O irreversible Decrees of the Fates, that never swerve from your stated Course! Why did you ever advance me to an unstable Felicity, since the Punishment of lost Happiness is greater than the Sense of present Misery? The Remembrance of the Time when vast Numbers of Men obsequiously attended me at the taking of Cities and wasting the Enemies Countries, more deeply pierces my Heart, than the View of my present Calamity, which has exposed me to the Derision of those who formerly laid at my Feet. O Rage of Fortune! Shall I ever again see the Day, when I may be able to reward those according to their Deserts who have forsaken me in my Distress? How true was thy Answer, *Cordeilla*, when I asked thee concerning thy Love to me, *As much as you have, so much is your Value, and so much I love you*? While I had any Thing to give they valued me, being Friends not to me, but to my Gifts: They loved me then indeed, but my Gifts much more: When my Gifts ceased, my Friends vanished. But with what Face shall I presume to see you my dearest Daughter, since in my Anger I married you upon worse Terms than your Sisters, who, after all the mighty Favours they have received from me, suffer me to be in Banishment and Poverty?'

Weeping 'bitterly' at his poor condition, Cordeilla orders a retinue of servants to clothe and heal him, and in Chapter XIII she and Aganippus receive Leir 'honourably, and submitted to his Management the whole Power of *Gaul*'.

[In Chapter XIV,] *Leir* returned to *Britain* with his Son and Daughter and their Forces they had raised, where he fought with his Sons-in-Law, and routed them. Thus having reduced the whole Kingdom under his Power, he died in the third Year after. *Aganippus* also died; so that *Cordeilla* now obtaining the Government of the Kingdom, buried her Father in a certain Vault, which she ordered to be made for him under the River *Sore* in *Leicester*.

In Chapter XV, after five years' reign, Cordeilla is betrayed by her two nephews and kills herself in prison.

Figure I Holinshed's *Chronicles* (1577). A woodcut of King Leir. By permission of the British Library, 598. h. 3–4.

Figure 2 Holinshed's *Chronicles* (1577). Two woodcuts of Cordeilla, as the strong warrior and as the despondent suicide. By permission of the British Library, 598. h. 3–4.

From **Raphael Holinshed, *The Historie of England in The First and Second Volumes of Chronicles*** (London, 1587), Vol. 1, Book 2, pp. 12–13 (signature B1r)

> Shakespeare consulted Holinshed's *Chronicles*, the first volume of which was published in 1577, throughout his career. The *Chronicles* were expanded between 1577 and 1587, but the story of Leir and his family stayed substantially the same in the later text. We cannot be sure which edition Shakespeare used; the second edition is presented here. Holinshed follows Geoffrey in all of the key points. Compare especially Shakespeare's treatment of Lear and Cordelia's relationship in Key Passages on **pp. 105–13** and **165–73**

[. . .] Leir the sonne of Baldud was admitted ruler over the Britaines, in the yeare of the world 3105, at what time Joas reigned in Juda. This Leir was a prince of right noble demeanor, governing his land and subjects in great wealth. He made the towne of Caerleir now called Leicester, which standeth upon the river of Sore. It is written that he had by his wife three daughters without other issue, whose names were Gonorilla, Regan, and Cordeilla, which daughters he greatly loved, but specially Cordeilla the yoongest farre above the two elder. When this Leir therefore was come to great yeres, & began to waxe unweldie through age, he thought to understand the affections of his daughters towards him, and preferre hir whome he best loved, to the succession over the kingdome. Wherupon he first asked Gonorilla the eldest, how well she loved him: who calling hir gods to record, professed that she 'loved him more than hir owne life, which by right and reason should be most deere unto hir'. With which answer the father being well pleased, turned to the second, and demanded of hir how well she loved him: who answered (confirming hir saiengs with great othes) that she loved him more than toong could expresse, and farre above all other creatures of the world.'

Then called he his yoongest daughter Cordeilla before him, and asked of hir what account she made of him, unto whome she made this answer as followeth: 'Knowing the great love and fatherlie zeale that you have alwaies borne towards me (for the which I maie not answere you otherwise than I thinke and as my conscience leadeth me) I protest unto you, that I have loved you ever, and will continuallie (while I live) love you as my naturall father. And if you would more understand of the love that I beare you, assertaine your selfe, that so much as you have, so much you are worth, and so much I love you, and no more'. The father being nothing content with this answer, married his two eldest daughters, the one unto Henninus the duke of Cornewall, and the other unto Maglanus the duke of Albania, betwixt whome he willed and ordeined that his land should be divided after his death, and the one halfe thereof immediatelie should be assigned to them in hand: but for the third daughter Cordeilla he reserved nothing.

Nevertheles it fortuned that one of the princes of Gallia (which now is called France) whose name was Aganippus, hearing of the beautie, womanhood, and good conditions of the said Cordeilla, desired to have hir in marriage, and sent

over to hir father, requiring that he might have hir to wife: to whome answer was
made, that he might have his daughter, but as for anie dower he could have none,
for all was promised and assured to hir other sisters alreadie. Aganippus notwithstanding this answer of deniall to receive anie thing by way of dower with Cordeilla, tooke hir to wife, onlie moved thereto (I saie) for respect of hir person and
amiable vertues. This Aganippus was one of the twelve kings that ruled Gallia in
those daies, as in the British historie it is recorded. But to proceed.

After that Leir was fallen into age, the two dukes that had married his two
eldest daughters, thinking it long yer the government of the land did come to their
hands, arose against him in armour, and reft from him the governance of the land,
upon conditions to be continued for terme of life: by the which he was put to his
portion, that is, to live after a rate assigned to him for the maintenance of his
estate, which in processe of time was diminished as well by Maglanus as by
Henninus. But the greatest griefe that Leir tooke, was to see the unkindnesse of his
daughters, which seemed to thinke that all was too much which their father had,
the same being never so little: in so much that going from the one to the other, he
was brought to that miserie, that scarslie they would allow him one servant to
wait upon him.

In the end, such was the unkindnesse, or (as I maie saie) the unnaturalnesse
which he found in his two daughters, notwithstanding their faire and pleasant
words uttered in time past, that being constreined of necessitie, he fled the land, &
sailed into Gallia, there to seeke some comfort of his yongest daughter Cordeilla,
whom before time he hated. The ladie Cordeila hearing that he was arrived in
poore estate, she first set to him privilie a certeine summe of monie to apparell
himselfe withall, and to reteine a certeine number of servants that might attend
upon him in honorable wise, as apperteined to the estate which he had borne: and
then so accompanied, she appointed him to come to the court, which he did, and
was so joifullie, honorablie, and lovinglie received, both by his sonne in law
Aganippus, and also by his daughter Cordeilla, that his hart was greatlie comforted: for he was no lesse honored, than if he had beene king of the whole
countrie himselfe.

Now when he had informed his sonne in law and his daughter in what sort he
had beene used by his other daughters, Aganippus caused a mightie armie to be
put in a readinesse, and likewise a great navie of ships to be rigged, to passe over
into Britaine with Leir his father in law, to see him againe restored to his kingdome. It was accorded, that Cordeilla should also go with him to take possession
of the land, the which he promised to leave unto hir, as the rightfull inheritour
after his decesse, notwithstanding any former grant made to hir sisters or to their
husbands in anie manner of wise.

Hereupon, when this armie and navie of ships were readie, Leir and his daughter Cordeilla with hir husband tooke the sea, and arriving in Britaine, fought with
their enimies, and discomfited them in battell, in the which Maglanus and Henninus were slaine: and then was Leir restored to his kingdome, which he ruled
after this by the space of two yeeres, and then died, fortie yeeres after he first
began to reigne. His bodie was buried at Leicester in a vau[l]t under the channell
of the river of Sore beneath the towne.

[...] Cordeilla the yoongest daughter of Leir was admitted Q[ueen] and supreme governesse of Britaine, in the yeere of the world 3155, before the bylding of Rome 54, Uzia then reigning in Judea, and Jeroboam ouer Israell.

From **The True Chronicle Historie of King Leir and his three daughters, Gonorill, Ragan, and Cordella. As it hath beene diuers and sundry times lately acted** (London: printed by Simon Stafford for John Wright, 1605), signatures A3, A4ᵛ–B2, H1ᵛ–H3ᵛ, H4–H4ᵛ

THE
True Chronicle Hi.

ſtory of King LEIR, and his three
daughters, Gonorill, Ragan,
and *Cordella.*

As it hath bene diuers and ſundry
times lately acted.

LONDON,
Printed by Simon Stafford for Iohn
Wright, and are to bee ſold at his ſhop at
Chriſtes Church dore, next Newgate-
Market. 1605.

Figure 3 Anon., *The True Chronicle History of King Leir and his three daughters* (1605). Title page. By permission of the British Library, C. 34. L. 11.

This anonymous play was almost certainly written before Shakespeare's, and is probably the same 'King leare' play performed by the Queen's and Sussex's Men's acting companies on 8 April 1594, for which the theatrical entrepreneur Philip Henslowe records 26 shillings (an average amount of profit) as his total box office receipts.[1] *King Leir* more closely follows the histories of Geoffrey, Holinshed and others, and the poems of Higgins and Spenser (see below, **pp. 32–8**), than does Shakespeare's play, especially in presenting the happy ending of Lear's restoration to the throne and Cordelia's succession to her father as monarch of Britain. A synopsis follows.

1 *Henslowe's Diary*, ed. R. A. Foakes and R. T. Rickert (Cambridge: Cambridge University Press, 1961), p. 21.

Mourning the death of his beloved wife, King Leir ponders how to convince his three daughters to accept the suitors he will shortly choose for them. He knows that his stubborn but favourite daughter Cordella will only marry for love, so he contrives a love-test that he assumes will force her to accede to his choice of husband. Skalliger, a manipulative courtier, warns Gonorill and Ragan about the love-test, giving them the chance to rehearse their answers and to sabotage Cordella's response.

In the love-test, Gonorill and Ragan praise Leir and allow him to choose their husbands, while Cordella refuses to flatter him, so he disinherits her. Leir marries Ragan to the Duke of Cambria and Gonorill to the Duke of Cornwall (Shakespeare reverses this coupling). Leir divides his kingdom between his two sons-in-law by forcing them to draw lots, even though his courtier Perillus (the counterpart to Shakespeare's Kent) warns him that he is 'blind'. Disgraced, Cordella leaves the court but soon falls in love with the disguised Gallian (French) king, who had sailed to England with his courtier Mumford to woo her. She happily agrees to marry him and return to his country.

Leir sets off for his agreed visit to Gonorill and her husband but soon quarrels with her over his retinue. Weeping at her lack of filial devotion, he leaves for the safety of Ragan's home, unaware that the two daughters have begun to plot his murder. Leir expresses remorse for his treatment of Cordella; at the same time, Cordella, now the French queen, expresses concern for her father, but the ambassador whom her husband has sent to England does not succeed in protecting Leir from Gonorill and Ragan. After fighting with Ragan, Leir and Perillus flee but are soon pursued by the Messenger contracted to murder them. Leir assumes that Cordella has ordered his murder, but the Messenger reveals that Ragan and Gonorill have hired him. The Messenger offers Leir and Perillus the option of suicide, but they refuse. Leir eventually frightens the Messenger into dropping his daggers and fleeing by pointing out that, if he commits the murders, Gonorill and Ragan will have to kill him to ensure his silence and his soul will be eternally damned.

Weary and distraught, Leir and Perillus disguise themselves as sailors and travel to France. After landing they accidentally meet Cordella and her husband, disguised as country folk, who reveal themselves and rescue them from their distress. They unite to form an army and return to England where they triumph over the forces of Gonorill, Ragan and their husbands. Leir confronts Ragan about her letters ordering his murder, but allows her, Gonorill and their husbands to run away. Leir returns to the throne as king of Britain, makes Cordella and her husband his heirs, and invites them to stay with him until their return to France.

Below are four extracts from the play showing: (1) Leir's decision to set up a love-test; (2) the love-test; (3) Leir's reunion with Cordella; and (4) their final triumph. Compare these with Shakespeare's presentation of the same characters in the Key Passages on **pp. 102–9 and 165–79**), focusing particularly on his alterations of plot and dialogue.

1. From Act 1, Scene 1

LEIR.　I am resolv'd, and even now my mind　　　　　77
　　　Doth meditate a sudden stratagem,
　　　To try which of my daughters loves me best:
　　　Which till I know, I cannot be in rest.　　　　80
　　　This graunted, when they joyntly shall contend,
　　　Eche² to exceed the other in their love:
　　　Then at the vantage will I take *Cordella*,
　　　Even as she doth protest she loves me best,
　　　Ile say, Then, daughter, graunt me one request,
　　　To shew thou lovest me as thy sisters doe,
　　　Accept a husband, whom my selfe will woo.
　　　This sayd, she cannot well deny my sute,
　　　Although (poore soule) her sences will be mute:
　　　Then will I tryumph in my policy,　　　　　90
　　　And match her with a King of Brittany.

2. From Act 1, Scene 3

　　　　Enter Leir and Perillus [. . .] with the three daughters.
LEIR.　Deare *Gonorill*, kind *Ragan*, sweet *Cordella*,　　224
　　　Ye florishing branches of a Kingly stocke,
　　　Sprung from a tree that once did flourish greene,
　　　Whose blossomes now are nipt with Winters frost,
　　　And pale grym death doth wayt upon my steps,
　　　And summons me unto his next Assizes.³
　　　Therefore, deare daughters, as ye tender the safety　　230
　　　Of him that was the cause of your first being,
　　　Resolve a doubt which much molests my mind,
　　　Which of you three to me would prove most kind;
　　　Which loves me most, and which at my request
　　　Will soonest yeeld unto their fathers hest.
GON.　I hope, my gracious father makes no doubt
　　　Of any of his daughters love to him
　　　Yet for my part, to shew my zeale to you,
　　　Which cannot be in windy words rehearst,
　　　I prize my love to you at such a rate,　　　　240
　　　I thinke my life inferiour to my love.
　　　Should you injoyne me for to tye a milstone
　　　About my neck, and leape into the Sea,
　　　At your commaund I willingly would doe it:

2　Each.
3　Judgement, i.e. death.

Yea, for to doe you good, I would ascend
The highest Turret in all Brittany,
And from the top leape headlong to the ground:
Nay, more, should you appoynt me for to marry
The meanest vassayle in the spacious world,
Without reply I would accomplish it: 250
In briefe, commaund what ever you desire,
And if I fayle, no favour I require.

LEIR.   O, how thy words revive my dying soule!
COR.   O, how I doe abhorre this flattery!
LEIR.   But what sayth *Ragan* to her fathers will?
RAG.   O, that my simple utterance could suffice,
To tell the true intention of my heart,
Which burnes in zeale of duty to your grace,
And never can be quench'd, but by desire
To shew the same in outward forwardnesse.   260
Oh, that there were some other mayd that durst
But make a challenge of her love with me;
Ide make her soone confesse she never loved
Her father halfe so well as I doe you.
I then, my deeds should prove in playner case,
How much my zeale aboundeth to your grace:
But for them all, let this one meane suffice,
To ratify my love before your eyes:
I have right noble Suters to my love,
No worse then Kings, and happely I love one: 270
Yet, would you have me make my choyce anew,
Ide bridle fancy, and be rulde by you.

LEIR.   Did never *Philomel*[4] sing so sweet a note.
COR.   Did never flatterer tell so false a tale.
LEIR.   Speak now, *Cordella*, make my joyes at full,
And drop downe Nectar from thy hon[e]y lips.
COR.   I cannot paynt my duty forth in words,
I hope my deeds shall make report for me:
But looke what love the child doth owe the father,
The same to you I beare, my gracious Lord.   280
GON.   Here is an answere answerlesse indeed:
Were you my daughter, I should scarcely brooke it.
RAG.   Dost thou not blush, proud Peacock as thou art,
To make our father such a slight reply?
LEIR.   Why how now, Minion, are you growne so proud?
Doth our deare love make you thus peremptory?
What, is your love become so small to us,

---

4   i.e. the nightingale.

As that you scorne to tell us what it is?
Do you love us, as every child doth love
Their father? True indeed, as some, 290
Who by disobedience short their fathers dayes,
And so would you; some are so father-sick,
That they make meanes to rid them from the world;
And so would you: some are indifferent,
Whether their aged parents live or dye;
And so are you. But, didst thou know, proud gyrle,
What care I had to foster thee to this,
Ah, then thou wouldst say as thy sisters do:
Our life is lesse, then love we owe to you.
COR.   Deare father, do not so mistake my words, 300
Nor my playne meaning be misconstrued;
My toung was never usde to flattery.
GON.   You were not best say I flatter: if you do,
My deeds shall shew, I flatter not with you.
I love my father better then thou canst.
COR.   The prayse were great, spoke from anothers mouth
But it should seeme your neighbours dwell far off.
RAG.   Nay, here is one, that will confirme as much
As she hath sayd, both for my selfe and her.
I say, thou dost not wish my fathers good. 310
COR.   Deare father.—
LEIR.   Peace, bastard Impe, no issue of King *Leir*,
I will not heare thee speake one tittle more.
Call not me father, if thou love thy life,
Nor these thy sisters once presume to name:
Looke for no helpe henceforth from me nor mine;
Shift as thou wilt, and trust unto thy selfe:
My Kingdome will I equally devide
'Twixt thy two sisters to their royall dowre,
And will bestow them worthy their deserts: 320
This done, because thou shalt not have the hope,
To have a childs part in the time to come,
I presently will dispossesse my selfe,
And set up these upon my princely throne.
GON.   I ever thought that pride would have a fall.
RAG.   Plaine dealing, sister: your beauty is so sheene,[5]
You need no dowry, to make you be a Queene.

---

5   Bright.

3. From Act 1, Scene 24

[In France] *Enter the Gallian King and Queene, and Mumford, with a basket, disguised like Countrey folke.*

They stand aside and eavesdrop.

> *Enter Leir & Perillus very faintly. [. . .]*
LEIR. Ah, *Gonorill*, was halfe my Kingdomes gift   2142
 The cause that thou dist seeke to have my life?
 Ah, cruell *Ragan*, did I give thee all,
 And all could not suffice without my bloud?
 Ah, poore *Cordella*, did I give thee nought,
 Nor never shall be able for to give?
 O, let me warne all ages that insueth,
 How they trust flattery, and reject the trueth.
 Well, unkind Girles, I here forgive you both,   2150
 Yet the just heavens will hardly do the like;
 And only crave forgivenesse at the end
 Of good *Cordella*, and of thee, my friend;
 Of God, whose Majesty I have offended,
 By my transgression many thousand wayes:
 Of her, deare heart, whom I for no occasion
 Turn'd out of all, through flatterers perswasion:
 Of thee, kind friend, who but for me, I know,
 Hadst never come unto this place of wo.
COR. Alack, that ever I should live to see   2160
 My noble father in this misery.
KING. Sweet Love, reveale not what thou art as yet,
 Untill we know the ground of all this ill.

Without revealing their identities Cordella and the King feed Leir and Perillus.

COR. My selfe a father have a great way hence,   2291
 Usde me as ill as ever you did her;
 Yet, that his reverend age I once might see,
 Ide creepe along, to meet him on my knee.
LEIR. O, no mens children are unkind but mine.
COR. Condemne not all, because of others crime:
 But looke, deare father, looke behold and see
 Thy loving daughter speaketh unto thee.   [*she kneeles.*
LEIR. O, stand thou up, it is my part to kneele,

And aske forgivenesse for my former faults.   [he kneeles.
COR.   O, if you wish I should injoy my breath,
    Deare father rise, or I receive my death.   [he riseth.
LEIR.   Then I will rise to satisfy your mind,
    But kneele againe, til pardon be resignd.   [he kneeles.   2300
COR.   I pardon you: the word beseemes not me:
    But I do say so, for to ease your knee.
    You gave me life, you were the cause that I
    Am what I am, who else had never bin.
LEIR.   But you gave life to me and to my friend,
    Whose dayes had else had an untimely end.   2310
COR.   You brought me up, when as I was but young,
    And far unable for to helpe my selfe.
LEIR.   I cast thee forth, when as thou wast but young,
    And far unable for to helpe thy selfe.
COR.   God, world and nature say I do you wrong,
    That can indure to see you kneele so long.
PER.   Let me breake off this loving controversy,
    Which doth rejoyce my very soule to see.
    Good father, rise, she is your loving daughter,   [He riseth.
    And honours you with as respective duty,   2320
    As if you were the Monarch of the world.
COR.   But I will never rise from off my knee,   [She kneeles.
    Untill I have your blessing, and your pardon
    Of all my faults committed any way,
    From my first birth unto this present day.
LEIR.   The blessing, which the God of *Abraham* gave
    Unto the trybe of *Juda*, light on thee,
    And multiply thy dayes, that thou mayst see
    Thy childrens children prosper after thee.
    Thy faults, which are just none that I do know,   2330
    God pardon on high, and I forgive below.   [She riseth.

4. From Scene 32

Alarums and excursions, then sound victory. Enter Leir, Perillus,
King, Cordella, and Mumford.
KING.   Thanks be to God, your foes are overcome,
    And you againe possessed of your right.   2633
LEIR.   First to the heavens, next, thanks to you, my sonne,
    By whose good meanes I repossesse the same:
    Which if it please you to accept your selfe,
    With all my heart I will resigne to you:
    For it is yours by right, and none of mine.
    First, have you raisd, at your owne charge, a power   2640

Of valiant Souldiers; (this comes all from you)
Next have you ventured your owne persons scathe.[6]
And lastly, (worthy *Gallia* never staynd)
My kingly title I by thee have gaynd.
KING.   Thank heavens, not me, my zeale to you is such,
Commaund my utmost, I will never grutch.[7]
COR.   He that with all kind love intreats his Queene,
Will not be to her father unkind scene.
LEIR.   Ah, my *Cordella*, now I call to mind,
The modest answere, which I tooke unkind: 2650
But now I see, I am no whit beguild,
Thou lovedst me dearely, and as ought a child.
And thou (*Perillus*) partner once in woe,
Thee to requite, the best I can, Ile doe:
Yet all I can, I, were it ne're so much,
Were not sufficient, thy true love is such.
Thanks (worthy, *Mumford*) to thee last of all,
Not greeted last, 'cause thy desert was small;
No, thou hast Lion-like layd on to day,
Chasing the Cornwall King and Cambria;   2660
Who with my daughters, daughters did I say?
To save their lives, the fugitives did play.
Come, sonne and daughter, who did me advaunce,
Repose with me awhile, and then for Fraunce.
            Sound Drummes and Trumpets.   [*Exeunt.*

Secondary Sources

The story of Lear and his daughters appeared in poems, prose romances (the Renaissance equivalent of novels) and pamphlets (the equivalent of modern newspapers) as well as history books. Here are extracts from these texts as well as two others from which Shakespeare indirectly or directly drew.

From **John Higgins, *The First Parte of the Mirour for Magistrates containing the falles of the first infortunate Princes of this lande*** (London: Thomas Marshe, 1574), Fol. 47ᵛ–48ʳ

First published in 1574, this long poem presents the stories of famous British monarchs on whom Renaissance rulers could model themselves. Here, uniquely

---

6   Hurt.
7   Complain.

among the sources, the tragic Cordelia narrates the story of Lear and his family from her own perspective. Subsequent editions of this poem, including that of 1587, show heavy revisions, but as both the 1574 and 1587 editions show particular correspondences to lines in Shakespeare's play (and to his main source, *The True Chronicle Historie of King Leir*) it is uncertain if he used only one or both editions. Compare Shakespeare's treatment of the causes of Lear's madness and his rejection of Cordelia in Key Passages on **pp. 141–9** and **102–13**.

Cordila shewes how by despaire when she was in prison she slue herselfe. the yeare before Christe. 800.

> . . . [Leire] had three daughters, first and eldest hight[1] *Gonerell:*
> Next after hir, my sister *Ragan* was begote:
> The thirde and last was, I the yongest namde,
> And of us all, our father *Leire* in age did dote.
> So minding her that lov'd him best to note,
> Because he had no sonne t'enjoye[2] his lande:
> He thought to give, where favour most he fande.[3]

> What though I yongest were, yet men me judgde more wise   50
> Then either *Gonorell*, or *Ragan* had more age,
> And fayrer farre: wherefore my sisters did despise
> My grace, and giftes, and sought my praise t'swage[4]
> But yet though vice gainst vertue die with rage,
> It cannot keepe her underneath to drowne,
> But still she flittes above, and reapes renowne.

> Yet nathelesse, my father did me not mislike:
> But age so simple is, and easye to subdue:
> As childhode weake, thats voide of wit and reason quite:
> They thincke thers nought you flater fainde, but all is true: 60
> Once olde and twice a childe, tis said with you,
> Which I affirme by proofe, that was definde:
> In age my father had a childishe minde.

> He thought to wed us unto nobles three, or Peres:[5]
> And unto them and theirs, devide and part the lande:

---

1 Called.
2 To enjoy.
3 Put to the test.
4 To assuage.
5 Peers of the realm.

For both my sisters first he sent as first their yeares
Requirde their mindes, and love, and favour t'understand.
(Quod[6] he) all doubtes of duty to abande,[7]
I must assaye[8] and eke[9] your frendships prove:
Now tell me eche how much you do me love.   70

    Which when they aunswered, they lovde him wel and more
Then they themselves did love, or any worldly wight:[10]
He praised them and said he would againe therefore,
The loving kindnes they deservde in fine requite:[11]
So found my sisters favour in his sight,
By flatery fayre they won their fathers hart:
Which after turned him and mee to smart.[12]

    But not content with this he minded me to prove,
For why he wonted was to love me wonders well:
How much dost thou (quoth he) *Cordile* thy father love?   80
I will (said I) at once my love declare and tell:
I lovde you ever as my father well,
No otherwise, if more to know you crave:
We love you chiefly for the goodes you have.

    Thus much I said, the more their flattery to detect,
But he me answered therunto again with Ire,
Because thou dost thy fathers aged yeares neglect,
That lovde the more of late then thy desertes require,
Thou never shalt, to any part aspire
Of this my realme, emong[13] thy sisters twayne,[14]   90
But ever shalt undoted[15] ay[16] remayne.

> Cordila then reveals that Lear denied her a dowry and married Gonerell to the
> King of Albany and Ragan to the Prince of Camber and Cornwall. The King of
> France hears of her virtues, and she accepts his offer of marriage.

---

6   Said.
7   Abandon.
8   Test.
9   Also.
10 Person.
11 Requital.
12 Hurt.
13 Among.
14 Two.
15 Unloved.
16 Always.

But while that I these joyes enjoyd, at home in *Fraunce*   120
My father *Leire* in *Britayne* waxed aged olde,
My sisters yet them selves the more aloft t'advaunce,
Thought well they might, be by his leave, or sans so bolde,
To take the realme & rule it as they wold.
They rose as rebels voyde of reason quite,
And they deprivde him of his crowne and right.

    Then they agreed, it should be into partes equall
Devided: and my father threscore knightes & squires
Should alwayes have, attending on him still at cal.
But in six monthes so much encreasid hateful Ires,   130
That *Gonerell* denyde all his desires,
So halfe his garde she and her husband refte:[17]
And scarce alowde the other halfe they lefte.

    Eke[18] as in *Scotlande* thus he lay lamenting fates,
When as his daughter so, sought all his utter spoyle:
The meaner upstarte gentiles,[19] thought themselves his mates
And better eke, see here an aged prince his foyle.
Then was he faine for succoure his, to toyle,
With all his knightes, to *Cornewall* there to lye:
In greatest nede, his *Raganes* love to trye.   140

    And when he came to *Cornwall*, *Ragan* then with joye,
Received him and eke hir husbande did the lyke:
There he abode a yeare and livde without anoy,[20]
But then they tooke, all his retinue from him quite
Save only ten, and shewde him dayly spite,
Which he bewailde complayning durst not strive,
Though in disdayne they laste alowde but five.

    On this he deemde him selfe was far that tyme vnwyse,
When from his doughter *Gonerell* to *Ragan* hee
Departed erste[21] yet eache did him poore king despise,   150
Wherfore to *Scotlande* once againe with hir to bee
And bide[22] he went: but beastly cruell shee,
Bereavde him of his servauntes all save one,
Bad[23] him content him self with that or none.

17 Took away.
18 Also.
19 Gentlemen.
20 Annoyance.
21 Right away.
22 Abide.
23 Bade.

Eke at what time he askte of eache to have his garde,
To garde his grace where so he walkte or wente:
They calde him doting foole and all his hestes[24] debarde,
Demaunded if with life he could not be contente.
Then he to late his rigour did repente,
Gainst me and sayde, *Cordila* now adieu: 160
I finde the wordes thou toldste me to to true.

And to be short, to *Fraunce* he came alone to mee,
And tolde me how my sisters him our father usde
Then I besought my king with teares upon my knee,
That he would aide my father thus by them misusde
Who nought at all my humble heste[25] refusde:
But sent to every coste of *Fraunce* for ayde,
Wherwith my father home might be conveide.

                              [. . .]

This had: I partid with my father from my fere,[26]   176
We came to *Britayne* with our royall campe to fight:
And manly fought so long our enemies vanquisht were
By martiall feates, and force by subjectes sword and might.
The Britishe kinges were fayne[27] to yelde our right,   180
And so my father well this realme did guide,
Three yeares in peace and after that he dide.

Cordila then talks of her five-year reign after Leire's death, her overthrow by
her nephews, and her suicide in prison.

From **Edmund Spenser**, *The Faerie Queene* (London: William Ponsonbie, 1596), Book II, Canto X, Stanzas 27–32, pp. 332–4

In *The Faerie Queene*, consisting of six books and the 'Mutability' cantos, Spenser attempted to trace the glorious history of the British kingdom, all in celebration of his patron Queen Elizabeth I. This epic poem serves as a kind of blueprint for Renaissance thought, politics, society and religion, while demonstrating the poetic fluency of the English language. In teaching 'by example', Spenser presented such troubled monarchs as Lear as a warning to his audience of 'noble'

---

24 Requests.
25 Request.
26 Husband.
27 Glad.

[. . .] Next him king *Leyr* in happie peace long raind,[1]
But had no issue male him to succeed,
But three faire daughters, which were well uptraind,[2]
In all that seemed fit for kingly seed:
Mongst whom his realme he equally decreed
To have divided. Tho when feeble age
Night to his utmost date he saw proceed,
He cald his daughters; and with speeches sage
Inquyrd, which of them most did love her parentage.

The eldest *Gonorill* gan[3] to protest,
That she much more then her owne life him lov'd:
And *Regan* greater love to him profest,
Then all the world, when ever it were proov'd;
But *Cordeill* said she lov'd him, as behoov'd:
Whose simple answere, wanting colours faire
To paint it forth, him to displeasance moov'd,
That in his crowne he counted her no haire,
But twixt the other twaine[4] his kingdome whole did shaire.

So wedded th' one to *Maglan* king of Scots,
And th'other to the king of *Cambria*,
And twixt them shayrd his realme by equall lots:
But without dowre[5] the wise *Cordelia*
Was sent to *Aganip* of *Celtica*.
Their aged Syre, thus eased of his crowne,
A private life led in *Albania*,
With *Gonorill*, long had in great renowne,
That nought him griev'd to bene from rule deposed downe.

But true it is, that when the oyle[6] is spent,
The light goes out, and weeke is throwne away;
So when he had resignd his regiment,

---

1 Reigned.
2 Brought up.
3 Began.
4 Two.
5 Dowry.
6 Oil.

His daughter gan despise his drouping day,
And wearie waxe[7] of his continuall stay.
Tho to his daughter *Regan* he repayrd,
Who him at first well used every way;
But when of his departure she despayrd,
Her bountie she abated, and his cheare empayrd.[8]

The wretched man gan then avise[9] too late,
That love is not, where most it is profest,
Too truely tryde in his extreamest state;
At last resolv'd likewise to prove the rest,
He to *Cordelia* him selfe addrest,
Who with entire affection him receav'd,
As for her Syre and king her seemed best;
And after all an army strong she leav'd,
To war on those, which him had of his realme bereav'd.

So to his crowne she him restor'd againe,
In which he dyde, made ripe for death by eld,[10]
And after wild, it should to her remaine:
Who peaceably the same long time did weld:[11]
And all mens harts in dew obedience held:
Till that her sisters children, woxen[12] strong
Through proud ambition, against her rebeld,
And overcommen kept in prison long,
Till wearie of that wretched life, her selfe she hong.[13] [. . .]

From **Sir Philip Sidney, *The Countesse of Pembroke's Arcadia***
(London: William Ponsonbie, 1590), Book 2, Chapter 10, pp. 143–4, 146–7

The intrigues in the Gloucester family, including Edmund's betrayal of his father and his innocent brother Edgar, do not appear in the other sources that Shakespeare used. For this subplot, he turned to Sidney's pitiful 'storie of the *Paphlagonian* unkinde King and his kind sonne, first related by: the son, then by the blind father'. Compare Shakespeare's presentation of the Gloucester family, especially in Key Passages on **pp. 115–20, 149–56 and 158–62.**

---

7 Grew.
8 Impaired.
9 Learn.
10 Old age.
11 Wield.
12 Grew.
13 Hanged.

[. . . The two princes Pyrocles and Musidorus encounter Leonatus who tells them:] 'This old man (whom I leade) was lately rightfull Prince of this countrie of *Paphlagonia*, by the hard-harted ungratefulnes of a sonne of his, deprived, not onely of his kingdome (whereof no forraine[1] forces were ever able to spoyle him) but of his sight, the riches which Nature grauts to the poorest creatures. Whereby, and by other his unnaturall dealings, he hath bin driven to such griefe, as even now he would have had me to have led him to the toppe of this rocke, thence to cast himselfe headlong to death: and so would haue made me (who received my life of him) to be the worker of his destruction. But noble Gentlemen (said he) if either of you have a father, and feele what duetifull affection is engraffed[2] in a sonnes hart, let me intreate you to convey this afflicted Prince to some place of rest and securitie. Amongst your worthie actes it shall be none of the least, that a King, of such might and fame, and so unjustly oppressed, is in any sort by you relieved'.

But before they could make him answere, his father began to speake, 'Ah my sonne (said he) how evill an Historian are you, that leave out the chiefe knotte of all the discourse! my wickednes, my wickednes. And if thou doest it to spare my ears, (the onely sense nowe left me proper for knowledge) assure thy selfe thou dost mistake me. And I take witnesse of that Sunne which you see (with that he cast up his blinde eyes, as if he would hunt for light,) and wish my selfe in worse case then I do wish my selfe, which is as evill as may be, if I speake untruely; that nothing is so welcome to my thoughts, as the publishing of my shame. Therefore know you Gentlemen (to whom from my harte I wish that it may not prove ominous foretoken of misfortune to have mette with such a miser as I am) that whatsoever my sonne (O God, that trueth binds me to reproch him with the name of my sonne) hath said, is true. But besides those truthes, this also is true, that having had in lawful mariage, of a mother fitte to beare royall children, this sonne (such one as partly you see, and better shall knowe by my shorte declaration) and so injoyed the expectations in the world of him, till he was growen to justifie their expectations (so as I needed envie no father for the chiefe comfort of mortalitie, to leave an other ones-selfe after me) I was caried by a bastarde sonne of mine (if at least I be bounde to beleeve the words of that base woman my concubine, his mother) first to mislike, then to hate, lastly to destroy, to doo my best to destroy, this sonne (I thinke you thinke) undeserving destruction. What waies he used to bring me to it, if I should tell you, I should tediously trouble you with as much poysonous hypocrisie, desperate fraude, smoothe malice, hidden ambition, and smiling envie as in any living person could be harbored'. [. . .]

[T]he blind King (having in the chief cittie of his Realme, set the crowne upon his sonne *Leonatus* head) with many teares (both of ioy and sorrow) setting forth to the whole people, his owne fault and his sonnes vertue, after he had kist him, and forst his sonne to accept honour of him (as of his newe-become subject) even in a moment died, as it should seeme: his hart broken with unkindnes and afflic-tion, stretched so farre beyond his limits with this excesse of comfort, as it was

---

1   Foreign.
2   i.e. engraved.

able no longer to keep safe his roial spirits. But the new King (having no lesse lovingly performed all duties to him dead, then alive) pursued on the siege of his unnatural brother, as much for the revenge of his father, as for the establishing of his owne quiet. In which siege truly I cannot but acknowledge the prowesse of those two brothers, then whom the Princes never found in all their travell two men of greater habilitie to performe, nor of habler[3] skill for conduct.

But *Plexirtus* finding, that if nothing els, famin would at last bring him to destruction, thought better by humblenes to creepe, where by pride he could not march [. . .] though no man had lesse goodnes in his soule then he, no man could better find the places whence arguments might grow of goodnesse to another: though no man felt lesse pitie, no man could tel better how to stir pitie: no man more impudent to deny, where proofes were not manifest; no man more ready to confesse with a repenting manner of aggravating his owne evil, where denial would but make the fault fouler. Now he tooke this way [. . .] with a rope about his necke, barefooted, came to offer himselfe to the discretion of *Leonatus*. [. . .] though at first sight *Leonatus* saw him with no other eie, then as the murderer of his father; and anger already began to paint revenge in many colours, ere long he had not only gotten pitie, but pardon. [. . .]

From **Samuel Harsnett, A Declaration of Egregious Popish Impostures** (London: James Roberts, 1603), Chapter 10, p. 49, 'The strange names of their devils'.

> From this book, Shakespeare borrowed the names of the devils conjured by Edgar as Poor Tom (see Key Passages on **pp. 147–9** and **154–6**).

[. . .] *Frateretto, Fliberdigibbet, Hoberdidance, Tocobatto* were foure devils of the round, or Morrice, whom *Sara* in her fits, tuned together, in measure and sweet cadences. And least you should conceive, that the devils had no musicke in hell, especially that they would goe a maying without theyr musicke, the Fidler comes in with his Taber, & Pipe, and a whole Morice after him, with motly visards for theyr better grace. These foure had forty assistants under them, as themselves doe confesse.

From **James I, The True Law of Free Monarchies: or the Reciprok[al] dutie betwixt a free King and his naturall subjects** (Edinburgh: Robert Waldegrave, 1598), signatures B4ᵛ–B5ʳ, D4ʳ

> James's political treatise on the responsibilities of monarchs and subjects was first published in 1598 when he was King of Scotland and reprinted in 1603 to

---

3 Abler.

[. . .] By the law of Nature the King becomes a naturall Father to all his Lieges[1] at his Coronation. And as the Father of his fatherly duety is bounde to care for the nourishing, education, and vertuous government of his children: even so is the King bounde to care for all his subjects [. . .] As the kindly father ought to foresee all inconvenients & dangers that may aryse towardes his children, and though with the hazard of his owne person presse to prevente the same: So ought the King towardes his people. As the Fathers wrath and correction upon any of his children, that offendeth, ought to be a fatherly chastizement seasoned with pittie, as long as there is any hope of amendment in them: So ought the King towardes any of his lieges that offendes in that measure. [. . .]

[. . .] consider I pray you, what duty his children owe to him, and whether, upon any pretext whatsoever, it wil not be thoght monstrous and unnaturall to his sonnes to rise up against him, to controll him at their appetite, and when they thinke good to slay him, or to cut him off, and adopt to themselves any other [way] they please in his room. Or can any pretence of wickednes or rigour on his parte be a just excuse for his children to put hand into him? And although we see by the course of nature that love ever useth to descend more then to ascend: in case it were true, that the father hated and wronged the children never so much, will any man endued[2] with the leaste sponke[3] of reason think it lawfull for them to meete him with the like? [. . .]

From **James I, *Basilikon Doron* [*The King's Gift*]: or His Majesties Instructions to his dearest sonne, Henry the Prince** (Edinburgh: Robert Waldegrave, 1603), Books 2–3, signatures H1^v–H2^r, H8^r, I4^v.

1 Subjects.
2 Endowed.
3 Amount.

the kingdoms. A few generations later, as James most certainly knew, the historical King Leir inherited the problems caused by Brutus' disastrous division. James also advises Henry how to use a king's 'wrath', the same term used by Shakespeare's Lear (see Key Passages on **pp. 105–9, 123–9** and **135–40**).

[. . .] If God send you succession [i.e. children], be carefull for their vertuous education: love them as ye ought, but let them knowe as much of it, as the gentlenesse of their nature will deserve; contayning them ever in a reverent love and feare of you. And in case it please God to provide you to all these three kingdomes, make your eldest sonne Issac,[1] leaving him all your kingdomes; and provyde the rest with private possessions. Otherwaies by dividing your kingdomes, ye shall leave the seede of division & discorde among your posteritie: as befell to this Ile, by the division & assignement thereof, to the three sonnes of *Brutus, Locrine, Albanact,* and *Camber.* [. . .]

Embrace true Magnanimitie, not in being vindictive, which the corrupted judgements of the worlde thinkes to be true Magnanimitie; but by the contrary, in thinking your offender not worthie of your wrath, empyring[2] over your owne passion, and triumphing in the commanding of your selfe to forgive [. . .] where ye finde a notable injury, spare not to give course to the torrents of your wrath. *The wrath of a King, is like the roaring of a Lyon.* [. . .]

Tis a true old saying, That a King is as one set on a stage, whose smallest actions and gestures, all the people gazinglie doe beholde [. . .]

1   Oldest son of the biblical figure Abraham and sole inheritor of his property.
2   Reigning.

2

Interpretations

Critical History

Due to the seemingly relentless portrayal of cruelty and the apparent lack of any concluding redemption in *King Lear*, its critical 'reception', that is, the way it has been treated by critics and reading audiences, has often been grim. Those critics who have recognised Shakespeare's dramatic skill in the play, especially his extraordinary presentations of language, character and setting, and his shaping of the plot, have also felt it necessary to apologise for admiring him. For example, in the early nineteenth century, in analysing each of the plays, William Hazlitt marvelled at Shakespeare's brilliance, but of *King Lear* he began: 'We wish that we could pass this play over, and say nothing about it' (**pp. 51–2**).

King Lear raises a series of 'taboo' subjects that could make an audience, including critics, uncomfortable, squeamish or repulsed. While his early plays such as *Titus Andronicus* are replete with characters that commit gratuitous murders, rapes, maimings and other bloody acts of retribution, Shakespeare keeps his audience from bonding with these one-dimensional characters, and therefore we can keep some distance from them. However, Shakespeare fills his later tragedies with sympathetic characters whose inner turmoil, emotions and guilt we must share. Their most gruesome and 'most foul' acts are usually presented in narration only, as in the ghost of Old Hamlet reporting the story of his murder to his son, or Macbeth leaving the stage to murder Duncan and then returning to describe his success to his wife. Other murders in *Hamlet*, *Macbeth* and *Othello*, for example, are staged for the audience, but Shakespeare seems to provide enough recovery time afterwards for the traumatised audience to continue watching the plays. In *King Lear* Shakespeare offers far too many acts of cruelty in succession, not in narration, but acted out onstage, leaving the audience increasingly breathless with anxiety, fear or disgust. We must watch Lear's rejection of Cordelia and Kent, his abuse at the hands of Goneril and Regan, his painful psychological breakdown in its entirety and his loving reunion with Cordelia cut short by her murder, his own death and the murder-suicide of his other two daughters, not to mention too many parallel events in the lives of the Gloucester family, especially Gloucester's blinding and his attempted suicide. There are no drunken porters or bumbling gravediggers to provide comic relief, just increasing barbarity; even the court-jester figure of the Fool who 'hath much pined away', and who disappears altogether half-way through the play, is more 'bitter' than comic.

By forcing us as the audience to watch such successive acts of physical and psychological cruelty, Shakespeare makes us complicit. We do not rise from our seats demanding the play cease but are numbed into accepting such behaviour as ordinary or appropriate. In this way, we aid and abet Shakespeare's characters in their evil and instability. We do not avert our eyes but watch willingly, gawking the same way we would when encountering the bloody aftermath of a real-life car accident. Thus, in *King Lear* Shakespeare makes us confront the subjects that we are ashamed to think about, including parent–child grudges and old hurts, thoughts of incest and uncontrolled sexuality, and sibling resentment and rivalry, provoking feelings which we normally work so hard to repress from our conscious into our unconscious mind. For these reasons, the play has disturbed critics, readers and audiences.

We know nothing of its reception as a literary or theatrical text until after the Restoration when *King Lear* was considered so distressing that the playwright Nahum Tate rewrote it in 1681 to suit a new kind of audience (**pp. 75–6**). He returned to the sources to provide the happy ending of the survival both of Lear and Cordelia, and invented the star-crossed romance and eventual betrothal of Cordelia and Edgar. For the next 150 years, critics, readers and theatrical audiences preferred Tate's version to Shakespeare's, which languished in obscurity. Tate's astonishing success distressed some critics but justified the complaint of others that Shakespeare's language, plots and morality were too barbarous or uncivilised for the more refined taste of those in the Restoration and the age of Enlightenment.

None were as distressed as his editors, including Dr Samuel Johnson, charged with the task of making his now obscure plays readable by later audiences. The eighteenth century saw a huge increase in the number of collected editions of Shakespeare's plays being printed; each editor offered his own adapted or reconstructed texts, claiming preceding editors had been sloppy, but also blaming Shakespeare for his inconsistent style and ignorance. At the same time, these editors insisted that Shakespeare should serve as the writer by whom all other great writers were to be measured. In fact, our modern conceptions of how to practise literary criticism began with the publication of Dr Johnson's 'Preface' to his 1765 edition of Shakespeare's plays (**pp. 49–50**). It was not until the early nineteenth century, and the rise of Romanticism, which appreciated natural and spontaneous sensibility and 'passion', that critics such as Charles Lamb, William Hazlitt and Samuel Taylor Coleridge (**pp. 50–1, 51–2 and 53**) fully accepted Shakespeare's naturalism as appropriate for his own time and admirable for later generations of scholars. Thus Romantic poets such as John Keats (**pp. 53–4**) could celebrate 'the fierce dispute/Betwixt damnation and impassioned clay' that *King Lear* offered as inspiration. Not surprisingly, it is in this period that Tate's version of the play finally disappears and Shakespeare's returns to the professional London stage.

Shakespeare's worth has often been measured through the success of his characters, rather than through any other single element in his plays, probably because the enormity of his accomplishments is too much to comprehend or measure in its entirety. In the early twentieth century, A. C. Bradley used the character of Lear to propound a very influential theory of tragedy and its effects on the audience, finally concluding that *King Lear* was 'Shakespeare's greatest work', but not 'the best of his plays' (**pp. 55–6**). Bradley's qualified reaction was echoed by later critics until the revolutionary re-assessment of the play by Jan Kott, living in the Eastern-bloc country of Poland under a repressive Soviet regime. Kott argued that Shakespeare's treatment of *King Lear* could be seen for the first time as immediate, modern and 'contemporary' (**pp. 56–7**). His vision changed the direction of Shakespearean criticism and had a profound effect in the theatre, particularly through the influence of the extraordinary British director Peter Brook, who now works primarily in France. Brook's 1962 stage production of the play with Paul Scofield as Lear forced Shakespearean performance into a new era. For Brook, *King Lear* is not 'unactable' as Lamb claimed, or 'too huge for the stage' as Bradley claimed, but 'directly related to the most burning themes of our time' (**pp. 58–9**).

As a result, *King Lear* has displaced *Hamlet* as the single most representative embodiment of Shakespeare's genius and accomplishment, both to critics and to reading and theatrical audiences. According to R. A. Foakes (**pp. 59–60**), those in the post-nuclear age could better understand the bleak, grim vision offered at the conclusion of *Lear* than the more redemptive ending of *Hamlet*. That is, Hamlet's sacrificial pain and death seem to promise a better world, an optimistic view that has now become obsolete. Lear's pain and death are not sacrificial but futile, and both confirm that such suffering will continue. With the subsequent rise of 'theory', critics brought their own private concerns to the play, seeing it, for example, as a depiction not of Shakespeare's age or culture but of his personal support for suffocating patriarchy or liberating subversion. At the same time, 'new revisionist' textual scholars and editors expanded old arguments that Shakespeare heavily revised *King Lear* between its first composition (as printed in the1608 first quarto) and some later point (as printed in the 1623 First Folio) to intensify its bleakness, grimness and anarchy. Below is a selection of early and later critical discussions that covers the full range of these significant and central issues.

Early Critical Reception

From **Charles Gildon, 'Remarks on the Plays of Shakespear'**, in *The Works of Mr William Shakespear*, ed. Nicholas Rowe (London: printed for E. Curll and E. Sanger, 1710), Volume 7, p. 406.

> Gildon, a critic and playwright, is typical of those in this period who dismissed Shakespeare's presentation of tragedy in *King Lear* and defended Tate's 1681 adaptation of the play.

[. . .] The King and *Cordelia* ought by no means to have dy'd, and therefore Mr *Tate* has very justly alter'd that particular, which must disgust the Reader and Audience to have Vertue and Piety meet so unjust a Reward. So that this Plot, tho' of so celebrated a Play, has none of the Ends of Tragedy moving neither Fear nor Pity. We rejoice at the Death of the *Bastard* and the two Sisters, as of Monsters in Nature under whom the very Earth must groan. And we see with horror and Indignation the Death of the King, *Cordelia* and *Kent* [who implies at the play's conclusion that he will 'journey' towards death]; tho' of the Three the King only cou'd move pity if that were not lost in the Indignation and Horror the Death of the other two produces, for he is a truly *Tragic* Character not supremely Virtuous nor Scandalously vicious he is made up of *Choler*, and the Obstinacy, Frailties pardonable enough in an Old Man, and yet what drew on him all the Misfortunes of his Life. [. . .]

From **Lewis Theobald, Notes on *King Lear***, in *The Works of Shakespeare*, ed. Lewis Theobald (London: printed for A. Bettesworth *et al.*, 1733), Volume 5, p. 217

> Here Theobald, a literary critic and editor, comments on Shakespeare's use of sources.

[. . .] Our Poet has taken the Liberty in the Catastrophe of this Play to depart from the *Chronicles*; in which *Lear* is said to be reinstated in his Throne by *Cordelia*, and to have reign'd upwards of two Years after his Restoration. He might have done This for two reasons. Either, to heighten the Compassion towards the poor old King: or to vary from another, but most execrable, Dramatic Performance upon this Story [i.e. *The Chronicle History of King Leir*]; which I certainly believe to have preceded our Author's Piece, and which none of our Stage-Historians appear to have had any Knowledge of. [. . .]

From **Samuel Johnson, Notes on** *King Lear*, in *The Plays of William Shakespeare*, ed. Samuel Johnson, Volume 6 (London: J. and R. Tonson *et al.*, 1765), pp. 158–9

The literary criticism of Dr Johnson, an author, editor, and compiler of the first English dictionary (1755), still influences modern scholars and students. The preface and notes to his 1765 edition of Shakespeare's plays, from which this extract is taken, have especially been cited by succeeding generations of Shakespearean critics, scholars, directors, and actors as the first fundamental examination of Shakespeare as author and dramatist.

[. . .] The Tragedy of *Lear* is deservedly celebrated among the dramas of *Shakespeare*. There is perhaps no play which keeps the attention so strongly fixed; which so much agitates our passions and interests our curiosity. The artful involutions of distinct interests, the striking opposition of contrary characters, the sudden changes of fortune, and the quick succession of events, fill the mind with a perpetual tumult of indignation, pity, and hope. There is no scene which does not contribute to the aggravation of the distress or conduct of the action, and scarce a line which does not conduce to the progress of the scene. So powerful is the current of the poet's imagination, that the mind, which once ventures within it, is hurried irresistibly along.

On the seeming improbability of *Lear's* conduct it may be observed that he is represented according to histories at that time vulgarly received as true. And perhaps if we turn our thoughts upon the barbarity and ignorance of the age to which this story is referred, it will appear not so unlikely as while we estimate *Lear's* manners by our own. Such preference of one daughter to another, or resignation of dominion on such conditions, would yet be credible, if told of a petty prince of *Guinea* or *Madagascar*. *Shakespeare*, indeed, by the mention of his Earls and Dukes, has given us the idea of times more civilised, and of life regulated by softer manners; and the truth is, that though he so nicely discriminates, and so minutely describes the characters of men, he commonly neglects and confounds the characters of ages, by mingling customs ancient and modern, *English* and foreign.

My learned friend Mr *Warton*, who has in the *Adventurer* very minutely criticized this play, remarks, that the instances of cruelty are too savage and shocking, and that the intervention of *Edmund* destroys the simplicity of the story. These objections may, I think, be answered by repeating that the cruelty of the daughters is an historical fact, to which the poet has added little, having only drawn it into a series by dialogue and action. But I am not able to apologize with equal plausibility for the extrusion of *Gloucester's* eyes, which seems an act too horrid to be endured in dramatic exhibition, and such as must always compel the mind to relieve its distress by incredulity. Yet let it be remembered that our author well knew what would please the audience for which he wrote.

The injury done by *Edmund* to the simplicity of the action is abundantly recompensed by the addition of variety, by the art with which he is made to co-operate with the chief design, and the opportunity which he gives the poet of combining perfidy with perfidy, and connecting the wicked son with the wicked daughters, to impress this important moral, that villainy is never at a stop, that crimes lead to crimes and at last terminate in ruin.

But though this moral be incidentally enforced, *Shakespeare* has suffered the virtue of *Cordelia* to perish in a just cause, contrary to the natural ideas of justice, to the hope of the reader, and, what is yet more strange, to the faith of the chronicles. Yet this conduct is justified by the Spectator, who blames *Tate* for giving *Cordelia* success and happiness in his alteration, and declares, that, in his opinion, *the tragedy has lost half its beauty.* [. . .] A play in which the wicked prosper, and the virtuous miscarry, may doubtless be good, because it is a just representation of the common events of human life: but since all reasonable beings naturally love justice, I cannot easily be persuaded, that the observation of justice makes a play worse; or, that if other excellencies are equal, the audience will not always rise better pleased from the final triumph of persecuted virtue.

In the present case the publick has decided. *Cordelia*, from the time of *Tate*, has always retired with victory and felicity. And, if my sensations could add any thing to the general suffrage, I might relate, that I was many years ago so shocked by *Cordelia's* death, that I know not whether I ever endured to read again the last scenes of the play till I undertook to revise them as an editor. [. . .]

From **Charles Lamb, 'On the Tragedies of Shakespeare'** (1810), in *The Works of Charles Lamb in Two Volumes* (London: printed for C. and J. Ollier, 1818), Volume 2, pp. 25–6

Lamb's literary letters and essays had a profound influence on Romantic poets and critics such as William Wordsworth, William Hazlitt, and Samuel Taylor Coleridge. He and his sister Mary also became famous for *Tales from Shakespeare*, their adaptations of Shakespeare's plays into children's stories. Lamb's contention that the character of Lear 'cannot be acted' held sway for almost 150 years, until Laurence Olivier's and Paul Scofield's superb portrayals of Lear (see below, **pp. 84–5**) proved Lamb wrong. For Lamb's references to the play, see Key Passages on **pp. 141–7**.

[. . .] To see Lear acted, to see an old man tottering about the stage with a walking-stick, turned out of doors by his daughters in a rainy night, has nothing in it but what is painful and disgusting. We want to take him into shelter and relieve him. That is all the feeling which the acting of Lear ever produced in me. But the Lear of Shakespeare cannot be acted. The contemptible machinery by which they mimic the storm which he goes out in, is not more inadequate to represent the horrors of the real elements, than any actor can be to represent Lear: they might more easily propose to personate the Satan of Milton upon a stage, or one of Michael Angelo's terrible figures. The greatness of Lear is not in corporal dimension, but in intellectual: the explosions of his passion are as terrible as a volcano: they are storms turning up and disclosing to the bottom of that sea, his mind, with all its vast riches. It is his mind which is laid bare. This case of flesh and blood seems too insignificant to be thought on; even as he himself neglects it. On the stage we see nothing but corporal infirmities and weakness, the impotence of rage; while we read it, we see not Lear, but we are Lear, we are in his mind, we are sustained by a grandeur which baffles the malice of daughters and storms; in the aberrations of his reason, we discover a mighty irregular power of reasoning, immethodized from the ordinary purposes of life, but exerting its powers, as the wind blows where it listeth, at will upon the corruptions and abuses of mankind. What have looks, or tones, to do with that sublime identification of his age with that of the *heavens themselves*, when in his reproaches to them for conniving at the injustice of his children, he reminds them that 'they themselves are old'. What gesture shall we appropriate to this? What has the voice or the eye to do with such things? But the play is beyond all art, as the tamperings with it shew: it is too hard and stony, it must have love-scenes and a happy ending. It is not enough that Cordelia is a daughter, she must shine as a lover too. Tate has put his hook in the nostrils of this Leviathan, for Garrick and his followers, the showmen of the scene, to draw the mighty beast about more easily. A happy ending! as if the living martyrdom that Lear had gone through, the flaying of his feelings alive, did not make a fair dismissal from the stage of life the only decorous thing for him. If he is to live and be happy after, if he could sustain this world's burden after, why all this pudder and preparation, why torment us with all this unnecessary sympathy? As if the childish pleasure of getting his gilt robes and sceptre again could tempt him to act over again his misused station, as if at his years, and with his experience, any thing was left but to die.

Lear is essentially impossible to be represented on a stage.

From **William Hazlitt, 'Characters of Shakespear's Plays: *King Lear*'** (1817), in *The Complete Works of William Hazlitt*, ed. P. P. Howe (London: J. M. Dent & Sons, Ltd, 1930), Volume 4, pp. 257–8, 271–2

Through the several series of lectures he delivered to the public and the wide-ranging sets of essays and other works he published in magazines and other journals, Hazlitt, a contemporary of Coleridge and Lamb, developed his renown as one of the chief literary critics of his age. In this extremely influential essay, Hazlitt echoes the concerns of the Romantic poets and demonstrates the Romantic concern with the 'passion' of Shakespeare's poetry in *King Lear*.

[. . .] We wish that we could pass this play over, and say nothing about it. All that we can say must fall far short of the subject; or even what we ourselves conceive of it. To attempt to give a description of the play itself or of its effect upon the mind, is mere impertinence: yet we must say something:—It is then the best of all Shakespear's plays, for it is the one in which he was the most in earnest. He was here fairly caught in the web of his own imagination. The passion which he has taken as his subject is that which strikes its root deepest into the human heart; of which the bond is the hardest to be unloosed; and the canceling and tearing to pieces of which gives the greatest revulsion to the frame. This depth of nature, this force of passion, this tug and war of the elements of our being, this firm faith in filial piety, and the giddy anarchy and whirling tumult of the thoughts at finding this prop failing it, the contrast between the fixed, immoveable basis of natural affection, and the rapid, irregular starts of imagination, suddenly—wrenched from all its accustomed holds and resting-places in the soul, this is what Shakespear has given, and what nobody else but he could give. So we believe.—The mind of Lear, staggering between the weight of attachment and the hurried movements of passion, is like a tall ship driven about by the winds, buffetted by the furious waves, but that still rides above the storm, having its anchor fixed in the bottom of the sea; or it is like the sharp rock circled by the eddying whirlpool that foams and beats against it, or like the solid promontory pushed from its basis by the force of an earthquake.

[. . .] Four things have struck us in reading LEAR:

1. That poetry is an interesting study, for this reason, that it relates to whatever is most interesting in human life. Whoever therefore has a contempt for poetry, has a contempt for himself and humanity.

2. That the language of poetry is superior to the language of painting; because the strongest of our recollections relate to feelings, not to faces.

3. That the greatest strength of genius is strewn in describing the strongest passions: for the power of the imagination, in works of invention, must be in proportion to the force of the natural impressions, which are the subject of them.

4. That the circumstance which balances the pleasure against the pain in tragedy is, that in proportion to the greatness of the evil, is our sense and desire of the opposite good excited; and that our sympathy with actual suffering is lost in the strong impulse given to our natural affections, and carried away with the swelling tide of passion, that gushes from and relieves the heart. [. . .]

From **Samuel Taylor Coleridge, Records of his Lecture on** *King Lear* (28 January 1819), in *The Collected Works of Samuel Taylor Coleridge: Lectures 1808–1819 On Literature*, ed. R. A. Foakes (London & Princeton, NJ: Routledge & Kegan Paul/Princeton University Press, 1987), Volume 2, pp. 325–8

In a lecture in 1819, Coleridge, whose powerful poetry often explored the power of supernatural evil, considered Shakespeare's representation of evil in a more natural form (see Key Passages on **pp. 113–15, 126–9, 135–40, 149–54, 157–8** and **168–73**). Here is a brief summary of that lecture, taken down by a member of the audience.

[. . . In] this Tragedy the story or fable constrained Shakespear to introduce wickedness in an outrageous form, in Regan and Goneril. He had read Nature too heedfully not to know, that Courage, Intellect, and strength of Character were the most impressive Forms of Power: and that to Power in itself, without reference to any moral end, an inevitable Admiration & Complacency appertains. [. . .] But in the display of such a character it was of the highest importance to prevent the guilt from passing into utter *monstrosity*—which again depends on the presence or absence of causes and temptations sufficient to *account* for the wickedness, without the necessity of recurring to a thorough fiendishness of nature for its origination – For such are the appointed relations of intellectual Power to Truth, and of Truth to Goodness, that it becomes both morally and poetic[ally] unsafe to present what is admirable—what our nature compels to admire—in the mind, and what is most detestable in the Heart, as co-existing in the same individual without any apparent connection, or an modification of the one by the other. [. . .]

John Keats, 'On Sitting Down to Read *King Lear* Once Again'
(1818) in *The Poetical Works and Other Writings of John Keats*, ed. H. Buxton Forman, with revisions by M. B. Forman, 6 Vols (New York: Scribner's Sons, 1939), 4: 76–7.

Keats, the extraordinary Romantic poet and author of *Endymion*, *Lamia*, and *The Eve of St Agnes* among other works, died at the age of twenty-six. In this sonnet, he offers a sublime and stunning representation of his reaction to reading the play. He first wrote the poem on 22 January 1818 in the text of his copy of Shakespeare's plays, and the next day sent a copy of it in a letter to his brothers. The sonnet was first published in 1838 and then throughout the nineteenth century in slightly differing versions. This is a version of the text corrected from Keats's manuscripts.

O golden-tongued Romance, with serene lute!
   Fair plumed Siren, Queen of far-away!
   Leave melodizing on this wintry day,
Shut up thine olden pages, and be mute:
Adieu! for, once again, the fierce dispute
   Betwixt damnation and impassioned clay
   Must I burn through; once more humbly assay
The bittersweet of this Shakespearian fruit:
Chief poet! and ye clouds of Albion,
   Begetters of our deep eternal theme!
When through the old oak forest I am gone,
   Let me not wander in a barren dream,
But, when I am consumèd in the fire,
Give me new phoenix wings to fly at my desire.

Modern Criticism

From **A. C. Bradley, Shakespearean Tragedy: Hamlet, Othello, King Lear and Macbeth** (1904; rpt New York, NY: Meridian Books, 1960), pp. 200–1

Bradley had a long and distinguished career as a literary critic, writing, for example, on Alfred, Lord Tennyson and other poets of the nineteenth century. However, he is now best known for his book on Shakespearian tragedy (from which this extract has been taken), which has almost certainly been the single most influential critical work ever written on Shakespeare. Bradley's theories on the nature of tragedy, as drawn from his analyses of Shakespeare's presentation of characters (see Key Passages on **pp. 126–9, 135–40 and 165–8**), are still regarded as definitive by many scholars. Here Bradley draws heavily on the critical traditions established by Lamb and Hazlitt.

[. . .] The stage is the test of strictly dramatic quality, and *King Lear* is too huge for the stage. Of course, I am not denying that it is a great stage-play. It has scenes immensely effective in the theatre; three of them—the two between Lear and Goneril and between Lear, Goneril and Regan, and the ineffably beautiful scene in the Fourth Act between Lear and Cordelia—lose in the theatre very little of the spell they have for imagination; and the gradual interweaving of the two plots is almost as masterly as in *Much Ado*. But (not to speak of defects due to mere carelessness) that which makes the peculiar greatness of *King Lear*,—the immense scope of the work; the mass and variety of intense experience which it contains; the interpenetration of sublime imagination, piercing pathos, and humour almost as moving as the pathos; the vastness of the convulsion both of nature and of human passion; the vagueness of the scene where the action takes place, and of the movements of the figures which cross this scene; the strange atmosphere, cold and dark, which strikes on us as we enter this scene, enfolding these figures and magnifying their dim outlines like a winter mist; the half-realised suggestions of vast universal powers working in the world of individual fates and passions,—all this interferes with dramatic clearness even when the play is read, and in the theatre not only refuses to reveal itself fully through the senses but seems to be almost in contradiction with their reports. This is not so with the other great tragedies. No doubt, as Lamb declared, theatrical representation gives only a part of what we imagine when we read them; but there is no conflict between the representation and the imagination, because these tragedies are, in essentials, perfectly dramatic. But *King Lear*, as a whole, is imperfectly dramatic, and there is something in its very essence which is at war with the senses, and demands a purely imaginative realization. It is therefore Shakespeare's greatest work, but it is not what Hazlitt called it, the best of his plays; and its comparative unpopularity is due, not merely to the extreme painfulness of the catastrophe, but in part to its dramatic defects, and in part to a failure in many readers to catch the peculiar effects to which I have referred,—a failure which is natural because the appeal is made not so much to dramatic perception as to a rarer and more strictly poetic kind of imagination. For this reason, too, even the best attempts at exposition of *King Lear* are disappointing; they remind us of attempts to reduce to prose the impalpable spirit of the *Tempest*. [. . .]

From **Jan Kott, Shakespeare Our Contemporary**, trans. Boleslaw Taborski (second edition, London: Methuen, 1967), pp. 296–8

Kott, a native of Poland, spent much of his career protesting against the Soviet domination of his country. In 1964, he joined with others in condemning government censorship in Poland, finally leaving for the United States in 1966 and requesting political asylum there in 1969. A specialist in drama and tragedy, he here considers the ways in which Shakespeare could be seen as our political contemporary in the post-modern age. His discussions of *King Lear* with theatre director Peter Brook profoundly influenced both modern criticism and modern theatre.

[. . .] A tale of two bad daughters and one good daughter, or a story about the druid king. The opening of *King Lear* compels the producer to make an absurd choice between a fairy tale and a Celtic mystery. By being reduced to a fable or to archaeology, *King Lear* had always been deprived of both its great seriousness and its great buffo [i.e., comical] tone. Thus the play used to lose stature at the outset. To my mind, Peter Brook's first discovery consisted in finding an historical situation in which *King Lear* could at last be set; a situation in which it became a history brutal and tragic, serious and grotesque, with real people and real objects taking part.

Let us recall the Polish borderland princes and magnates, all those seventeenth-century Wisniowieckis, Radziwills, Potockis with their courts that wanted to equal the royal court in splendour, with their customs in which, as at Lear's court, courtly manners mingled with cruelty, exquisite elegance with coarseness, high politics with family interests.

They were very much alike, those sixteenth- and seventeenth-century nobles, whether in England or in the Ukraine, in Scotland or in Lithuania. Too small, this Lear, to be a king, but his characteristics can easily be found in Border country nobles anywhere. By a whim of old age he suddenly divides his lands among his daughters and sons-in-law and demands of them rhetorical displays of filial love. Having given away his power and treasury, he drags with him the drunken horde of his bodyguards from estate to estate. He comes with them to reside with his daughters in turn, devastating everything on his way like a swarm of locusts. There is in *King Lear*—and Mr Brook was the first to discover it—a combination of madness, passion, pride, folly, imperiousness, anarchy, humanity and awe, which all have their exact place and time in history.

The first three acts almost belong to epic theatre. There are few objects, but every one of them is real and means something: the orb and the sword, the map drawn on leather, old Gloster's astrolabe, stocks, even the chain-spoon carried by Oswald as the court steward. *King Lear* is a play about the disintegration of the world. But, in order to show the world disintegrating, one has first to prove that it exists. Until it falls, it has to exist, with its hierarchy of power, with its faiths, rituals and ceremonies, with its mutually entangled relationships of power and family, marriage and adultery, legitimate and illegitimate children, violence and law. To my mind, it was more difficult to show the continued existence of the world in *King Lear* than its disintegration. The disintegration had already been shown by the theatre of the absurd. It sufficed to discover [the playwright Samuel] Beckett in Shakespeare.

The scenes of Lear's madness are like a plummet thrown from a boat to fathom the lowest depths. These people of flesh and blood have now been reduced to trunks, to crippled torsos. Then, from the fourth act onwards, the world slowly begins, as it were, to grow together again. Ceremonies and rituals begin anew, wars are waged somewhere, with someone, for something. But for Lear, for Gloster, those are just the incomprehensible noises of a world which has ceased to exist.

In my conversations with Peter Brook I once tried to persuade him to show how all the characters of this drama descended lower and lower. I wanted the early acts to be performed on a large platform placed high up on the stage and to demonstrate physically, materially, visibly as it were, the disintegration and descent. Brook did not need any of these naïve metaphors. The disintegrated world does not grow together in is this production, just as it does not grow together in Shakespeare's play. Human wrecks find their humanity again, but this only means that they refuse to accept suffering, torture and death. They refuse to accept the absurdity of the world in which one lives in order to breed, murder and die.

A brother throws over his shoulder the body of the brother he has killed. This is all there is. There will not be another king. The stage remains empty. Like the world.

From **Peter Brook,** *The Empty Space* (New York, NY: Atheneum, 1968),
pp. 91–4

A distinguished theatre, opera and film director, Brook began his professional
career in 1942. He was a co-director of the Royal Shakespeare Theatre in
Stratford-upon-Avon for a number of years, and his grim, spare and extremely
powerful 1962 production there of *King Lear* revolutionised modern theatre. This
production later toured the world, inspiring Jan Kott and the Russian film director
Grigori Kozintsev, among others who have shaped modern representations of
Shakespeare. Brook filmed his production in 1971. In his productions, essays and
interviews, he has continued to offer innovative ideas on staging Shakespeare.
Here he concentrates on moral issues (see Key Passages on **pp. 168–79**).

[. . .] Experimentally, we can approach Lear not as a linear narrative, but as a
cluster of relationships. First, we try to rid ourselves of the notion that because the
play is called *King Lear* it is primarily the story of one individual. So we pick an
arbitrary point in the vast structure – the death of Cordelia, say, and now instead
of looking towards the King we turn instead towards the man who is responsible
for her death. We focus on this character, Edmund, and now we begin to pick our
way to and fro across the play, sifting the evidence, trying to discover who this
Edmund is. He is clearly a villain, whatever our standards, for in killing Cordelia
he is responsible for the most gratuitous act of cruelty in the play – yet if we look
at our first impression of him in the early scenes, we find he is by far the most
attractive character we meet. [. . .] Not only do we sympathize with Goneril and
Regan for falling in love with him, but we tend to side with them in finding
Edmund so admirably wicked, because he affirms a life that the sclerosis of the
older people seems to deny. Can we keep this same attitude of admiration
towards Edmund when he has Cordelia killed? If not, why not? What has
changed? Is it Edmund who has changed, through outside events? Or is it just the
context that is different? [. . .]

[. . .] Indeed, it is clearly shown to us in the unfolding of the play that Lear
suffers most and 'gets farthest'. Undoubtedly his brief moment of captivity with
Cordelia is as a moment of bliss, peace and reconciliation, and Christian com-
mentators often write as though this were the end of the story – a clear tale of the
ascent from the inferno through purgation to paradise. Unfortunately for this
neat view the play continues, pitilessly, away from reconciliation.

'We that are young
Shall never see so much, nor live so long.'

The power of Edgar's disturbing statement – a statement that rings like a half-
open question – is that it carries no moral overtones at all. He does not suggest for
one moment that youth or age, seeing or not seeing, are in any way superior,
inferior, more desirable or less desirable one than the other. In fact we are com-
pelled to face a play which refuses all moralizing – a play which we begin to see
not as a narrative any longer, but as a vast, complex, coherent poem designed to

study the power and the emptiness of nothing – the positive and negative aspects latent in the zero. So what does Shakespeare say? What is he trying to teach us? Does he mean that suffering has a necessary place in life and is worth cultivating for the knowledge or inner development it brings? Or does he mean us to understand that the age of titanic suffering is now over and our role is that of the eternally young? Wisely, Shakespeare refuses to answer. But he has given us his play, and its whole field of experience is both question and answer. In this light, the play is directly related to the most burning themes of our time, the old and the new in relation to our society, our arts, our notions of progress, our way of living our lives. If the actors are interested, this is what they will bring out. If we are interested, that is what we will find. Fancy dress, then, will be left far behind. The meaning will be for the moment of the performance. [. . .]

From **R. A. Foakes, *Hamlet versus Lear: Cultural Politics and Shakespeare's Art*** (Cambridge: Cambridge University Press, 1993), pp. 70–1, 73–4.

Foakes, a critic, editor and theatre historian, deftly outlines here the ways in which literary critics and theorists since 1945 have insisted that *King Lear* replace *Hamlet* as Shakespeare's most important, most representative and, to use Kott's term, most 'contemporary' work.

[. . .] Only after the outbreak of the Second World War was serious attention given to the 'political chaos' shown in the play, and Edmund, Goneril and Regan began to be seen as precursors of the machiavellian 'realpolitik' associated with fascism and Nazism. The mythological distancing of Lear as embodying 'Man's tragic fate' or pilgrimage towards redemption insulated him from any direct link with modern tyrannies, and his world was identified with an old order (a benevolent medieval one in John Danby's view) which was under attack by new forces representing a ruthless, competitive capitalism. It was not until about 1960 and after that the play began to be considered in direct relation to a new political consciousness engendered by the Cold War, the rediscovery of the Holocaust, the renewed interest in Hiroshima, and the development of the hydrogen bomb, and then the building of the Berlin Wall. In this context the tyranny and obsession with power of Lear himself became more noticeable, and the similarity between his behaviour and that of Goneril and Regan, emphasized by Peter Brook in his 1962 production, turned the play, as noted earlier, into a bleak vision of negation. During the 1960s critics found confirmation of bleakness in their readings of the text in the various editions of the full play, usually a composite version amalgamating Quarto and Folio texts. Their emphasis tended to be less political than Brook's (he saw a Stalinist figure in Lear), and more concerned with the indifference of the gods and the frailty of human life. In other words, the new political emphasis fostered by Kott and Brook was transmuted into metaphysical terms, with Lear progressing towards despair rather than towards redemption.

Since the culmination of nihilistic readings of *King Lear* in Edward Bond's reworking of the play (1970) as celebrating violence in a contemporary world perceived as dedicated to violence, there has been a retreat from such essentially pessimistic interpretations. Deconstructive critics have found a radical instability in the play that permits no confidence in any particular reading, and the sense of instability has been reinforced by the revival of interest by textual scholars in the differences between the Quarto and Folio texts, and the evidence that Shakespeare or someone else revised the play, effectively creating two different but perhaps equally valid versions. [. . .]

[. . .] During the 1980s all four approaches, political/nihilistic, deconstructive, revisionary and feminist, whatever their differences, have contributed to a redefining of the nature and status of *King Lear*, in what they see as a process of liberating us from an allegiance to such static notions as the truth or autonomy or coherence of the play, into a recognition of contradictions in it, of ranges of possible meanings, indefiniteness, and the clash of ideological stances. [. . .]

But if the reaction of critics from the 1960s to the 1980s can be seen, however indirectly, as affected by the political situation of those decades, what can be said of the earlier criticism of *King Lear*? How could criticism remain so apparently unconcerned with political issues for so long, roughly from 1800 to the 1950s? Perhaps that is the wrong question to ask, though it is implicit in the assumption of some cultural materialists that earlier critics used texts like *King Lear* to perpetuate an imperialist ideology: 'Shakespeare, as a central component of British culture, has inevitably been incorporated into the dominant ideology and made an instrument of hegemony.'[1] A more sophisticated view is presented by Jonathan Dollimore, who argues that both traditional Christian redemptionist readings of *King Lear*, and liberal humanist interpretations that emphasize instead Lear's growth in stature through heroic endurance of suffering, are two sides of the same coin, and both need to be contested by a materialist account that stresses the play's concern with 'power, property and inheritance'.[2]

From **Kathleen McLuskie, 'The Patriarchal Bard'** (1985), in *Political Shakespeare: Essays in Cultural Materialism*, ed. Jonathan Dollimore and Alan Sinfield, 2nd edn (Manchester: Manchester University Press, 1994), pp. 98–9, 102

At the forefront of feminist criticism for the last two decades, McLuskie was one of the first critics to examine *King Lear* in terms of what it tells us about Shakespeare's, and our own, views on gender differences (see Key Passages on pp. 102–9, 113–15, 126–9, 135–40, 147–54 and 157–8).

1 [Foakes's note.] David Margolies, 'Teaching a Handsaw to Fly: Shakespeare as a Hegemonic Instrument', in Holderness, ed., *The Shakespeare Myth*, pp. 42–53, citing p. 43.
2 [Foakes's note.] Jonathan Dollimore, *Radical Tragedy* (Brighton: Harvester Press, 1984; 2nd edn, 1989), p. 197.

[. . .] In *Measure for Measure* the pleasure denied is the pleasure of comedy, a pleasure many feminists have learned to struggle with as they withhold their assent from the social approval of sexist humour. A much more difficult pleasure to deny is the emotional, moral and aesthetic satisfaction afforded by tragedy. Tragedy assumes the existence of 'a permanent, universal and essentially unchanging human nature'[1] but the human nature implied in the moral and aesthetic satisfactions of tragedy is most often explicitly male. In *King Lear* for example, the narrative and its dramatisation present a connection between sexual insubordination and anarchy, and the connection is given an explicitly misogynist emphasis.

The action of the play, the organisation of its point of view and the theatrical dynamic of its central scenes all depend upon an audience accepting an equation between 'human nature' and male power. In order to experience the proper pleasures of pity and fear, they must accept that fathers are owed particular duties by their daughters and be appalled by the chaos which ensues when those primal links are broken. Such a point of view is not a matter of consciously-held opinion but it is a position required and determined by the text in order for it to make sense. It is also the product of a set of meanings produced in a specific way by the Shakespearean text and is different from that produced in other versions of the story.

The representation of patriarchal misogyny is most obvious in the treatment of Goneril and Regan. In the chronicle play *King Leir*, the sisters' villainy is much more evidently a function of the plot. Their mocking pleasure at Cordella's downfall takes the form of a comic double act and Regan's evil provides the narrative with the exciting twist of an attempt on Lear's life.[2] In the Shakespearean text by contrast, the narrative, language and dramatic organisation all define the sisters' resistance to their father in terms of their gender, sexuality and position within the family. Family relations in this play are seen as fixed and determined, and any movement within them is portrayed as a destructive reversal of rightful order (see I.iv). Goneril's and Regan's treatment of their father merely reverses existing patterns of rule and is seen not simply as cruel and selfish but as a fundamental violation of human nature – as is made powerfully explicit in the speeches which condemn them (III.vii.101–3; IV.ii.32–50). Moreover when Lear in his madness fantasises about the collapse of law and the destruction of ordered social control, women's lust is vividly represented as the centre and source of the ensuing corruption (IV.vi.110–28). The generalised character of Lear's and Albany's vision of chaos, and the poetic force with which it is expressed, creates the appearance of truthful universality which is an important part of the play's claim to greatness. However, that generalised vision of chaos is present in gendered terms in which patriarchy, the institution of male power in the family and the State, is seen as the only form of social organisation strong enough to hold chaos at bay. [. . .]

---

1   [McLuskie's note.] Raymond Williams, *Modern Tragedy* (London: Chatto, 1966), p. 45.
2   [McLuskie's note.] See *The True Chronicle History of King Lear*, ed. Geoffrey Bullough, *The Narrative and Dramatic Sources of Shakespeare*, vol. VII (London: Routledge, 1973), 337–402.

[. . .] A feminist reading of the text cannot simply assert the countervailing rights of Goneril and Regan, for to do so would simply reverse the emotional structures of the play, associating feminist ideology with atavistic selfishness and the monstrous assertion of individual wills. Feminism cannot simply take 'the woman's part' when that part has been so morally loaded and theatrically circumscribed. Nor is any purpose served by merely denouncing the text's misogyny, for *King Lear*'s position at the centre of the Shakespeare canon is assured by its continual reproduction in education and the theatre and is unlikely to be shifted by feminist sabre-rattling.

From **Coppélia Kahn, 'The Absent Mother in *King Lear*'** in *Rewriting the Renaissance: The Discourses of Sexual Difference in Early Modern Europe*, eds Margaret W. Ferguson, Maureen Quilligan and Nancy J. Vickers (Chicago: Ill.: University of Chicago Press, 1986), pp. 33–6.

A specialist in psychoanalytic criticism, Kahn offers here a very modern response to Shakespeare's treatment of the female, and the feminine, in *King Lear* (see Key Passages on **pp. 105–13, 126–9, 133–40** and **149–54**). Her persuasive theories about the effect of the 'absent mother' have since been used by numerous critics to examine many of Shakespeare's other plays, including his early comedies and late romances.

[. . .] By calling his sorrow hysterical ['*Hysterica passio*' in 2.2, Key Passage on p. 135] Lear decisively characterizes it as feminine, in accordance with a tradition stretching back to 1900 B.C. when an Egyptian papyrus first described the malady. Fifteen hundred years later in the writings of Hippocrates, it was named, and its name succinctly conveyed its etiology. It was the disease of the *hyster*, the womb. From ancient times through the nineteenth century, women suffering variously from choking, feelings of suffocation, partial paralysis, convulsions similar to those of epilepsy, aphasia, numbness, and lethargy were said to be ill of hysteria, caused by a wandering womb. What sent the womb on its errant path through the female body, people thought, was either lack of sexual intercourse or retention of menstrual blood. In both cases, the same prescription obtained: the patient should get married. A husband would keep that wandering womb where it belonged. If the afflicted already had a husband, concoctions either noxious or pleasant were applied to force or entice the recalcitrant womb to its proper location.[1]

In Shakespeare's time, hysteria was also called, appropriately, 'the mother.' Although Shakespeare may well have consulted a treatise by Edward Jordan called *A Brief Discourse of a Disease Called the Suffocation of the Mother*,

---

1 [Kahn's note.] See Ilza Veith, *Hysteria: The History of a Disease* (Chicago, Ill.: University of Chicago Press, 1965).

published in 1603, like anyone in his culture he would have understood 'the mother' in the context of notions about women. For hysteria is a vivid metaphor of woman in general, as she was regarded then and later, a creature destined for the strenuous bodily labours of childbearing and childrearing but nonetheless physically weaker than man. Moreover, she was, like Eve, temperamentally and morally infirm:—skittish, prone to err in all senses. Woman's womb, her justification and her glory, was also the sign and source of her weakness as a creature of the flesh rather than the mind or spirit. The very diversity of symptoms clustering under the name of hysteria bespeaks the capricious nature of woman. And the remedy—a husband and regular sexual intercourse—declares the necessity for male control of this volatile female element.[2] [. . .]

Now, it is interesting that there is no literal mother in *King Lear*. The earlier anonymous play that is one of Shakespeare's main sources opens with a speech by the hero lamenting the death of his 'dearest Queen'.[3] But Shakespeare, who follows the play closely in many respects, refers only once in passing to this queen. In the crucial cataclysmic first scene of his play, from which all its later action evolves, we are shown only fathers and their godlike capacity to make or mar their children. Through this conspicuous omission the play articulates a patriarchal conception of the family in which children owe their existence to their fathers alone; the mother's role in procreation is eclipsed by the father's, which is used to affirm male prerogative and male power.[4] The aristocratic patriarchal families headed by Gloucester and Lear have, actually and effectively, no mothers. The only source of love, power, and authority is the father—an awesome, demanding presence.

But what the play depicts, of course, is the failure of that presence: the failure of a father's power to command love in a patriarchal world and the emotional penalty he pays for wielding power.[5] Lear's very insistence on paternal power, in fact, belies its shakiness; similarly, the absence of the mother points to her hidden

---

2 [Kahn's note.] As Veith (ibid.) shows, during the Middle Ages, hysteria had ceased to be known as a disease and was taken as a visible token of bewitchment. Jordan wrote his treatise to argue for a distinction between the two. Both his work and the pamphlet by Samuel Harsnett denouncing the persecution of witches (from which Shakespeare took much of Poor Tom's language) have the effect of pointing up parallels between hysteria and witchcraft as deviant kinds of behavior associated with women, which are then used to justify denigrating women and subjecting them to strict control. [. . .]

3 [Kahn's note.] *The True Chronicle Historie of King Leir and His Three Daughters*, in *Narrative and Dramatic Sources of Shakespeare*, ed. Geoffrey Bullough, 7 vols. (New York, NY: Columbia University Press, 1973), 7: 337–402.

4 [Kahn's note.] In his brilliant and wide-ranging essay in [*Rewriting the Renaissance: The Discourses of Sexual Difference in Early Modern Europe*], '"Shaping Fantasies:" Figurations of Gender and Power in Elizabethan Culture', Louis Adrian Montrose explicates the patriarchal ideology threaded through *A Midsummer Night's Dream*, whereby the mother's part in procreation is occluded and men alone are held to 'make women, and make themselves through the medium of women'. He interprets this belief as 'an overcompensation for the natural fact that men do indeed come from women; an overcompensation for the cultural facts that consanguineal and affinal ties between men are established through mothers, wives, and daughters'.

5 [Kahn's note.] Murray Schwartz explored this idea in a series of talks given at the Center for the Humanities, Wesleyan University, February–April 1978.

presence, as the lines with which I began might indicate. When Lear begins to feel the loss of Cordelia, to be wounded by her sisters, and to recognize his own vulnerability, he calls his state of mind hysteria, 'the mother', which I interpret as his repressed identification with the mother. Women and the needs and traits associated with them are supposed to stay in their element, as Lear says, 'below'— denigrated, silenced, denied. In this patriarchal world, masculine identity depends on repressing the vulnerability, dependency, and capacity for feeling which are called 'feminine.'

From **Michael Warren, 'General Introduction', William Shakespeare: The Complete King Lear 1608–1623** (Berkeley, Calif./ London: University of California Press, 1989), p. xi

Warren, a textual critic, used his studies of the Quarto and Folio texts of *King Lear* to re-open in 1976 the centuries-old debate about Shakespeare's revision of his own plays. Warren's persuasive arguments led to a 'textual revolution' in the 1980s and 1990s that questioned the traditional concept of the 'mediating' editor who was required to reconstruct lost originals of Shakespeare's texts in order to produce an edition, rather than presenting the texts to readers as originally printed in Quarto and Folio form. Warren's *The Complete King Lear 1608–1623* offers unedited photographic facsimiles of the texts of Quartos 1 and 2 and the Folio.

No authorial manuscript of *King Lear* exists, and the earliest printed texts present scholars and editors with problems. The [1608] First Quarto prints approximately three hundred lines that are not in the [1623] First Folio; the First Folio prints approximately one hundred lines not in the First Quarto. There are, moreover, numerous individual verbal variants between the two texts. These complex variations make King Lear a crucial subject of study for bibliographers and textual critics, whose conclusions have important consequences for all who study and perform the play. What is the work called *King Lear*?

It has been the custom for textual critics and editors to posit an early single text of *King Lear*, applying critical principles 'to the textual raw material of the authoritative preserved documents in order to approach as nearly as may be to the ideal of the authorial fair [i.e. clean] copy by whatever necessary process of recovery, independent emendation, or conflation of authorities'.[1] In recent years, however, many scholars have challenged this objective, arguing that the single ideal text is not an object that can be reconstituted in this case; they have instead posited that the two relatively different texts called *King Lear* may be evidence for two stages in the existence of that work. The case for the First Folio text as an

---

1   [Warren's note.] Fredson Bowers, *Textual and Literary Criticism* (Cambridge, 1959), p. 120.

authorial revision of an earlier version represented by the First Quarto has been strongly argued.[2] [. . .]

From **Terence Hawkes, *William Shakespeare: King Lear*** (Plymouth: Northcote House, 1995), pp. 61–2

> Hawkes, a 'Cultural Materialist' who examines Shakespeare's works through a cultural, sociological and political perspective, is one of the leading figures in modern theoretical studies of literature. Here he politicises the views of Michael Warren and his followers who argue against reconstructing lost original texts of Shakespeare's.

[. . .] There is no final 'play itself' to which we can at last turn, when all the different readings of it are done. There is no 'original' text which Shakespeare uncomplicatedly thought up, and wrote down, which remains always the same, and to which access is immediate and complete, regardless of time, place, or specific circumstance. That is, there is no 'ideal' *King Lear*.

What does exist is a material object, or set of objects, on which we can and do operate in order to produce a range of 'meanings' in aspects of which our society from time to time chooses to invest. The shift of emphasis involved here is crucial: it moves our attention from a concern with sameness to a concern with difference. That is, it abandons an idealized notion of an unchanging super-being called 'Shakespeare' who bequeathed us permanent masterpieces which speak to and derive from our enduring nature. In its place, it sets the proposition that all of us – even 'Shakespeare' – of necessity have our being in the flow of time called 'history', a situation whose main effect is to impose change and so differences upon us. To accept this alteration of emphasis is to propose that to some degree it is we who 'produce' King Lear, we who 'construct' it in whatever form the prejudices and pressures of our own time dictate. We, to that extent, and to stretch the point, for the sake of argument, almost to absurdity, are not far from being effectively the 'authors' of the play. As a result, the question 'what does King Lear mean?' makes much less sense than the more appropriate 'what do we mean by *King Lear*?'.

It should be made clear that 'we' here does not refer to us as individual beings. The argument is not that each of us constructs our own individual *King Lear* for our own individual purposes: far from it. 'We' refers to our culture at large, our way of life, the collective view of the world our society has arrived at and agreed upon in a particular place at a particular time. That notion of 'we' allows us to

2 [Warren's note.] Michael J. Warren, 'Quarto and Folio King Lear and the Interpretation of Albany and Edgar', in *Shakespeare, Pattern of Excelling Nature*, ed. David Bevington and Jay L. Halio (Newark, Del., 1978), pp. 95–107; Steven Urkowitz, *Shakespeare's Revision of "King Lear"* (Princeton, 1980); Gary Taylor, 'The War in *King Lear*', in *Shakespeare Survey 33*, ed. Kenneth Muir (Cambridge, 1980), pp. 27–34; *The Division of the Kingdoms: Shakespeare's Two Versions of 'King Lear'*, ed. Gary Taylor and Michael Warren (Oxford, 1983).

generalize about societies in a way that might begin to explain why a *King Lear* in the eighteenth century is something very different from a *King Lear* in the twentieth century and why, most importantly, neither of them can claim to be the 'real' or the 'right' one. There is, in this view, no such thing as the 'real' or the 'right' version of the play: not even 'Shakespeare's' version could make that claim.

This, of course, is a case made from a specific position and perhaps it is helpful at this stage broadly to label it a 'Cultural Materialist' one. The focus of such an approach will always, of course, be on the ways in which a play such as *King Lear* is processed by a society—whether an early modern society, an eighteenth-century one, or our own—rather than on any mythical 'play itself'.

The Work in Performance

King Lear on Stage

The performance of *King Lear* 'before the Kings Maiestie at Whitehall upon S[t]. Stephan's night in Christmas Holidayes' in 1606 may not have been its first. Whether the play was first performed at the public Globe theatre, used by the Chamberlain's (later the King's) Men from 1599, or at Whitehall or any other private residence, Shakespeare may have slightly altered it in moving it from one venue to another. From 1609, the King's Men also turned the old Blackfriars abbey banqueting hall (north across the River Thames from the Globe) into their private indoor theatre; however, they continued to use the outdoor Globe. Private audiences were used to more spectacular, and costly, stage effects, costumes and music than those used in public theatres, and it is tempting to wonder how the staging of *King Lear* changed in a private playhouse. For example, the storm scenes could probably have become more realistic and frightening at Blackfriars, which had the luxury of dimmable lighting (using candles) and better stage effects, than at the Globe, where all performances took place in the natural light of the afternoon. In its earliest performances, Richard Burbage, leading actor with the King's Men for a decade and no longer able to perform younger roles like Henry V, almost certainly performed as Lear, and Robert Armin, the resident comic actor, as the Fool, and other roles were taken by members of the company. The play's portrayal of the punishment of the wicked would have suited audiences and government officials who were becoming increasingly puritanical in their views. Thus the play was probably performed until the closing of the theatres in 1642.

After the reopening of the theatres in 1660, we know of at least two professional London productions, in 1664 and 1675, but as Restoration taste and sensibility were more 'refined' the text was probably heavily cut and perhaps altered. The printing of the First Folio in 1623 had been followed in the next fifty years by the publication of the Second, Third and Fourth Folios. Editors also began to prepare their own collected edition of Shakespeare's works, with the first appearing in 1709, and successive editions proliferated throughout the eighteenth century. As a result of this sudden increase in editions of Shakespeare, many of which claimed to present the latest version as acted in London, theatrical audiences in the Restoration period and eighteenth century held the majority of Shakespeare's plays, with the exception of *King Lear*, in high regard.

In 1681, Nahum Tate rewrote and sentimentalised *King Lear* (see **pp. 75–6**) to suit the sensibilities of those in his generation and to rescue Shakespeare, in his opinion, from his own shortcomings. After suffering through the actual horrors of the civil war and its aftermath from 1640 to 1660, Restoration and later audiences especially wanted to see comedies such as Aphra Behn's *The Rover* or R. B. Sheridan's *The Rivals* and not the kind of gruesome and continual horrors of *King Lear*. The introduction of actresses to the professional stage also meant that female roles, such as Cordelia, Goneril and Regan, could be enlarged and reshaped. The proscenium-arch theatre became the norm, with indoor lighting by candles and extravagant costumes and sets, including backdrop scenery, making productions more elaborate. Tate followed Shakespeare in showing the defeat and imprisonment of Lear and Cordelia but used the sources to justify Lear and Cordelia's eventual return to the throne after their rescue by the 'rebel' Edgar and Albany. Most strikingly, Tate cut the role of the Fool and increased Cordelia's role so that, contrary to Shakespeare's play, she remains a constant presence throughout and ultimately is betrothed to Edgar. This was also the age of the celebrity actor, and David Garrick and John Philip Kemble, among others, became famous for their portrayals of Tate's Lear.

Tate's revisions proved so successful that Shakespeare's text ceased to be performed on the London stage, and at least two other authors 'revived', to use Tate's word, the play with their own alterations. One was the writer George Colman, who claimed that Tate had desecrated Shakespeare's original play but none the less adapted it himself. Colman particularly objected to Cordelia and Edgar's love affair and to the intensified evil of Goneril and Regan, concluding in the preface to his 1768 edition, 'I have now endeavoured to purge the tragedy of Lear of the alloy of Tate, which has so long been suffered to debase it'.[1] But otherwise he followed Tate's revisions. From 1756, the great actor David Garrick had a memorable success in the title role of Colman's version of the play, although Garrick had earlier felt free to adapt Tate's version to suit himself and published it in 1786. Garrick's and Colman's revisions of Tate were apparently enough to satisfy those who objected to Tate. However, as noted by William Macready, the play was prohibited from performance for several years before the death of King George III in 1820, as the staged madness of King Lear too closely resembled the real madness of King George.

The success of these 'revived' and altered versions continued until the early nineteenth century, when, as Jacky Bratton and Christie Carson note in *The Cambridge 'King Lear' CD-ROM*,[2] some actors and directors began to reinsert Shakespeare's tragic ending into Colman's or Tate's version. Most famous of

1   Colman, 'Advertisement', *The History of King Lear. As it is performed at the Theatre Royal in Covent Garden, and Altered by George Colman* (Dublin: Printed for James Hoey and John Exshaw, 1768) p. vi.
2   Carson and Bratton, ed., *The Cambridge 'King Lear' CD-Rom: Text and Performance Archive* (Cambridge: Cambridge University Press, 2000).

these was Edmund Kean, an actor especially renowned for his tragic acting abilities and whose performance of Hamlet inspired John Keats to expound the theory of 'negative capability'. Finally, 153 years after Tate's revision appeared, Macready presented his first 'restored' version of Shakespeare's text in 1834 (see **pp. 79–80**). However, it was not until four years later that he returned the character of the Fool to Shakespeare's play, eventually travelling with this production to New York. By this time, with Romanticism's value of unbridled and spontaneous emotion, which the Fool represents, as well as the establishment by Romantic critics and poets of new principles for editing his texts, Shakespeare could fit firmly into cultural context and be appreciated for his accomplishments. The florid, exaggerated acting style of the eighteenth century also gave way to a quieter, more reflective style embodied by Kean, Macready and, in America, Edwin Booth (the brother of John Wilkes Booth, the assassin of Abraham Lincoln). Throughout the rest of the century, various combinations of Colman's, Tate's, Macready's and Shakespeare's versions of the play were performed on average at least once a year in England, the United States, Australia and other English-language countries.

By the beginning of the twentieth century, and the rise of the 'new bibliography', which set strict limits on importing dubious material or refining the text according to changing taste, Shakespeare's texts became standardised. Although scholars considered the printing of the 1608 Quarto 1 of *King Lear* to be unauthorised until Peter Blayney demonstrated otherwise in 1982,[3] they routinely created a 'conflated' (or patched-together) text of the play by combining the 'best' passages from the Quarto 1 and the First Folio texts. Although any editor's given text could vary slightly from another's, the text of the play became stable enough for actors, stage directors and film-makers generally to have the same material from which to work. The textual inventions of the seventeenth and eighteenth centuries were now a thing of the past, and actors and directors could concentrate, as the critic A. C. Bradley had, on the play's characters. John Gielgud (**pp. 82–3**), Donald Wolfit, Laurence Olivier (**pp. 84–5**), and Michael Redgrave, among others, acted the role in this traditional way. Peter Brook's 1962 searing production for the Royal Shakespeare Company with Paul Scofield as Lear toured the world and changed the approach of theatre directors, actors and audiences not only to *King Lear* but also to staging theatre in general. Extravagant sets, properties and costumes, and complicated bits of stage business were replaced by minimal sets, sometimes imaginary properties and dull or plain costumes, and the focus returned to the language and its meanings. As Richard Eyre and Nicholas Wright note below (**p. 85**), this was Shakespeare stripped bare. Although burdened with following Scofield, Michael Gambon, Brian Cox, Robert Stephens and, more recently, Ian Holm (**p. 92**) and Nigel Hawthorne have found their own postmodern interpretations of the role in English stage productions. In America, John Colicos, Lee J. Cobb and James Earl Jones also played Lear. But it was the actor Morris Carnovsky (blacklisted as a result of the McCarthy witch-hunt)

---

3   Blayney, *The Texts of King Lear and Their Origins* (Cambridge: Cambridge University Press, 1982).

who brought the real pathos of the Cold War age to Lear's suffering in a series of stage productions from 1963 to 1975, inspiring a new generation of American actors to train as Shakespeareans.

George Colman was not the last to adapt Shakespeare's play to suit his generation's sensibilities. Edward Bond's radical rewriting of the play in 1971 (**pp. 89–90**) shocked audiences with its graphic displays of torture, rape and other forms of physical brutality. Bond's *Lear*, almost certainly a product of the risks taken by Brook and his followers in postmodernising the staging of Shakespeare's play, may have contributed to the return in the 1980s and 1990s of more sedate or traditional productions of *King Lear*, including those using either the Quarto 1 or the Folio text of the play. However, most subsequent productions, however traditional, seem to be overlaid with Brook's influence, so that Lear now exists in a postmodern world of dysfunctional families, gender discrimination and a deep-seated suspicion of government in general and political hierarchy in particular.

King Lear on Screen

As noted by Bratton and Carson, the earliest film of *King Lear*, made in 1909 by the Vitagraph Company of America, was followed in the next year by French and Italian films. Due to the limitations of the period, these brief silent films used heavily cut texts. For example, the Italian film, *Re* [King] *Lear*, starring the stage actor Ermete Novelli and directed by Gerolamo Lo Savio, runs only about fifteen minutes, yet covers the main plot points, with the characters of Gloucester, Edgar and Edmund entirely cut. The film is tremendously moving, even though the actors use the exaggerated pantomime gestures common in silent films.

The first modern screen adaptation was a 1953 American production for television, at that time a fledgling industry which presented productions live, rather than on tape as is common today. The director of this pioneering film was, not surprisingly, Peter Brook. In the title role was Orson Welles, co-founder of the famous Mercury Theater acting company and director of his own films of *Macbeth*, *Othello* and *Chimes at Midnight*, a reworking of the *Henry IV* plays, as well as *Citizen Kane*. This production ran for only seventy-three minutes to suit the limitations of television, and as the characters of Edmund and Edgar had been cut Oswald replaced Edmund as villain. Brook departed from his usually modern or non-time-specific costuming style and dressed his actors in traditional Elizabethan clothes, possibly because his American audience had watched in the same year the televised coronation of Queen Elizabeth II, full of traditional English ritual and costume. Tony Howard credits 'Brook's interpretation, Welles's barnstorming presence, and the compromises forced by a commercial medium' for shaping the final product, which received mixed reviews.[4]

The most innovative film of the play, with a pounding score by Dmitry

---

4   Howard, 'When Peter Met Orson: The 1953 CBS *King Lear*', in *Shakespeare, the Movie: Popularising the Plays on Film, TV, and Video*, ed. Lynda E. Boose and Richard Burt (London: Routledge, 1997), pp. 122, 126–7.

Shostakovich, appeared in 1970 in Russian and was directed by the highly regarded Grigori Kozintsev (see **pp. 88–9**), whose 1964 film of *Hamlet* had already dazzled audiences. His black-and-white film of *King Lear* presented a lean, energetic Yuri Yarvet in the title role, ruling over a bleak, rocky countryside dominated by a fortress, outside which are the poor, sick subjects who have made a pilgrimage to seek his help. Kozintsev used Boris Pasternak's modern Russian translation of the text, although English subtitles provided Shakespeare's text when the play was eventually distributed. The director was heavily influenced by Brook's 1962 production, which he had seen in Moscow in 1964, and through him by the work of Jan Kott. Kozintsev emphasised Lear's crumbling world as resulting from the break-up of the feudal system, in which peasants are no longer willing to keep their assigned place and instead try to revolt. The very fortress that protects him from his starving peasants ultimately traps him, as he finds the dead Cordelia hanging from one of its towers. The film ends without any dialogue or even voice-overs after the death of Lear and his daughters, and instead the camera lingers on an overwhelmed Edgar watching the peasants scavenge through the rubble for food.

Kozintsev's 1970 film was not widely distributed outside the Soviet Union, and

Figure 4 **Grigori Kozintsev, dir., *King Lear* (1970 film). The capture of Cordelia (Valentina Shendrikova) and Lear (Yuri Yarvet) in Act 5, Scene 3. © Lenfilm. Courtesy of the Kobal Collection.**

thus it did not deflate the acclaim awarded to Brook's 1971 film, adapted from his stage production. As Kozintsev had done, Brook filmed his movie in black and white, but set it in the Celtic era, using bleak, frozen wintry locations in Jutland and a sharply cut and conflated text to give the story a sense of frigidity, sterility and repression. Lear's subjects were numbly and silently huddled together as labour-camp prisoners, and Paul Scofield's unemotional, spare performance set the tone for a drained, terse and abrupt series of catastrophes. His Lear is a ruthless dictator who needs a public display of obedience from his daughters not to reassure himself of their love but to instil fear in any of those watching who may be plotting his overthrow. Lear explodes into riotous behaviour at Goneril's home, his rage and impatience always threatening and absolute. He only becomes mad once he wanders on to the heath, especially in confronting Poor Tom, wearing a Christ-like crown of thorns. Brook succeeded in presenting the poetic language as everyday prose, relieving the film of the type of self-conscious verse technique common in stage productions in the early twentieth century.

In the film, Brook is particularly adept at intercutting the action with flashbacks in which we read the characters' internal thoughts; for example, during the mock-trial of Goneril and Regan, Brook briefly intercuts a scene from Lear's love-test

Figure 5 **Peter Brook, dir., *King Lear* (1971 film). Lear (Paul Scofield) confronts his huddled and silent subjects. © Filmways/ Athena/Lanterna. Courtesy of the Kobal Collection.**

with Cordelia in Act 1, Scene 1. We then see Lear recognise that his first mock-trial was of Cordelia, and that her crimes pale in comparison to her sisters'. Brook prepares his audience for the horrific cruelty of Gloucester's blinding by having Cornwall apply a branding iron to Gloucester's eye in darkness (his screams are audible) and then shows Cornwall pulling the other eye out in a close-up. Brook followed the conclusion as printed in the Folio which allows Lear to die believing that Cordelia is still breathing, and which gives the play's final lines to Edgar, and not to Albany, as in Quarto 1. Ultimately his film suggests some catharsis for the audience, which is denied in Kozintsev's film.

The esteemed Japanese film director Akiro Kurosawa followed these two films of *King Lear* with *Ran* in 1985, placing the story of Lear in a feudal Japan in which the king must use his samurai to battle the cruelty of his daughters. Kurosawa's international success with this film demonstrates that Shakespeare's text can be made fluid enough to suit any examination of family strife, regardless of time or place. For example, Jean-Luc Godard's 1987 film adaptation of the play, subtitled 'Fear and Loathing', offers a rambling series of monologues by Norman Mailer, as Don Learo, as well as Godard, Burgess Meredith and Woody Allen, among others, on how modern images are now 'born from reconciliation of two realities'. Despite the critical success of the Kozinstsev, Brook and Kurosawa films, later television adaptations (most of which are currently available on video or DVD) returned to more traditional productions of the play.

In 1982, the BBC Shakespeare series version followed the text faithfully, setting it not in the Jacobean period but in the one that followed, ruled by James's son Charles I, whose misrule would lead to his execution and the chaos of the civil war. The characters dress in the severe black clothing and white lace collars of the Puritans, and their close confinement within a dark, interior room and their almost frozen positions suggest that they are trapped within a baroque painting in the style of Rembrandt. The staging emphasises the restriction, darkness and severity of Lear's kingdom, with the actors portraying their characters as logical and rarely emotional. Michael Hordern's Lear is similarly contained as the play opens but increasingly suffers tantrums as it progresses. This television film offers no attempt at realism, as it does not use outdoor locations but remains within the same restricted set throughout, even in the heath scenes. This Lear is not particularly mad but badly behaved, and the mock-trial is portrayed in a calm, rational way. Lear dies believing that Cordelia is alive, Edgar speaks the final scenes and the claustrophobic production comes to an end.

Laurence Olivier's portrayal of Lear in a 1983 film for Granada Television was directed by Michael Elliot. This Lear rules over a Celtic Britain, holding court in a set resembling Stonehenge, as an over-indulgent father who speaks his responses of 'Nothing' so slowly and affectionately that he seems to be coaching Cordelia on how to respond properly in her love-test. Goneril and Regan also shower this Lear and Cordelia with affection in Act 1, Scene 1, and the film focuses more on the nature of hypocrisy than of pure evil. John Hurt plays the Fool as a young, very loving surrogate of Cordelia, moved by Lear's (and Olivier's) obvious physical frailty and confusion. Olivier's Lear is very emotional, his tears flowing freely, with the result that his reunion with Cordelia and his grief at her death are very moving. Yet the film follows Quarto 1 in having Lear die believing that Cordelia is dead, and although he is told that Goneril and Regan have also died he is not confronted with their bodies. The final scene is encircled by candles at Stonehenge, suggesting that Lear and Cordelia are the sacrifices to the gods being offered at this Druid temple.

It was not until 1998, when Richard Eyre's 1997 Royal National Theatre production of the play was televised on BBC2, that *King Lear* on screen again became exciting, immediate and mesmerising. Although the television adaptation did not carry the power of the stage production, which was truly electric in the close confines of the Cottesloe Theatre, there is no denying the force of Ian Holm's portrayal of Lear. Whether brandishing a whip at Cordelia and Kent as he strides across a table in the first act, or recognising his madness while being cradled by a shell-shocked Edgar as Poor Tom in the third act, or sinking into despair when laying the dead body of Cordelia on to a cart alongside those of his other two daughters in the fifth act, Holm seems to encapsulate traditional and postmodern visions of Lear and the world he has created.

As Peter Brook's film shows, *King Lear* can be made immediate and postmodern, offering the audience the chance to see it 'in the moment' if they are 'interested' (as he states in the extract from his book *The Empty Space* above, **pp. 58–9**). As Richard Eyre's later stage and TV productions show, *King Lear* can be made new and revelatory, even in 1997 and 1998. The 'barnacles of theatricality,

Figure 6 **Richard Eyre, dir., *King Lear* (1998 BBC television film). Lear (Ian Holm) and his troublesome daughters, from left, Cordelia (Victoria Hamilton), Regan (Amanda Redman) and Goneril (Barbara Flynn). By permission of the BBC Photograph Library.**

style, and interpretation' can still fall away, as Alastair Macaulay notes below (p. 92), so that the play can 'live' in the line, becoming 'spontaneous' and 'new-minted'. *King Lear* in performance still carries with it the stamp of Shakespeare's age, but it has been infinitely renewable and powerful for every age since.

1681–1834: Tate's *King Lear* in Performance

From **Nahum Tate, *The History of King Lear, Acted at the Duke's Theatre. Reviv'd with Alterations*** (London: printed for E. Flesher, 1681), signatures A2r–v, A3r

> Although Tate kept intact most of Shakespeare's original plot points, other than the ending, he altered the play's structure, changed, cut or added characters, and modernised the language to suit Restoration taste. Surprisingly, he retained Act 3, Scene 7 (on **pp. 149–54**), showing Gloucester's blinding by Regan and Cornwall, perhaps because Gloucester deserved such punishment for abusing Edgar, now the romantic hero who pines for and rescues Cordelia three times. Tate has Goneril and Regan poison each other and Albany return the kingdom to Lear, who will make Cordelia his queen and betroth her to Edgar. In the epilogue, Cordelia graciously reminds the audience: 'Still so many Master-Touches shine/Of that vast Hand that first laid this Design.' The first passage is from Tate's Dedication to Thomas Boteler; the second is from Act 3, Scene 2, in which Edgar, disguised as Poor Tom, rescues Cordelia and her servant Arante from two 'ruffians'.

[. . .] Nothing but the Power of your Perswasion, and my Zeal for all the Remains of *Shakespear*, cou'd have wrought me to so bold an Undertaking. I found that the New-modelling of this Story, wou'd force me sometimes on the difficult Task of making the chiefest Persons speak something like their Character, on Matter whereof I had no Ground in my Author. *Lear's* real and *Edgar's* pretended Madness have so much of *extravagant Nature* (I know not how else to express it) as cou'd never have started but from our *Shakespear's* Creating Fancy. The Images and Language are so odd and suprizing, and yet so agreeable and proper, that whilst we grant that none but *Shakespear* cou'd have form'd such Conceptions, yet we are satisfied that they were the only Things in the World that ought to be said on those Occasions. I found the whole to answer your Account of it, a Heap of Jewels, unstrung and unpolisht; yet so dazling in their Disorder, that I soon perceiv'd I had seiz'd a Treasure. 'Twas my good Fortune to light on one Expedient to rectifie what was wanting in the Regularity and Probability of the Tale, which was to run through the whole, a *Love* betwixt *Edgar* and *Cordelia*, that never chang'd word with each other in the Original. This renders *Cordelia's* Indifference and her Father's Passion in the first Scene probable. It likewise gives Countenance to *Edgar's* Disguise, making that a generous Design that was before a poor Shift to save his Life. The Distress of the Story is evidently heightned by it; and it particularly gave Occasion of a New Scene or Two, of more Success (perhaps) than Merit. This Method necessarily threw me on making the Tale conclude in a Success to the innocent distrest Persons: Otherwise I must have incumbred the Stage with dead Bodies, which Conduct makes many Tragedies conclude with unseasonable Jests.

[. . .]

EDG.   O *Cordelia!*
COR.   Ha!—Thou knowst my Name.
EDG.   As you did once know *Edgar's*.
COR.   *Edgar!*
EDG.   The poor Remains of *Edgar*, what your Scorn
   Has left him.
COR.   Do we wake, *Arante?*
EDG.   My Father seeks my Life, which I preserv'd
   In hopes of some blest Minute to oblidge
   Distrest *Cordelia*, and the Gods have giv'n it;
   That Thought alone prevail'd with me to take
   This Frantick Dress, to make the Earth my Bed,
   With these bare Limbs all change of Seasons bide,
   Noons scorching Heat, and Midnights piercing Cold,
   To feed on Offals, and to drink with Herds,
   To Combat with the Winds, and be the Sport
   Of Clowns, or what's more wretched yet, their Pity.
AR.   Was ever Tale so full of Misery!
EDG.   But such a Fall as this I grant was due
   To my aspiring Love, for 'twas presumptuous,
   Though not presumptuously persu'd;
   For well you know I wore my Flames conceal'd,
   And silent as the Lamps that Burn in Tombs,
   'Till you perceiv'd my Grief, with modest Grace
   Drew forth the Secret, and then seal'd my Pardon.
[. . .] COR.   Come to my Arms, thou dearest, best of Men,
   And take the kindest Vows that e're were spoke
   By a protesting Maid.
EDG.   Is't possible?

From **Thomas Davies, *Dramatic Miscellanies***, Volume 2 (Dublin: printed for S. Price *et al.*, 1784), pp. 168–70, 180, 213

An actor and theatrical critic, Davies compares the performances of David Garrick and Barton Booth as Lear in Tate's version of the play.

[. . .] Till Tate produced his alterations of this play, it had to all appearance been laid aside and neglected as unprofitable to the players [. . .] Even Mr. Colman was, after mature deliberation, obliged to make Lear end happily. [. . .] The passion of Edgar and Cordelia is happily imagined; it strongly connects the main plot of the play [. . .] After those turbulent scenes of resentment, violence, disobedience, ingratitude, and rage, between Lear and his two eldest daughters, with the king's consequent agony and distraction, the unexpected interview of Cordelia and Edgar in act III. gives a pause of relief to the harassed distressed minds of the audience. It is a gleam of sunshine and a promise of fair weather in the midst of storm and tempest. I have seen this play represented twenty or thirty times, yet I can truly affirm that the spectators always dismissed the two lovers with the most rapturous applause [. . .]

The judgment of [Joseph] Addison, who has flatly given his opinion against Tate's alteration of the catastrophe, is not to be implicitly relied on [. . .]

The pathetic [Samuel] Richardson, in his [book] Clarissa, has embraced Addison's opinion, relative to the catastrophe of Lear. [. . .] I have heard certain critics complain, that, in pronouncing this denunciation, Garrick was too deliberate, and not so quick in the emission of his words as he ought to have been; that he did not yield to that impetuosity which his particular situation required. But we should reflect, that Lear is not agitated by one passion only, that he is not moved by rage, by grief, and indignation, singly, but by a tumultuous combination of them all together [. . .]

[. . .] Upon the whole, [Barton] Booth rendered the character of Lear more amiable, or, to speak critically, less terrible, than Garrick.—The latter went more deeply into his author's meaning; and expressed the various passions of the character with such truth and energy, that no audience ever saw him without astonishment as well as rapture. [. . .]

From Elizabeth Inchbald, Comments on King Lear; a Tragedy in Five Acts; by William Shakespeare. As Performed at the Theatres Royal, Drury Lane and Covent Garden (London: Longman, Hurst, Rees & Orme, 1807), pp. 4–5

Mrs Inchbald, a famous actress who first performed the role of Cordelia in 1772, discusses Tate's King Lear in performance.

[. . .] Not one of Shakespeare's plays more violently agitates the passions than this Tragedy; parents and children are alike interested in every character, and instructed by each. There is, nevertheless, too much of ancient cruelty in many of the events. An audience finds horror prevail over compassion, on Gloster's loss of his eyes: and though Dr. Johnson has vindicated this frightful incident, by saying 'Shakespeare well knew what would please the audience for which he wrote;' yet this argument is no apology for the correctors of Shakspeare, who have altered the Drama to gratify spectators more refined, and yet have not expunged this savage and improbable act. [. . .]

From **George Daniel, *King Lear: A Tragedy in Five Acts, by William Shakespeare*.** Printed from the Acting Copy, with remarks, biographical and critical, in *Cumberland's British Theatre*, Volume 6 (London: John Cumberland, 1830), p. 8

> Daniel reviews the late-eighteenth- and early-nineteenth-century portrayals of Lear by John Henderson, David Garrick, John Philip Kemble, George Frederick Cooke and Charles Mayne Young in Tate's version of the play and the portrayal by Edmund Kean in an 1824 production, which attached Shakespeare's tragic ending to Tate's version (for the scenes discussed, see Key Passages on **pp. 137–40, 162–8** and **173–9**).

[. . .] It is not on record who was the original representative of Lear. Nor do we know what succeeding actor rendered himself celebrated in the character, until Garrick drew the tears of the town. Henderson played it contemporary with Garrick, and almost divided the critics. By the death of Henderson, this tragedy remained lost to the stage, until an actor arose who carried the glory of Shakespeare beyond any preceding effort.

Kemble's Lear was a study for Michael Angelo – the Lady Macbeth of [Sarah] Siddons was not a more awful impersonation. His figure, countenance, and manner all conspired to give truth to the resemblance. His angry impatience,—'*The fiery* duke;' his incredulity,—'*Does Lear walk thus? Speak thus? Speak thus?*' His bitter irony,—'Dear daughter, I confess that I am old.' Who but remembers Kemble's look and voice when he uttered these heart-breaking words—

'I gave you *all!*'

But the climax of *all* acting was the curse upon Goneril. On his knees, bare-headed, his white locks streaming like a meteor to the troubled air; with heavenward eye, quivering lip, and hands clasped together in convulsive agony, he pronounced that terrible curse. In this instance, the actor almost divided the crown with the poet. The daring presumption that marred this glorious drama, deprived us of Mr Kemble's exertions in the scene where Lear enters bearing in the dead body of Cordelia. What this would have been in the hands of *such* an actor, we can only anticipate. But we deeply regret that Mr Kemble's correct taste did not brush away this vile interpolation, and restore the original text of Shakespeare.

Cooke gave the more unnameable parts of Lear's character with great effect; but he lost much of the tenderness, and all the dignity. Young plays it with his voice completely in *falsetto*. He wants the plaintive tremulous tones in Kemble. Kean's is, in truth—

'A very foolish fond old man;'

But he is not—

'Ev'ry inch *a king*.'

With what grandeur and pathos did Kemble pronounce these lines,—

'*The king* would speak with Cornwall: the *dear father*
Would with his *daughter* speak, *commands* her service.'

Mr Kean's dying scene (for, to his credit be it spoken, he plays the character nearly as Shakspeare wrote it), though somewhat deficient in power, is deeply affecting. We felt, when the curtain fell, as if we were relieved from some dreadful calamity, so strongly did his dying looks and agonising tones impress us when he faintly exclaimed.—

'Pray you undo this button. Thank you sir.
Do you see this? Look, in her,—look—her lips—
Look there—look there!' [. . .]

The Nineteenth Century: The Return of Shakespeare's *King Lear* to the Stage

From **[William]** *Macready's Reminiscences, and Selections from his Diaries and Letters*, ed. F. Pollock (London: Macmillan and Co., 1876), pp. 155–6, 318–19

In the first passage, Macready assesses previous actors in the role of Lear; in the second, from his diary, he discusses his performance of Lear in the first London production (at the Theatre Royal, Drury Lane) to restore most of Shakespeare's text.

[. . .] The performance of Tate's miserable debilitation and disfigurement of Shakespeare's sublime tragedy of 'King Lear' (adopted by Garrick, Kemble, etc) had been for several years interdicted at the theatres, as suggesting in its principal character a resemblance to the actual condition of the reigning sovereign, George III. His death this year (January 29th, 1820) caused the restriction to be removed [. . .]

Most actors, Garrick, Kemble and Kean among others, seemed to have based their conception of the character on the infirmity usually associated with 'fourscore and upwards,' and have represented the feebleness instead of the vigour of old age. But Lear's was in truth a 'lusty winter:' his language never betrays imbecility of mind or body. He confers his kingdom indeed on 'younger strengths:' but there is still sufficient invigorating him to allow him to ride, to hunt, to run wildly through the fury of the storm, to slay the ruffian who murdered his Cordelia, and to bear about her dead body in his arms [. . .] Indeed the towering rage of thought with which his mind dilates, identifying the heavens themselves with his griefs, and the power of conceiving such vast imaginings, would seem incompatible with a tottering, trembling frame, and betoken rather one of 'mighty bone and bold emprise', in the outward bearing of a grand old man. [. . .]

[23 May 1834] Went to the theatre; dressed; became excessively nervous; took wine; went on the stage—as nervous as the first night I acted in London, without the overbearing ardour that could free me from the thraldom of my fears. My performance in the two first acts was so unlike my rehearsal that, although I goaded myself to resistance by suggestions of my own reputation, of my wife and children's claims upon me, still I sunk under the idea that it was a failure. In the third act the audience struck me as being interested and attentive, and in the fourth and fifth, they broke out into loud applause; the last scene went tamely, but I was called for by my friends, and went on, was much applauded, and said that 'Gratified as I was by their approbation, I hoped, when relieved from the nervousness of a first appearance, to offer them a representation more worthy of their applause.'

This is the last of the great characters of Shakespeare that I have left unattempted – I do not feel that I have yet succeeded, but it is consoling to me to believe that I have not failed. [. . .]

Figure 7 King Lear (1892 stage production). A plate from the souvenir programme, showing Cordelia (Ellen Terry) and the ill Lear (Henry Irving) lovingly reunited in Act 4, Scene 7. By permission of the British Library, 11763.ee.2.

Henry Irving, Preface to *King Lear: A Tragedy in Five Acts*, by William Shakespeare, as arranged for the stage by Henry Irving, and presented at the Lyceum Theatre on November 10th 1892 (London: Nassau Steam Press, Ltd, 1892), p. 5

Irving was the dominant actor-director of the late Victorian and early Edwardian age. His production of *King Lear*, in which he played the title role, featured the most famous actress of the period, Ellen Terry, as Cordelia.

This version of Shakespeare's tragedy, *King Lear*, has been made for practical use on the stage, the play being necessarily reduced to reasonable length to suit the exigencies of the present time. In the curtailment, all superfluous horrors have been omitted.

As the period of *King Lear* is fabulous, I have chosen, at the suggestion of Mr. Ford Madox Brown (who has kindly designed three scenes in the First and Second Acts), a time shortly after the departure of the Romans, when the Britons would naturally inhabit the houses left vacant.

Modern Performance: Traditional and Radical *King Lear*

From **Harley Granville-Barker, *Prefaces to Shakespeare*** (London: Sidgwick & Jackson, Ltd, 1927), pp. 149–50, 206, 210, 212

Granville-Barker was the most important British theatre director and producer in the first half of the twentieth century. His *Prefaces to Shakespeare* was begun in 1927 as a volume discussing issues in staging particular Shakespeare plays, including *King Lear*, and expanded to several other volumes over the years. The *Prefaces* are still enormously influential on modern stage productions. Here he concentrates on scenes in the first three acts of *King Lear* (see Key Passages on **pp. 115–54**).

[. . .] while Act III is at the height of its argument, Shakespeare is careful to keep alive the lower-pitched theme of Edmund's treachery, his new turn to the betrayal of his father. He affords it two scenes, of twenty-five lines each, wedged between the three dominant scenes of the storm and Lear's refuge from it. They are sufficient and no more for their own purpose; in their sordidness they stand as valuable contrast to the spiritual exaltation of the others. The supreme moment for Lear himself, the turning-point, therefore, of the play's main theme, is reached in the second of the three storm scenes, when the proud old king kneels humbly and alone in his wretchedness to pray. This is the argument's absolute height; and from now on we may feel (as far as Lear is concerned) the tension relax, through the first grim passage of his madness, slackening still through the fantastic scene of the arraignment of the joint-stools before that [. . .] bench of justices, to the moment of his falling asleep and his conveyance away—his conveyance, we find it to be, out of the main stream of the play's action. Shakespeare then deals the dreadful blow to Gloucester. The very violence and horror of this finds its dramatic justification in the need to match in another sort—since he could not hope to match it in spiritual intensity—the catastrophe to Lear. And now we may imagine him, if we please, stopping to consider where he was. Anti-climax, after this, is all but inevitable. Let the producer take careful note how Shakespeare sets out to avoid the worst dangers of it.

[. . .] Gloucester himself is the play's nearest approach to the average sensual man. The civilised world is full of Gloucesters. In half a dozen short speeches Shakespeare sets him fully before us: turning elderly but probably still handsome; nice of speech if a little pompous; the accomplished courtier (he seems to be Lear's master of ceremonies); vain, as his mock modesty shows, but the joking shamelessness that succeeds it is mainly swagger; an egotist, and blind knowing least of what he should know most, of his two sons. [. . .]

Edmund is, in wickedness, half-brother to Iago. Having no such great nature as Othello's to work on, Shakespeare has no need of such transcendent villainy; and he lessens and vulgarises his man by giving him one of those excuses [i.e. his bastardy] for foul play against the world which a knave likes to find as a point of departure. [. . .]

Edgar is a 'slow starter' and shows no promise at all as a hero. The worth of Edgar waits discovery, and trial and misfortune must help discover it – to himself above all. [. . .]

But Edgar's philosophy of indifference to fortune, of patience with life itself, of the good comfort of fellowship, is now, certainly, to dominate the play. [. . .]

From **John Gielgud, *An Actor and His Time*** (London: Penguin, 1981), pp. 110–12

> Gielgud first performed the role of Lear in 1931, then again in 1940, 1950 and 1955, and in a radio adaptation in 1993. Here he reflects on his acclaimed 1940 portrayal of Lear in a production directed by Lewis Casson and Harley Granville-Barker at the Old Vic Theatre, London (see Key Passages on **pp. 102–9 and 126–9**).

[. . .] Someone afterwards said that Granville-Barker spoiled my first entrance in *Lear* by ignoring the convention that the leading character should always come on from the centre. But in *Lear* the throne has to be in the centre for the opening scene. [Henry] Irving got round the problem by coming down a great staircase at the side of the throne, but I've seen a drawing showing that he also sat at one side of the stage. Granville-Barker put the throne dead centre, with the six seats, for the other principal characters, placed three on each side of Lear, and the whole

Figure 8 *King Lear* **(1960 RSC stage production). Lear (John Gielgud), holding the joint-stool, tells Edgar (Harry Andrews), the Fool (Alan Badel) and Kent (Andrew Cruikshank) how to conduct the mock-trial of Goneril and Regan in Act 3, Scene 6. Image: Angus McBean. © Royal Shakespeare Company.**

scene worked out in an absolutely symmetrical way. He declared that the much-held view that the first act of *Lear* is impossible, that Shakespeare wrote a ridiculous story, was nonsense. He told us to think of it as something from the Old Testament or one of the great fairy stories – 'Once upon a time there was an old king with three daughters' – and it illuminated it for us all. [. . .]

After rehearsal, Granville-Barker would say, 'You did some very good things today, I hope you know what they were,' and would then produce a page of shattering, critical notes, which I wrote down at the time. I once asked him about the scene when Goneril is cursed by Lear and he leaves the stage on a very high note. A few lines later he returns in a totally different mood, in tears. 'What! Fifty of my followers at a clap, Within a fortnight?' I asked Granville-Barker how Lear knows about the dismissal of his followers. Who told him? Granville-Barker replied that it does not matter. There is, he said, no off-stage time in Shakespeare: it did not come in until Ibsen, Pinero, Galsworthy and Shaw. In their plays you leave the stage to write a letter, stay off the stage for exactly the ten minutes it takes to write the letter and then come back. But Shakespeare knew how to convey an effect of time passing without realism. In this particular case the audience accepts the fact at once that somebody has told Lear the news offstage. In the same way Macbeth and Hamlet become older during the course of the plays, but we are not sure of their exact ages – whether Hamlet is very young, or thirty, as the grave-digger says – or of the actual lapse of time, though it is obvious in *Hamlet* that a considerable time passes during the action. In *Macbeth*, also, the last act is usually played as if months, or possible a year or two, have passed. Shakespeare does it in a very simple way, knowing that the audience will not be aware of such exact details while they are watching, whereas critics, students and experts have spent years trying to work out the niceties of time – whether Cassio could actually have had time to seduce Desdemona, and so on.

For this privileged production we had a splendid cast – Fay Compton [as Regan], Jessica Tandy [as Cordelia], Cathleen Nesbitt [as Goneril], Robert Harris, Jack Hawkins, Stephen Haggard – and there was a tremendous feeling of urgency and excitement. It seemed to take our minds off the awful things that were happening in France. When people used to come round I would say: 'How can you stand seeing so agonizing a play when such terrible things are going on in the world?' and they would answer that it gave them a kind of courage. It was a catharsis; you felt at the end of the play that the old man had learnt something from all the ghastly things that had happened to him, and the glory of the play and its magnificent poetry took you out of yourself. Shakespeare has always had that extraordinary appeal for every kind of audience. [. . .]

From **Ivor Brown, 'The Old Vic *King Lear*'** (1946), starring Laurence Olivier, in *The Masque*, 1 (1946), pp. 3, 14–15

> Here Brown considers the impact of Laurence Olivier's production of *King Lear* on an audience that has survived the global traumas of the Second World War (see Key Passages on **pp. 126–40 and 168–79**).

When the New Theatre opened for the booking of seats for the 'Old Vic's' production of *King Lear* in the autumn of 1946 some enthusiasts insisted on queueing all night and the house was soon sold far ahead. That may have been a salute directed more towards Laurence Olivier than towards William Shakespeare; but it was certainly a sign of the times, of times, that is to say, in which *Lear* is no longer dismissed as unactable or treated as endurable only in a completely garbled text. We live in harder years and amid more horrifying circumstances than our forefathers, who found this huge, relentless tragedy either too fierce a thistle to be grasped by the actor or too ugly a cactus to be enjoyed by a public which preferred its theatre to be orchidaceous. Now with the terrors of the atom bomb on one side, and with the magnetism of Mr Olivier on the other, we have altered all that. Let the hurricane whistle and roar, let Gloucester's eyes be gouged out like jellies, let mortals die like flies beneath the thumbs of wanton boys; Britain can take it.

[. . .] The part of Cordelia is bound to be a little dull, at least until the death-scene: one could note how beautifully Mr Olivier played the finale with Miss Joyce Redman. The positions of that pathetic pair were beautifully devised. The Goneril and Regan of Miss Pamela Brown and Miss Margaret Leighton were more carefully developed; no slurring of the parts, as being just bits of the plot, was allowed. Both actresses created studies in evil that were memorably keen and livid, and this section of the play, sometimes cut and hurried through, were given full value. This was the tale of Lear and his daughters – all of them.

Then the Fool; a Fool out of France, a timid, plaintive, endearing fragment of pathetic clownship, a magnificent Fool. Mr Alec Guinness [. . .] gave us a most memorable performance of a part which nearly always defeats the actor. [. . .] This Fool, who looked like something strayed from a medieval French mumming [i.e. a dumb show], was immensely human too, a creature living beyond time and place, the tragic clown of all ages, the he-who-gets-slapped, a wind-and-the-rain outcast, living and jesting on a diet of bitter herbs, sometimes finding favour and reward, sometimes the whip. [. . .]

And Mr Olivier himself? Always he touches nothing he does not humanise. Here was an old and testy curmudgeon of a king, veritably breaking and wounding himself on the flints of his own folly, most believable in his vanity and petulance, infinitely pathetic in his final collapse. [. . .]

From **Richard Eyre and Nicholas Wright, *Changing Stages: A View of British Theatre in the Twentieth Century*** (London: Bloomsbury, 2000), p. 50

Eyre, an extremely successful theatre, film, TV and opera director, and former Artistic Director of the Royal National Theatre in London, and the playwright Wright succinctly discuss the enormous impact of Brook's stage production of *King Lear*.

[. . .] Peter Brook's 1962 production of *King Lear* with Paul Scofield redefined the play for several generations. 'I think for me everything shifted around the time of *King Lear*,' said Peter Brook. 'Just before rehearsals were due to begin, I destroyed the set.' The production was 'the thing itself'—a bare stage, stripped of its pseudo-Celtic costumes and bric-à-brac, with the violently energetic Lear (Scofield was forty). The play was revealed in all its elemental force in a production that refused the audience the comfort of making judgements on the characters. Their universe was without moral absolutes, a permanent condition of fallibility, moral ambiguity and frailty: Shakespeare as Beckett's contemporary. [. . .]

From **Dennis Kennedy, '*King Lear* and the Theatre'**, in *Educational Theatre Journal*, 28 (1976), p. 42

Kennedy, a performance critic and scholar, discusses some of Brook's more radical decisions in his 1962 production of the play (see Key Passages on **pp. 149–54** and **173–9**).

Figure 9 King Lear (1962 stage production). **Paul Scofield (Lear) warns the blinded Gloucester (Alan Webb), 'Hark in thine ear!' as Edgar (Brian Murray) watches. Image: Gordon Goode. By permission of the Shakespeare Centre Library.**

[. . .] When Peter Brook took Kott's cue and brought it on the stage in 1962 he was, in effect, presenting a modern adaptation of the play. Because he followed an invisible 'subtext' it was not necessary for Brook to rewrite the play (though that possibility was considered for the film version; [the poet] Ted Hughes prepared a script, then tossed it out[1]); instead the 'revision' of the play was accomplished by emphases and cutting. Take the blinding scene, for example. Shakespeare (in the Quarto text) provides us with an indication of the moral norm and of the persistence of human dignity in the dialogue of two servants at the end of the scene who sympathize with Gloucester and agree to assist him. Brook followed the Folio in omitting the attendants' speeches, but left the characters on stage; his scene ended with the old man blindly stumbling into the servants, who push and shove him, then leave him to grope off alone. Similarly, Brook cut the speech in the final scene in which Edmund repents his order for the deaths of Lear and Cordelia ('some good I mean to do,/Despite of mine own nature'), thereby undercutting the humane, almost noble end Shakespeare gives to the Bastard. The characters in general tended to be dehumanized, were often treated as puppets or automatons.

---

1   [Kennedy's note.] Roger Manvell, *Shakespeare and the Film* (New York, 1971), p. 137.

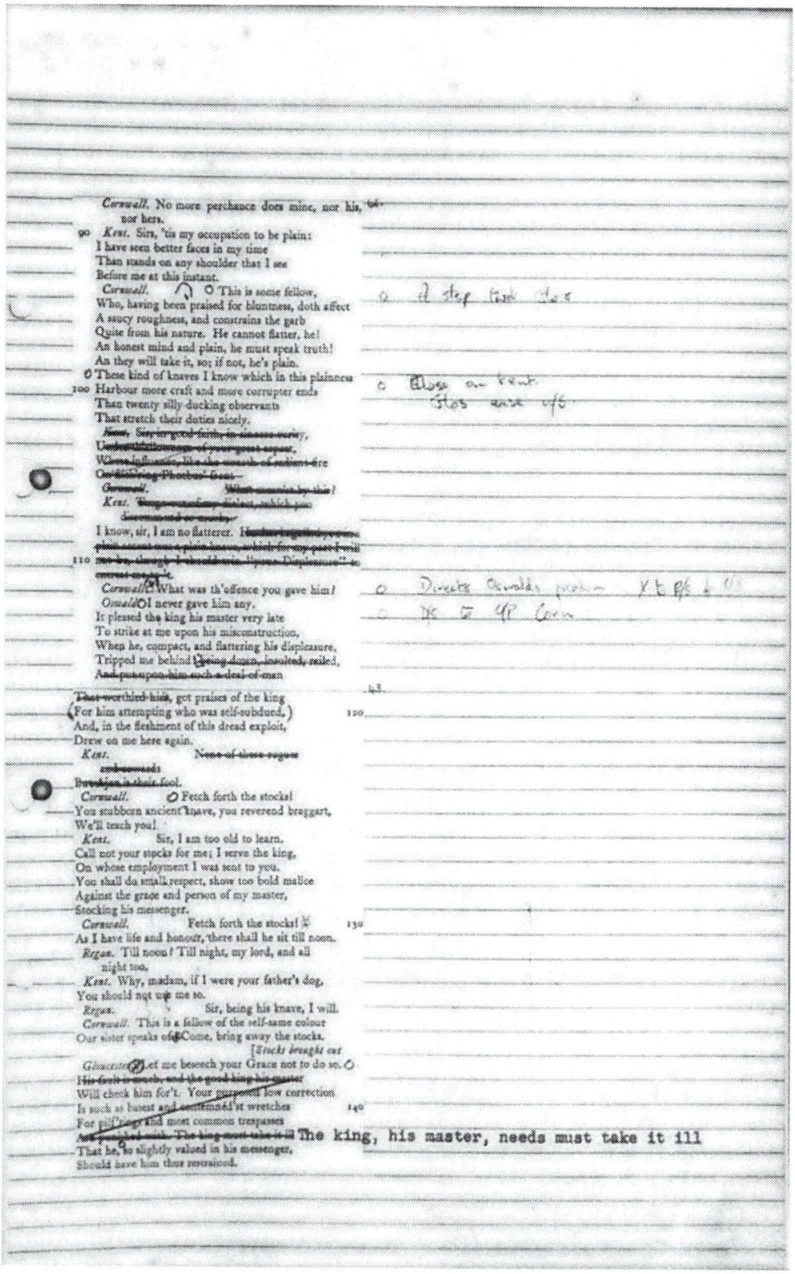

Figure 10 **King Lear (1962 stage production). A page from the director Peter Brook's promptbook, showing the types of cuts and blocking and lighting cues made for performance as Kent is stocked in Act 2, Scene 2. © Royal Shakespeare Company.**

The impulse of the production was to remove the audience's sympathy for the characters, especially for the King himself, in order to achieve a sense of 'epic objectivity': we are all playthings of the gods.[2] The point is that Brook narrowed the range of Shakespeare's theme in order to make coherent theatrical sense. He didn't 'destroy' the play, as often charged; he merely limited it, much as Tate limited it so that it would be understandable within the context of a current world-view. Tate's adaptation may have been more accepted because the world-view he appealed to was more accepted. If our century did not respect Shakespeare so much, Brook's version might have received less violent criticism. [. . .]

From **Grigori Kozintsev, King Lear: The Space of Tragedy. The Diary of a Film Director** (1973), trans. Mary Mackintosh (London: Heinemann, 1977), pp. 36–7, 74

Kozintsev notes throughout this book that his acclaimed 1970 film of the play was heavily influenced by Brook's stage production, which he saw in Moscow in 1964. Here Kozintsev discusses a director's concerns about the play (see Key Passages on **pp. 110–13** and **168–73**).

[. . .] The work of a director lies in selection and restriction. Directors of epics seek out from ancient customs and mores (or rather from books which describe them) all that is most effective, that will be interesting for its own sake on the screen: beautiful to look at and unusual. The producers spare no expense in the preparation of what is 'effective', money is its own justification: apart from the story of the film, the audience is interested in seeing with their own eyes how people lived in ancient times—the magnificence of the dress, the pageantry of the ceremonies. They pay in order to be distracted from life. I wanted to bring *Lear* as close as possible to life. This is why I was not interested in the unusual or the beautiful, but on the contrary, in everything which had been completely deprived of interest for its own sake. We needed a style of costume which would not attract attention, customs which were not remarkable in any way. There should be nothing to admire.

I did not want to shoot the film in colour for this very reason. I do not know what colour grief is, or what shades suffering has. I wanted to trust Shakespeare and the audience: it is shameful to sugar *Lear* with beautiful effects. [. . .]

It turned out we would shoot in detail some small part of the life of each of the characters, sometimes even a part which is mentioned only indirectly in the play or not even mentioned at all; on the other hand certain famous places in the play would be quickly passed over or even dropped altogether in the film.

---

2   [Kennedy's note.] A description of the general principles of Brook's production is given by his associate Charles Marowitz in 'Lear Log', *Theatre at Work*, ed. Marowitz and Simon Trussler (London, 1967).

This was not just a whim. The people whom Shakespeare wrote about demand this treatment; all we did was to listen hard to their voices. Cordelia insists that we linger over her departure and show her marriage to the King of France; the Duke of Albany thinks that his every change of facial expression is important during the division of the kingdom; the elder sisters do not want to talk out loud about their passion for Edmund, or about their jealousy of each other; they want not talk but to act, to meet with their lover in dirty castle courtyards in the heat of war.

Just you try controlling them. [. . .]

From **Edward Bond, Lear** (1971) (London: Methuen, 1972), pp. 34–5

Bond adapts Shakespeare's play to present a nihilistic world in which the ruler Lear is overthrown, put on trial and imprisoned by his two daughters, Bodice and Fontanelle, who have him blinded. Cordelia, the raped wife of a young man whom Lear had befriended, leads a revolutionary army against the two sisters and their husbands and executes them. Lear is released but eventually begins to speak out against Cordelia's brutal government. He is finally shot when attempting to dismantle the wall that he had earlier erected to confine his subjects. Although *Lear* represents Bond's political and artistic concerns, it shows the influence of Kott's and Brook's radical views of Shakespeare's play.

In this passage from Lear's trial in Act 2, Scene 1 of Bond's play, he inverts Shakespeare's presentation of various images in *King Lear*, including Lear's mock trial of Goneril and Regan in Act 3, Scene 6 (Key Passage on **pp. 147–9**) and his promise in Act 5, Scene 3 (Key Passage on **pp. 173–9**) to Cordelia that in prison they 'will sing like birds i'th' cage' and 'laugh/At gilded butterflies' as if they were 'God's spies'.

JUDGE. Take the oath first.

LEAR. You have no right to sit there!

JUDGE. Take the oath.

LEAR. I gave you your job because you were corrupt!

JUDGE. Take the oath.

LEAR. The king is always on oath! (*He stares down at the mirror.*) No that's not the king . . . This is a little cage of bars with an animal in it. (*Peers closer.*) No, no, that's not the king! (*Suddenly gestures violently. The* Usher *takes the mirror.*) Who shut that animal in that cage? Let it out. Have you seen its face behind the bars? There's a poor animal with blood on its head and the tears running down its face. Who did that to it? Is it a bird or a horse? It's lying in the dust and its wings are broken. Who broke its wings? Who cut off its hands so that it can't shake the bars? It's pressing its snout on the glass. Who shut that animal in a glass cage? O god, there's no pity in this world. You let it lick the blood from its hair in the corner of a cage with nowhere to hide from its tormentors. No shadow, no hole! Let that animal out of its cage! (*He takes the mirror and shows it round.*) Look! Look! Have pity. Look at its claws trying to open the cage. It's dragging its broken body over the floor. You are cruel! Cruel! Look at it lying in its corner! It's shocked and cut and shaking and licking the blood on its sides (Usher *again takes the mirror from* Lear.) No, no! Where are they taking it now! Not out of my sight! What will they do to it? O God, give it to me! Let me hold it and stroke it and wipe its blood! (Bodice *takes the mirror from the* Usher.) No!

BODICE. I'll polish it every day and see it's not cracked.

LEAR. Then kill it. Kill it. Kill it. Don't let her torment it. I can't live with that suffering in the world.

JUDGE. See the king's madness.

    [. . .]

From **Antony Sher, *Beside Myself: An Autobiography*** (London: Hutchinson, 2001), pp. 164–5.

> A distinguished stage, film and television actor and author, Sher discusses his portrayal of the Fool in the Royal Shakespeare Company's acclaimed 1982 production of *King Lear*. Directed by Adrian Noble and featuring Michael Gambon as Lear, the production was notable for, among other things, Lear's accidental murder of the Fool during the mock trial in Act 3, Scene 6 (see Key Passages on **pp. 123–9 and 144–9**).

[. . .] And there I was – playing the Fool again – and *battling* again. I showed Adrian the little shuffling figure with the underbite [from Sher's previous portrayal of the Fool in the 1972 Liverpool Everyman Theatre production]. He wasn't convinced. 'The Fool's speeches may seem obscure', he said, 'but *he* knows what he means. He's the one speaking the truth – he speaks Truth to Power – and I simply can't hear you clearly when you speak like that.'

So back to the drawing board. I tried this, I tried that, I visited the London Zoo one Sunday to study the chimps – later discovering that Gambon was there the same day, gazing at the gorillas – but nothing yielded results. Rehearsals were invigorating nevertheless. [. . .] I tried to play the Fool in neutral for these sessions, but he kept turning into that little cheeky-chappie jester who appears in traditional productions of Shakespeare comedies, and who makes me throw up. Then one day Adrian said, 'Let's try a series of experiments. Tomorrow play him with a red nose, the next day with a white face, the day after . . .'

We never got past the red nose.

Masks are very liberating – with your face hidden or partly hidden you suddenly have new access to your courage and emotions – and a red nose is simply a miniature mask. Things started to fall into place. My research into court jesters had revealed that they were often cripples or freaks, their disability regarded as

Figure 11 *King Lear* (1982 RSC production). The Fool (Antony Sher) tries to avoid being whipped by Lear (Michael Gambon), who wears the Fool's bowler hat, in Act 1, Scene 4. Image: Joe Cocks Studio Collection. © Shakespeare Birthplace Trust.

funny. I scrunched up the Fool and gave him inward-twisting legs. A wretched figure, but plonk on some clown accoutrements – a battered bowler and elongated shoes as well as the red nose – and the mix becomes interesting. Adrian suggested adding a tiny violin [. . .] I never learned more than a few basic sawings and pluckings but it didn't matter. Or that I couldn't sing. For once this was a positive advantage. My tuneless chantings became part of this particular Fool's style, part of his anarchy.

As I'd already learned at the Everyman, the role of the Fool only works in relation to Lear. The Fool is the King's sidekick, his whipping boy, his pet, his shadow. Gambon, himself a superb clown, took to my new character with relish. We began doing our interchanges as little music-hall routines, the tackier the better: me on his knee as a ventriloquist's dummy, or the two of us doing double-act patter, marking the punch lines with a *ta-dah!* gesture to the audience. (Later, Adrian would actually light these like front-cloth scenes with footlights and giant shadows.) Then, with the onset of madness and the arrival of a darker soulmate – Poor Tom – Lear lost interest in his Fool. During the hovel scene he began stabbing a pillow that the Fool was holding – 'Let them anatomise Regan!' – a cloud of feathers arose and Lear never even noticed that he'd delivered a mortal blow. This was our solution to a mysterious (or lazy) piece of writing in the play: after that scene the Fool vanishes completely.

Gambon was magnificent at the final run-through. His ability to switch from clowning with his Fool to the terrible rages with his daughters, and then the disintegration into confusion and vulnerability . . . this was astonishing. [. . .]

From **Alastair Macaulay, Review of the Royal National Theatre's 1997 production of** *King Lear, Financial Times*, 1 April 1997, p. 21

> Macaulay's review of Richard Eyre's 1997 stage production, filmed in 1998 for BBC television, is typical of the response of nearly all the other critics, especially in its praise of Ian Holm's portrayal of Lear (see Key Passages on **pp. 126–9** and **141–9**)

The barnacles of theatricality, style, and interpretation seem to fall away from *King Lear* in the National Theatre's new staging. I envy anyone for whom this is his or her first *King Lear*. Often, wonderful to say, I felt as if it were mine.

Two features make this *Lear* exceptional: its location and its protagonist. The director, Richard Eyre, has placed it in the intimate Cottlesloe Theatre, so that – whereas we have grown used to having *Lear* oracularly hurled at us across some mighty distance – we here are easily encompassed by its volcanic flow of detail. The grand manner, which can elevate Shakespeare's purple passages but bog down the drama, is wonderfully absent.

Ian Holm's Lear is this production's ideal centrepiece. He can growl: 'Who am I?' quietly, like a lion. He addresses the elements ('Let fall/Your horrible pleasure') as if the lightning and thunder were passing through him like grim shocks that he craved. To talk of Holm's conception or characterisation of Lear is almost to miss the point. Indeed, he seems to miss his own point in two physical respects: the short-stepping old-man plod and the gumless chewing motion he occasionally deploys are the kind of characterising effects that here seem superficial, inorganic. No, the marvel of his performance is the way it lives in the line – the way it makes you feel anew the surprising developments of Shakespeare's thought in every word, and yet makes these sound spontaneous, new-minted.

Suddenly amid the storm and the onset of madness, he contemplates Poor Tom, and asks: 'Is man no more than this? Consider him well,' with a flash of Hamlet-like philosophical inquiry out of nowhere. I have never been so aware of how quickly Lear's mind shuttles between intemperate explosiveness and the quest for patience; or, later, of how seamlessly it shuttles between sanity and madness.

This is much the finest Shakespeare that Eyre, during his time at the National, has given us. Bob Crowley, designing, provides a few scenic *coups du théâtre* as when the set's two tall walls fall smack on the floor between them as the storm commences – and the best thunder and lightning for years; but, in general, the visual simplicity is very gratifying. [. . .]

3

Key Passages

Introduction

Note on the Text

King Lear exists in three early texts: Q1, the 1608 Quarto 1 text (the only one printed in Shakespeare's lifetime); Q2, the 1619 Quarto 2 text (now discounted as a surreptitious reprint of Quarto 1, falsely dated 1608); and F, the 1623 Folio 1 text. Q1 contains about 300 lines not in F, and F contains about 100 lines not in Q1, so the variants between them are significant. Many scholars believe that most of the variants were the result of Shakespeare revising the play between its original composition in 1606 and some later point before his death in 1616. Other variants, made either as corrections or inadvertent errors, may be due to non-authorial agents such as actors, the censor or printers. For example, the 1606 Act Against Abuses prohibited printed texts from containing the names of God, Jesus Christ, the Holy Spirit and other sacred figures; however, these names may have been used on stage. If so, these 'oaths' may have been purged from the Q1, Q2 and F texts when they were printed.

In creating editions of the play for modern audiences to read, editors usually choose from either Q1 or F as the copy-text (that is, the base text). A more recent option is to reproduce both of the original texts separately as first printed as Q1 or F. But the majority of modern editors prefer to follow standard principles of editing and choose one copy-text and incorporate (or 'interpolate') into it variant passages from the other text when those variants make more sense (or seem 'more Shakespearean') than those in the copy-text. This process of occasionally replacing words or passages from the copy-text with those of another text is known as conflation. Modern editions of the play that use Q1 as copy-text usually interpolate some or many F variants (for example, extra lines in Lear's confrontation of Cordelia in Act 1, Scene 1), while editions that use F as copy-text usually interpolate some or many Q variants (for example, the 'mock-trial' episode in Act 3, Scene 6). No one editor chooses exactly the same set of variables, so no two editors produce exactly the same text of the play. Hence other editions of *King Lear* that you read (or hear acted onstage) may vary slightly or significantly from the one presented below or any other available text of the play.

Note on the Key Passages

King Lear is now considered to be Shakespeare's greatest play, and indeed each and any passage of it can be, and has been, considered 'key', as evidenced by the variety of passages discussed by literary and performance critics above. It is simply not possible to divide the play into a handful of scenes or passages and still represent it in any way similar to Shakespeare's rendering of it or even to make sense of its enormous impact on past, present, and future audiences. Thus in the Key Passages I present as much as possible of this important play in order to keep intact its structure, settings, themes, characters and language. I fully summarise any passages or scenes that do not appear in their entirety. A list of the Key Passages appears below after the synopsis of the play.

Working as a modern editor does, I have constructed my own edition of the play for the Key Passages, using Q1 as the copy-text because it was almost certainly printed from Shakespeare's own manuscript. However, my edition also interpolates some single-word or longer corrections, as well as probable authorial revisions, made in the F text, probably printed from a later acting text (a combination of an annotated copy of Q2 and a theatrical manuscript showing at some remove Shakespeare's revisions). Thus the text below is a conflated text, which uses one substantive text, Q1, as its base while incorporating variants from another substantive text, F. Major interpolations from F, as well as significant variants between Q and F, are noted as appropriate in the annotations to the passage. I have regularised spelling, punctuation and other features, and have expanded or added stage directions as necessary. The analyses offered in the annotations are suggested, and not definitive, ways of thinking about the passages and are designed to challenge readers and to provoke further analyses, comparisons and contrasts.

In any edition of a play, the editor assigns a 'through' number to each line of verse or prose, beginning with '1' and then numbering through consecutively to the end of the play. Line numbers vary among any given editions depending on type size, spacing, and other features of page layout, so that no two editions will have exactly the same line numbering. As the text presented below is set from my own edition, and as it contains only passages rather than the entire text of the play, it is not possible to 'through' line-number the passages. Thus, each of the key passages has been individually numbered. However, references to the line numbers in a complete, published edition, in this case R. A. Foake's Arden edition of *King Lear* (Walton on Thames: Thomas Nelson & Sons, 1997) are given in parentheses at the beginning of each key passage. In this way, readers can easily turn from the key passages to a complete edition of the play.

Synopsis of the Play

Lear, king of a Celtic and pre-Christian Britain, announces that he will abdicate his kingship due to ill health and age, and will divide his kingdom among his three daughters and their spouses. He demands that his daughters compete for their shares by measuring in speech how much each loves him. His elder daughters Goneril, wife of the Duke of Albany, and Regan, wife of the Duke of Cornwall, equally flatter Lear by claiming they love him 'all', and each receives one-third of the kingdom. Cordelia, his unmarried, youngest and most beloved daughter, offers 'nothing' extra to her sisters' speeches, stating that she loves her father according to her bond, 'no more, nor less'.

Outraged, Lear disinherits Cordelia, dividing her portion of land between her two sisters and denying her the dowry announced to her two suitors, the Kings of France and Burgundy. Lear claims that he will keep the trappings but not the power of kingship and move between his two elder daughters' homes each month, accompanied by a retinue of one hundred knights. The Earl of Kent chastises Lear for rejecting Cordelia, but Lear angrily banishes him. Before she leaves with her new fiancé, the King of France, who prefers her honesty to a dowry, Cordelia warns her sisters that their lies will be revealed in time.

Meanwhile, the Earl of Gloucester is tricked by his illegitimate and villainous son Edmund into believing that his legitimate and loyal son Edgar plans to kill him and steal his title. Edmund convinces Edgar to flee, and the distraught Edgar resolves to wander the kingdom as the madman Poor Tom of Bedlam. Gloucester places all his trust in Edmund, who continues to plot against him.

As agreed, Lear arrives to stay with Goneril with his retinue, including his Fool and his new servant, Caius (the disguised Kent, who has remained loyal to Lear). Goneril demands that Lear reduce his 'riotous' train from one hundred to fifty knights; he refuses, quarrels with her and decides to stay with Regan. After finding her and her husband at Gloucester's home, Lear complains to Regan about Goneril's insulting behaviour, but Goneril soon arrives, and she and Regan coldly try to convince him to obey their commands, including reducing his train from fifty to twenty-five knights, and finally to none, if he expects their hospitality.

Lear, fearing the onset of madness, realises that his two eldest daughters lied in their claims to love him 'all' and that Cordelia told the truth. He flees to wander on a stormy heath. There he encounters the mad Poor Tom (the disguised Edgar, his godson) and discovers that man is nothing but 'a poor, bare, forked animal' and that his own royal robes and furs hide his true, base nature. Now completely mad, Lear makes the Fool, Kent and Poor Tom try and convict Goneril and Regan *in absentia*.

In defiance of Goneril and Regan's order, Gloucester has sheltered Lear from the storm and confides to Edmund that he will send Lear to the safety of Dover (where Cordelia has arrived as the head of the invading French army). Edmund betrays his father to Goneril, Regan and Cornwall, who capture Gloucester; and, as Regan and her servants watch, Cornwall plucks out Gloucester's eyes as punishment for his treachery. When Gloucester calls out for Edmund's help, he learns that Edmund has betrayed him and that Edgar was innocent of any conspiracy against him. A servant who attempts to save Gloucester fatally wounds Cornwall. Regan then kills the servant.

The blinded, wandering Gloucester soon encounters Poor Tom, not realising that he is his loving son Edgar. Poor Tom promises to take Gloucester to the

Dover cliffs so that he can commit suicide but instead leads him to low ground, from which Gloucester falls without injury. Disguised as a peasant, Edgar rescues Gloucester, claiming to have found him at the bottom of the cliffs and marvelling at his escape from certain death. Gloucester agrees to be led by the disguised Edgar.

The mad Lear is reunited with his loving daughter Cordelia, who claims to have 'no cause, no cause' to hate her father. Her French army fights the British army of Edmund, Regan, Goneril and Albany (now suspicious of his wife Goneril), but Cordelia's forces are defeated, and she and Lear go to prison, where Edmund arranges for their secret execution. The disguised Edgar accuses his brother Edmund of villainy and challenges him to a duel. Edgar fatally wounds Edmund, reveals his true identity and tells of the death of his father from a 'burst' heart shortly after their brief reunion as father and son.

Edmund dies repentant for his treachery against his family and Lear's, but he is too late to save Cordelia from execution by hanging. Lear, distraught and weak, enters with the dead Cordelia in his arms and is told that Goneril, jealous of Regan's love for Edmund, has poisoned Regan and then slain herself. Confronted by the bodies of three children, Lear also dies of a burst heart, possibly convincing himself that Cordelia is still breathing and thus alive. Albany is left to rule the divided and shattered kingdom with Edgar.

List of Key Passages

M. William Shak-ſpeare:

HIS
True Chronicle Hiſtorie of the life and
death of King L E A R and his three
Daughters.

With the vnfortunate life of Edgar, *ſonne*
and heire to the Earle of Gloſter, and his
ſullen and aſſumed humor of
ToM of Bedlam :

As it was played before the Kings Maieſtie at Whit·hall vpon
S. Stephans *night in Chriſtmas Hollidayes.*

By his Maieſties ſeruants playing vſually at the Gloabe .
on the Bancke-ſide.

LONDON,
Printed for *Nathaniel Butter,* and are to be ſold at his ſhop in *Pauls*
Church-yard at the ſigne of the Pide Bull neere
Sᵗ. *Auſtins* Gate. 1608.

Key Passages

Act 1, Scene 1: Lear tests the love of his daughters (1–82)

This opening presents the play's most important issues, themes and relationships in the language that will dominate the play. Father–child relationships are subject to careful measurement, with the patriarch Lear's relationships with two sons-in-law measured in the same way as those between the patriarch Gloucester and his two sons. The passage also offers motivation for the illegitimate Edmund's loathing of his father and jealousy of his legitimate half-brother Edgar, a plot device not provided to explain the animosity of Lear's daughters to him or to each other.

The notions here of the politics of power, nature versus nurture, illicit sexuality and procreation, the whorish nature of women and only the ghostly presence of mothers will also reverberate in the later plotting among sisters and in Lear's anxiety about the true parentage of his daughters. Gloucester's nasty question in discussing Edmund's bastardy here, – 'Do you smell a fault?' – will be echoed in Regan's cruel comment in Act 3, Scene 7 to the blinded Gloucester – 'Let him smell/His way to Dover'. The words of measurement, 'more', 'most', 'weighed' and 'neither' will appear throughout the play and foreshadow the crisis caused by Cordelia's use of 'nothing' in the rest of the scene.

Lear enters behind an attendant carrying a coronet, a lesser crown than that of a monarch. This symbolic entrance suggests a devaluing of the crown, as well as a dangerous division between ruler and the trappings of office, or between the king's two bodies, the body politic (his royal power) and his body natural (his human frailty). His politically disastrous 'division of the kingdoms' will mirror his division of his family. Lear's immediate dismissal of Gloucester, with his son Edmund remaining onstage, prevents his chief courtier from witnessing the effects of playing one child off against another, while his son watches all too closely.

In the anonymous source play, *The True Chronicle Historie of King Leir* (see above, **pp. 25–32**), Lear sets up the love-test among his daughters in order to cajole a reluctant Cordelia into marrying the French monarch he has already chosen for her. He assumes that once she had declared she loves him all and will do anything to please him she will accept his choice of husband. Shakespeare appears to have begun writing the scene with this intention in mind; thus, Lear notes that the princes of France and Burgundy must be answered just before he begins his test by asking his three daughters which loves him most. Shakespeare seemed less interested in this obvious reason for the love-test and offers a much more ambiguous test into the nature of human emotion.

Goneril's and Regan's immediate replies are smooth and polished, as if they are used to performing such public shows of devotion or at least anticipated such a test and rehearsed their replies (as in the source play; see above, **pp. 27–9**). But we can also question whether we see any hint of or motivation for their manipulative cruelty or deliberate malice later in the play in being asked to voice here what cannot be easily explained in words.

Only Cordelia's worried asides suggest either that such public protestations are not routine in the Lear court or that Cordelia knows herself to be a bad actress when pressed to speak flattery. Such a test is moot, as Lear has already decided before each daughter's profession of love how much and which part of his kingdom he will give her, saving the largest portion of his recklessly divided kingdom for his favourite, Cordelia. Truly their father's daughters, Goneril and Regan use his precise words of measurement and comparison – 'more', 'dearer', 'beyond', 'as much', 'no less', 'poor', 'short', 'most' – to persuade him of their devotion. The anxious Cordelia does the same in considering her responses.

To compare Shakespeare's treatment of the Lear story with his sources, see Geoffrey of Monmouth (**pp. 19–22**), Raphael Holinshed (**pp. 23–5**), John Higgins (**pp. 32–6**) and Edmund Spenser (**pp. 36–8**). On the importance of the play's structure, see Jan Kott (**pp. 56–7**). On John Gielgud's concerns with how to perform the role of Lear in the opening scene, see **pp. 82–4**.

Enter KENT, GLOUCESTER, *and* EDMUND

KENT   I thought the king had more affected[1] the Duke of Albany than Cornwall.

GLOUCESTER   It did always seem so to us, but now in the division of the kingdoms, it appears not which of the dukes he values most, for equalities are so weighed that curiosity in neither can make choice of either's moiety.[2]

KENT   Is not this your son, my lord?

GLOUCESTER   His breeding,[3] sir, hath been at my charge. I have so often blushed to acknowledge him, that now I am brazed to it.

---

1   Favoured.
2   Share.
3   Upbringing, with pun on 'conception'.

KENT   I cannot conceive you.   10

GLOUCESTER   Sir, this young fellow's mother could, whereupon she
grew round-wombed and had indeed, sir, a son for her cradle ere she
had a husband for her bed. Do you smell a fault?

KENT   I cannot wish the fault undone, the issue of it being so proper.

GLOUCESTER   But I have a son, sir, by order of law,[4] some years elder
than this, who yet is no dearer in my account. Though this knave
came something saucily[5] into the world before he was sent for, yet was
his mother fair, there was good sport at his making, and the whoreson
must be acknowledged. [*To* EDMUND] Do you know this noble
gentleman, Edmund?   20

EDMUND   No, my lord.

GLOUCESTER   My lord of Kent; remember him hereafter as my honourable friend.

EDMUND   My services to your lordship.

KENT   I must love you and sue[6] to know you better.

EDMUND   Sir, I shall study[7] deserving.

GLOUCESTER   He hath been out[8] nine years, and away he shall again.
The king is coming.

Sound a sennet.[9] Enter one bearing a coronet,[10] then LEAR, *then the Dukes of*
ALBANY *and* CORNWALL, GONERIL, REGAN, CORDELIA, *with followers*

LEAR   Attend the lords of France and Burgundy, Gloucester.

GLOUCESTER   I shall, my leige.   [*Exit* 30

LEAR   Meantime we will express our darker purposes.
Give me the map there. Know: we have divided
In three our kingdom, and 'tis our fast intent
To shake all cares and business of our state,
Confirming them on younger years.
The two great princes, France and Burgundy,
Great rivals in our youngest daughter's love,
Long in our court have made their amorous sojourn,
And here are to be answered. Tell me, my daughters,
Which of you shall we say doth love us most,   40
That we our largest bounty may extend
Where nature doth with merit challenge it?
Goneril, our eldest born, speak first.

GONERIL   Sir, I do love you more than words can wield the matter,

4   i.e. legitimate.
5   Impertinently.
6   Work.
7   Study to be.
8   Away from home.
9   Trumpet notes used for ceremonial entrance.
10   An inferior version of the type of crown worn by the monarch.

Dearer than eyesight, space, or liberty,
Beyond what can be valued rich or rare,
No less than life, with grace, health, beauty, honour,
As much as child e'er[11] loved, or father found,
A love that makes breath poor, and speech unable,
Beyond all manner of so much I love you.   50
CORDELIA [*Aside*]   What shall Cordelia do? Love, and be silent.
LEAR   Of all these bounds, even from this line to this,
With shady forests and with champains[12] riched,
With plenteous rivers and wide-skirted meads,
We make thee lady. To thine and Albany's issue
Be this perpetual.[13] What says our second daughter,
Our dearest Regan, wife to Cornwall? Speak.
REGAN   Sir, I am made of the self-same mettle[14] as my sister,
And prize me at her worth. In my true heart
I find she names my very deed of love.   60
Only she comes too short, that I profess
Myself an enemy to all other joys
Which the most precious square of sense possesses,
And find I am alone felicitate
In your dear highness' love.
CORDELIA   [*Aside*] Then poor Cordelia,
And yet not so, since I am sure my love's
More richer than my tongue.
LEAR [*To* REGAN]   To thee and thine hereditary ever
Remain this ample third of our fair kingdom,
No less in space, validity, and pleasure   70
Than that confirmed on Goneril.

Act 1, Scene 1: Lear tests Cordelia (82–167)

As the scene continues, Lear faces his most anxious combatant of the play, the blunt, outspoken and stubborn Cordelia, who reveals herself here as possessing those qualities we will soon see in Lear throughout the next three acts. Although the play is set in Celtic, pre-Christian England, it relies heavily on Christian values such as mercy, compassion and redemption from sin. Lear's comment that 'Nothing can come of nothing' is an allusion to the Greek philosophical and scientific tenet of *ex nihilo nihil fit* (from nothing, nothing

---

11 Contraction of 'ever' to suit the metre (used throughout the text).
12 Plains.
13 i.e. owned in perpetuity.
14 i.e. metal and mettle (meaning both tough enduring substance and strong spirit).

comes), an argument contradicted by the Bible's claim that God created the world from nothing (see Genesis 1:1).

We can see Cordelia here as either the honest, loving young woman who refuses, for his own good, to flatter her father, or as the spoiled, selfish child who cannot consider the anxious feelings of a short-tempered and ill old man, or as a combination of the two. Whether Lear has already begun his descent into madness is unclear. Yet his unrecognised repudiation in 'Nothing will come of nothing' of the same Christian beliefs that he will call on throughout the play suggests a man who cannot connect language with meaning, as his daughter Cordelia can. The irony is that she does indeed do what her father asks: she uses precise measurement to tell him exactly how much she loves him – 'According to my bond, no more nor less'.

Shakespeare probably revised this play between its original composition, as printed in Q1, and some later performance, as printed in F (see Michael Warren above, **pp. 64–5**). In the original text, Cordelia's 'Nothing, my Lord' was followed by Lear's 'How? Nothing can come of nothing, speak again'. In the revision, Shakespeare added the two lines in which Lear asks, 'Nothing?' and Cordelia responds, 'Nothing' (as printed below), intensifying the use of this word of measurement and their verbal duel. The word 'nothing' will re-appear frequently throughout the rest of the play, particularly in the speech of Lear and those directly addressing him, such as the Fool. Thus Shakespeare demonstrates both that the word 'nothing' will beget repeated uses of the word 'nothing' later (so that nothing can come of nothing, as Lear tries to predict here) and that the word 'nothing' will beget much more than nothing, in fact, far too much suffering and pain.

'Nothing' or 'no thing' (sometimes represented by an 'O') was also slang for 'vagina' (thus Hamlet's crude pun in *Hamlet*, Act 3, Scene 2 on Ophelia's use of the word 'nothing': 'That's a fair thought to lie between a maid's legs'). Although the word may not have that direct meaning here, Lear is clearly perturbed about Cordelia's honesty (meaning both 'truthfulness' and 'chastity') and divorces himself from her, as if she were his wife, rather than his daughter. Some critics have suggested that Lear's irrational anger derives from his fear of his incestuous feelings for his daughters (see Kathleen McLuskie and Coppélia Kahn above, **pp. 60–2 and 62–4**). Unlike the author of the source play, who portrays Lear mourning his late, beloved wife, Shakespeare provides no information about the absent mother of Lear's daughters or the state of his relationship with or his treatment of them before Act 1, Scene 1. Instead Shakespeare leaves us to draw our own conclusions about whether such division between father and daughter, and such collusion between sisters, stems from their innate evil natures or from their nurture by him thus far.

Lear disinherits Cordelia in excoriating her 'pride, which she calls plainness', yet Kent, who will be placed in the stocks in Act 2, Scene 2 for being 'plain', responds here, 'To plainness honour's bound,/When majesty stoops to folly'. Lear faces his second love-test here in his argument with Kent, who, as his surrogate son, offers him the same terms of endearment as Cordelia has, with the same result: banishment. Throughout the play, the blunt Kent and the outspoken Fool will recall and remind Lear of the absent Cordelia. Kent's warning, 'See better, Lear', introduces the play's concern with sight versus insight, a lesson both Lear and Gloucester will later learn; it also suggests that Lear blinds himself in this scene long before others will blind Gloucester.

After his quarrel with Cordelia, Lear reconfigures the terms of his abdication: he will now divide his kingdom in two between Goneril and Regan and their husbands as long as he can move between their households each month with a retinue of one hundred knights which his hosts will accommodate. The silence from his daughters and their husbands in response implies their consent to his conditions. That the two daughters will later try to ignore these conditions suggests that silence is no more expressive of consent or love than spoken words.

LEAR   [*To* CORDELIA] But now our joy,
    Although the last, not least, in our dear love,
    What can you say to win a third more opulent
    Than your sisters?
CORDELIA Nothing, my lord.
LEAR Nothing?
CORDELIA Nothing.
LEAR How? Nothing can come of nothing, speak again.
CORDELIA Unhappy that I am, I cannot heave
    My heart into my mouth. I love your majesty   10
    According to my bond, no more nor less.
LEAR Go to, go to,[1] mend your speech a little,
    Lest it may mar your fortunes.
CORDELIA   Good my lord,
    You have begot me, bred me, loved me. I
    Return those duties back as are right fit:
    Obey you, love you, and most honour you.
    Why have my sisters husbands, if they say
    They love you all? Haply,[2] when I shall wed,
    That lord whose hand must take my plight shall carry
    Half my love with him, half my care and duty.   20
    Sure, I shall never marry like my sisters,
    To love my father all.
LEAR But goes this with thy heart?
CORDELIA   Ay, my good lord.

1 i.e. Enough, enough.
2 By chance, with pun on 'happily'.

LEAR   So young, and so untender?[3]
CORDELIA   So young, my lord, and true.[4]
LEAR   Well, let it be so, thy truth then be thy dower.[5]
   For by the sacred radiance of the sun,
   The mysteries[6] of Hecate[7] and the night,
   By all the operation of the orbs[8]
   From whom we do exist and cease to be,   30
   Here I disclaim all my paternal care,
   Propinquity[9] and property of blood,
   And as a stranger to my heart and me
   Hold thee from this forever. The barbarous Scythian,[10]
   Or he that makes his generation messes[11]
   To gorge his appetite, shall be as well
   Neighboured, pitied, and relieved
   As thou my sometime[12] daughter.
KENT   Good my liege—
LEAR   Peace, Kent, come not between the dragon and his wrath.
   I loved her most, and thought to set my rest   40
   On her kind nursery.[13] Hence and avoid my sight!
   So be my grave my peace, as here I give
   Her father's heart from her. Call France. Who stirs?
   Call Burgundy. [*Exit an Attendant.*] Cornwall and Albany,
   With my two daughters' dowers digest[14] this third.
   Let pride, which she calls plainness, marry her.
   I do invest you jointly in my power,
   Pre-eminence, and all the large effects
   That troop with majesty. Ourself by monthly course,
   With reservation of an hundred knights   50
   By you to be sustained, shall our abode
   Make with you by due turns; only we still retain
   The name and all th'additions[15] to a king.
   The sway, revenue, execution of the rest,[16]
   Belovèd sons, be yours; which to confirm,

---

3   Unkind (meaning both ungentle and unnatural).
4   Meaning both honest and faithful.
5   Dowry.
6   Secret rituals.
7   Goddess of witchcraft.
8   Planets and stars.
9   Kinship.
10 Native of Scythia, a country in Asia; their warriors were noted for barbarism (see Marlowe's
    Tamburlaine plays).
11 i.e. he who eats his progeny (his 'generation').
12 Former.
13 Nursing.
14 Absorb.
15 Titles.
16 i.e. the remaining royal control (sway), income (revenue) and power (execution).

This coronet part betwixt you. [LEAR *hands* ALBANY *and* CORNWALL
  the coronet]
KENT   Royal Lear,
  Whom I have ever honoured as my king,
  Loved as my father, as my master followed,
  As my great patron thought on in my prayers—
LEAR   The bow is bent and drawn, make from the shaft.[17]   60
KENT   Let it fall rather, though the fork[18] invade
  The region of my heart. Be Kent unmannerly[19]
  When Lear is mad. What wilt thou do, old man?
  Think'st thou that duty shall have dread to speak
  When power to flattery bows? To plainness honour's bound
  When majesty stoops to folly. Reverse thy doom,
  And in thy best consideration check
  This hideous rashness. Answer my life, my judgement:
  Thy youngest daughter does not love thee least,
  Nor are those empty-hearted whose low sounds   70
  Reverb[21] no hollowness.
KENT   Kent, on thy life, no more.
KENT   My life I never held but as a pawn
  To wage against thy enemies, nor fear to lose it,
  Thy safety being the motive.
LEAR   Out of my sight!
KENT   See better, Lear, and let me still remain
  The true blank[22] of thine eye.
LEAR   Now by Apollo[23]—
KENT   Now by Apollo, king, thou swear'st thy gods in vain.
LEAR   Vassal![24] Recreant![25]
KENT   Do, kill thy physician,
  And the fee bestow upon the foul disease.
  Revoke thy doom, or whilst I can vent clamour   80
  From my throat, I'll tell thee thou dost evil.

---

17 Lear uses an archery metaphor here, warning Kent to get to the point.
18 Arrow point.
19 Rude.
20 i.e. banishment of Cordelia.
21 Reverberate.
22 The centre of the archer's target.
23 God of the sun and an archer.
24 Lowest form of servant.
25 Coward.

Act 1, Scene 1: Lear bargains with Cordelia's suitors (189–268)

After Lear pronounces Kent's banishment, Kent congratulates Cordelia, who 'rightly thinks, and hast most justly said', chastises her two sisters in the hope that 'good effects may spring from words of love' and exits. Gloucester enters with the Kings of Burgundy and France. The scene continues with yet another love-test: having set his daughters as rivals against each other and himself, he now sets the two suitors against each other and himself.

After hearing the King of Burgundy complain that she is worth 'less' than promised, Cordelia delivers a measured and precise defence of her reputation, but it is unclear whether she has been inspired by Kent's courage or has belatedly come to realise the importance of public shows in Lear's court. Iron-ically, Cordelia has been angered by a response by Burgundy that sounded very much like her own to Lear. Burgundy demands of Lear, 'I crave no more than what your highness offered,/Nor will you tender less', an echo of Cordelia's 'I love your majesty/According to my bond, no more nor less'.

The King of France offers the first rational arguments of the play (see his presentation in Holinshed above, **pp. 23–5**). He astutely notes that 'love is not love / When it is mingled with respects that stands/Aloof from the entire point', that is, love is not love that can be measured into words or altered to suit demands. Shakespeare also explored these points earlier in Sonnet 116 ('Love is not love/Which alters when it alteration finds') and later in *Antony and Cleopatra* (to Cleopatra's plea in Act 1, Scene 1, 'If it be love indeed, tell me how much', Antony replies, 'There's beggary in the love that can be reckoned' (i.e. measured)).

When Burgundy repeats his demand for the promised dowry, Lear announces, perhaps with a withering glance at Cordelia, 'Nothing, I have sworn', using her own words to rob her. In his revision in F, Shakespeare has added after these words the line 'I am firm'. Not surprisingly the passage is so littered with the very words Lear cherishes, 'more', 'less', 'most', 'least', 'rich', 'poor', that they have lost their meaning or have become oxymoronic.

Flourish. Enter FRANCE *and* BURGUNDY *with* GLOUCESTER *and Attendants*

GLOUCESTER   Here's France and Burgundy, my noble lord.
LEAR   My lord of Burgundy,
    We first address towards you, who with a king
    Hath rivalled for our daughter. What in the least
    Will you require in present dower[1] with her,
    Or cease your quest of love?

---

1   Dowry.

BURGUNDY   Royal majesty,
I crave no more than what your highness offered,
Nor will you tender less?
LEAR   Right noble Burgundy,
When she was dear to us, we did hold her so,
But now her price is fallen. Sir, there she stands.   10
If aught² within that little seeming substance,
Or all of it, with our displeasure pieced,
And nothing else, may fitly like your grace,
She's there, and she is yours.
BURGUNDY   I know no answer.
LEAR   Sir, will you, with those infirmities she owes,³
Unfriended,⁴ new-adopted to our hate,
Covered with our curse, and strangered⁵ with our oath,
Take her, or leave her?
BURGUNDY   Pardon me, royal sir,
Election⁶ makes not up on such conditions.
LEAR   Then leave her, sir, for by the power that made me,   20
I tell you all her wealth. [To FRANCE] For you, great king,
I would not from your love make such a stray
To match you where I hate; therefore beseech you
To avert your liking a more worthier way
Than *on a wretch whom nature is ashamed*
Almost to acknowledge hers.
FRANCE   This is most strange,
That she—that even but now was your best object,
The argument of your praise, balm of your age,
Most best, most dearest—should in this trice of time
Commit a thing so monstrous to dismantle   30
So many folds of favour. Sure, her offence
Must be of such unnatural degree
That monsters it, or your fore-vouched⁷ affections
Fall'n into taint;⁸ which to believe of her
Must be a faith that reason without miracle
Could never plant in me.
CORDELIA   I yet beseech your majesty
If for I want⁹ that glib and oily art

2   Anything.
3   Owns.
4   Friendless.
5   Disowned.
6   Choice.
7   Previously declared.
8   Become tainted.
9   Lack.

To speak and purpose not,[10] since what I well intend
I'll do't before I speak, that you make known   40
It is no vicious blot, murder, or foulness,
No unclean action or dishonoured step
That hath deprived me of your grace and favour,
But even for want of that for which I am rich:
A still-soliciting[11] eye, and such a tongue
As I am glad I have not; though not to have it,
Hath lost me in your liking.[12]
LEAR   Go to, go to. Better thou hadst not been born
Than not to have pleased me better.
FRANCE   Is it no more but this, a tardiness in nature   50
That often leaves the history unspoke
That it intends to do? My lord of Burgundy,
What say you to the lady? Love is not love
When it is mingled with respects that stands
Aloof from the entire point. Will you have her?
She is herself a dower.[13]
BURGUNDY   Royal Lear,
Give but that portion which yourself proposed,
And here I take Cordelia by the hand,
Duchess of Burgundy.
LEAR   Nothing, I have sworn. I am firm.   60
BURGUNDY [To CORDELIA]   I am sorry then you have so lost a father
That you must lose a husband.
CORDELIA   Peace be with Burgundy. Since that respects[14]
Of fortune are his love, I shall not be his wife.
FRANCE   Fairest Cordelia, that are most rich being poor,
Most choice forsaken, and most loved despised,
Thee and thy virtues here I seize upon.
Be it lawful I take up what's cast away.
Gods, gods! 'Tis strange, that from their cold'st neglect
My love should kindle to inflamed respect.   70
Thy dowerless daughter, king, thrown to my chance,
Is queen of us, of ours, and our fair France.
Not all the dukes in wat'rish[15] Burgundy
Shall buy this unprized precious maid of me.
Bid them farewell, Cordelia, though unkind,
Thou losest here a better where[16] to find.

---

10 i.e. to speak without meaning to do what I say.
11 Always soliciting or begging.
12 Favour.
13 Dowry.
14 Considerations.
15 Watery, superficial.
16 Place.

LEAR   Thou hast her, France, let her be thine, for we
Have no such daughter, nor shall ever see
That face of hers again. Therefore, be gone,
Without our grace, our love, our benison.[17]   80
Come, noble Burgundy.

[*Flourish. Exeunt* LEAR and BURGUNDY, ALBANY, CORNWALL, GLOUCESTER,
EDMUND, *followers and Attendants.*

Act 1, Scene 1: Cordelia confronts Goneril and Regan (269–309)

The scene continues with Cordelia, the King of France, Goneril and Regan left on stage. Thus we have the play's first and only private interaction among the sisters. Cordelia bids farewell to her sisters, an act she might not have committed without her fiancé's mediation, her words echoing Kent's earlier chastisement of the two sisters' empty words in the love-test. The passage suggests that Cordelia has long been the object of her sisters' jealousy because of their father's obvious preference for her; he has evidently loved her 'most'.

After Cordelia and the King of France leave, Goneril and Regan are the first to elucidate the reasons for Lear's irrational and rash behaviour in exiling Cordelia and Kent. As Regan explains, ''Tis the infirmity of his age; yet he hath ever but slenderly known himself'. Lear's advancing senility as well as his latent madness will dominate the rest of the play. Cordelia's remark to her sisters, 'I know you what you are', also suggests that this is a world in which people slenderly know themselves but others can see them precisely as they are.

We can begin to search here for the signs of evil that Goneril and Regan will display by the end of the play. Were they born evil, as Lear will later suggest, or do they have a reason to be evil – do they harbour grudges against his treatment of them in the past? Do they begin here to take advantage of their father's worsening condition, in effect, choosing evil? Or are they simply corrupted by the course of events set in place early in this scene by their father and continuing over the next few acts? In this passage, Shakespeare allows his audience to answer these questions; unlike their father, the sisters are each shrewd interpreters of human behaviour. For contrasting views of the causes for Goneril and Regan's behaviour, see Samuel Taylor Coleridge and Kathleen McLuskie above, **p. 53** and **60–2**.

17 Blessing.

FRANCE   Bid farewell to your sisters.

CORDELIA   The jewels of our father, with washed[1] eyes
Cordelia leaves you. I know you what you are,
And like a sister am most loath to call
Your faults as they are named. Use well our father:
To your professèd[2] bosoms I commit him.
But yet, alas, stood I within his grace,
I would prefer him to a better place.
So, farewell to you both.

GONERIL   Prescribe not us our duties.

REGAN   Let your study   10
Be to content your lord, who hath received you
At fortune's alms.[3] You have obedience scanted,[4]
And well are worth the want that you have wanted.[5]

CORDELIA   Time shall unfold what plighted[6] cunning hides;
Who covers faults, at last shame them derides.[7]
Well may you prosper.

FRANCE   Come, fair Cordelia.

[*Exeunt* FRANCE and CORDELIA

GONERIL   Sister, it is not a little I have to say of what most nearly
appertains to us both. I think our father will hence[8] tonight.

REGAN   That's most certain, and with you; next month with us.

GONERIL   You see how full of changes his age is; the observation we   20
have made of it hath not been little. He always loved our sister most,
and with what poor judgement he hath now cast her off appears too
grossly.[9]

REGAN   'Tis the infirmity of his age; yet he hath ever but slenderly
known himself.

GONERIL   The best and soundest of his time[10] hath been but rash. Then
must we look to receive from his age not alone the imperfection of
long-engrafted condition,[11] but therewithal[12] unruly waywardness[13]
that infirm and choleric[14] years bring with them.

REGAN   Such unconstant starts[15] are we like to have from him as this of   30
Kent's banishment.

GONERIL There is further compliment[16] of leave-taking between France and him. Pray, let's hit together. If our father carry authority with such dispositions as he bears,[17] this last surrender of his will but offend us.

REGAN We shall further think on't.

GONERIL We must do something, and i'th'heat.   [*Exeunt*

Act 1, Scene 2: Edmund deceives Gloucester (1–117)

Scene 2 opens with a soliloquy by Edmund. He and his brother Edgar are among the few characters allowed soliloquies, designed to give the audience a clear idea of a character's true nature (Lear is never allowed a soliloquy as he is accompanied by at least one other character at all times). Here we see a repetition of the major theme of the first scene: a father who has set his children against each other. But Gloucester, unlike Lear, does not love one better than the other (as we know from Gloucester's comments early in Act 1, Scene 1, Edgar is 'no dearer' to him than Edmund), but society values one child more than the other for being 'legitimate' rather than 'illegitimate'.

For Edmund, 'bastard', the usual epithet others apply to him, is empty precisely because it attempts to measure something that cannot be measured: his natural or nurtured character. We also see clear motivation for his later behaviour, for he argues here that evil men are not born but made. The final irony is Shakespeare's: while Edmund claims words should not be used as a form of power, his powerful speech bonds him to the audience, offering him more sympathy than the standard villain should expect (see Peter Brook above, **pp. 58–9**).

We may find it incredible that Gloucester so willingly accepts that Edgar, heretofore a blameless son, whose nature, Edmund will tell us, 'is so far from doing harms/That he suspects none', could so quickly turn against his father. Gloucester's irrational fear, of course, mirrors Lear's earlier rashness in dismissing the similarly innocent Cordelia (hence Gloucester's echo here of Lear's words: 'the quality of nothing hath not such need to hide itself'). That these two fathers know their grown children so little suggests they live in an alienating world. This is confirmed by Edgar's immediate acceptance of Edmund's lies; Edmund also shrewdly gambles that Edgar will not want to speak to his father but will flee instead. Not ironically, Edgar will soon adopt the disguise of the 'abhorred villain, unnatural, detested, brutish villain, worse than brutish' that Gloucester erroneously brands him here. To compare the source for this subplot, see Philip Sidney above, **pp. 38–40**.

---

16 Ceremony.
17 i.e. if he continues to show poor judgement in his decisions.

Enter EDMUND, *solus*[1]

EDMUND   Thou, Nature, art my goddess; to thy law
My services are bound. Wherefore should I
Stand in the plague of custom and permit
The curiosity of nations to deprive me?
For that I am some twelve or fourteen moonshines[2]
Lag[3] of a brother? Why 'bastard'? Wherefore[4] 'base'?[5]
When my dimensions are as well compact[6]
My mind as generous,[7] and my shape as true
As honest madam's[8] issue? Why brand they us   10
With 'base', 'baseness', 'bastardy'? Base, base?
Who in the lusty stealth of nature take
More composition and fierce quality
Than doth within a dull, stale tired bed
Go to the creating a whole tribe of fops
Got 'tween a sleep and wake?[9] Well, the
'Legitimate' Edgar, I must have your land.
Our father's love is to the bastard, Edmund,
As to the legitimate. Fine word, 'legitimate'!
Well, my legitimate, [*holding up a letter*] if this letter speed   20
And my invention thrive, Edmund the base
Shall to[10] th'legitimate. I grow, I prosper.
Now gods, stand up for bastards!

Enter GLOUCESTER

GLOUCESTER   Kent banished thus, and France in choler[11] parted,
And the king gone tonight, subscribed[12] his power,
Confined to exhibition,[13] all this done
Upon the gad![14] Edmund, how now? What news?
EDMUND   So please your lordship, none. [*Puts letter in his pocket*]
GLOUCESTER   Why so earnestly seek you to put up[15] that letter?

---

1   Alone.
2   i.e. months.
3   Behind.
4   Why.
5   Illegitimate, low.
6   i.e. my body is as well-built.
7   Large, capable.
8   Faithful wife's, with a pun on 'mistress'.
9   i.e. the children begotten in lust are better than the fools ('fops') begotten in marriage.
10 Overcome.
11 Anger.
12 Given away.
13 i.e. a financial allowance.
14 A wandering of the mind.
15 Put away.

EDMUND   I know no news, my lord.

GLOUCESTER   What paper were you reading?   30

EDMUND   Nothing, my lord.

GLOUCESTER   No? What needs then that terrible dispatch of it into
your pocket? The quality of nothing hath not such need to hide itself.
Let's see. Come, if it be nothing, I shall not need spectacles.

EDMUND   I beseech you, sir, pardon me; it is a letter from my brother
that I have not all o'erread; for so much as I have perused, I find it not
fit for your liking.

GLOUCESTER   Give me the letter, sir.

EDMUND   I shall offend either to detain or give it. The contents, as in
part I understand them, are too blame.[16]

GLOUCESTER   Let's see, let's see.   40

EDMUND   I hope for my brother's justification he wrote this but as an
essay[17] or taste of my virtue. [*Gives him the letter*]

GLOUCESTER   [*Reads*] 'This policy of age makes the world bitter to the
best of our times, keeps our fortunes from us till our oldness cannot
relish them. I begin to find an idle and fond[18] bondage in the oppres-
sion of aged tyranny, who sways not as it hath power, but as it is
suffered. Come to me, that of this I may speak more. If our father
would sleep till I waked him,[19] you should enjoy half his revenue
orever and live the beloved of your brother. Edgar.' Hum! Conspir-   50
acy! 'Slept till I waked him, you should enjoy half his revenue'. My
son Edgar, had he a hand to write this, a heart and brain to breed[20] it
in? When came this to you? Who brought it?

EDMUND   It was not brought me, my lord; there's the cunning of it. I
found it thrown in at the casement[21] of my closet.[22]

GLOUCESTER   You know the character[23] to be your brother's?

EDMUND   If the matter were good, my lord, I durst[24] swear it were his:
but in respect of that, I would fain[25] think it were not.

GLOUCESTER   It is his?

EDMUND   It is his hand, my lord, but I hope his heart is not in the   60
contents.

GLOUCESTER   Hath he never heretofore sounded[26] you in this business?

EDMUND   Never, my lord. But I have often heard him maintain it to be

---

16 Worthy of blame.
17 Trial.
18 Useless and senile.
19 i.e. if he died.
20 Nurture.
21 Window.
22 Dressing room.
23 Handwriting.
24 Dare.
25 Prefer to.
26 Involved with.

fit that, sons at perfect age and fathers declining, his father should be
as ward to the son,[27] and the son manage the revenue.

GLOUCESTER   O villain, villain his very opinion in the letter! Abhorred
villain, unnatural, detested, brutish villain, worse than brutish! Go,
sir, seek him; aye, apprehend him. Abominable villain! Where is he?

EDMUND   I do not well know, my lord. If it shall please you to suspend
your indignation against my brother till you can derive from him   70
better testimony of this intent, you should run a certain course,
where,[28] if you violently proceed against him, mistaking his purpose,
it would make a great gap in your own honour and shake in pieces the
heart of his obedience. I dare pawn[29] down my life for him. He hath
wrote this to feel[30] my affection to your honour and to no further
pretence of danger.

GLOUCESTER   Think you so?

EDMUND   If your honour judge it meet, I will place you where you
shall hear us confer of this and by an auricular assurance[31] have your
satisfaction, and that without any further delay than this very   80
evening.

GLOUCESTER   He cannot be such a monster.

EDMUND   Nor is not, sure.

GLOUCESTER   To his father, that so tenderly and entirely loves him.
Heaven and earth! Edmund, seek him out, wind me into him.[32] I pray
you, frame your business after your own wisdom. I would unstate[33]
myself to be in a due resolution.[34]

EDMUND   I shall seek him, sir, presently, convey the business as I shall
see means, and acquaint you withal.[35]

GLOUCESTER   These late eclipses in the sun and moon portend no good   90
to us. Though the wisdom of Nature can reason thus and thus, yet
nature finds itself scourged by the sequent[36] effects. Love cools,
friendship falls off, brothers divide; in cities, mutinies, in countries,
discords, in palaces, treason, the bond cracked between son and
father. Find out this villain, Edmund, it shall lose thee nothing. Do it
carefully. And the noble and true-hearted Kent banished, his offence
honest. Strange, strange!   [Exit

---

27 i.e. that the son should be the legal guardian of the father.
28 Whereas.
29 Hold in exchange.
30 Test.
31 Proof from hearing.
32 i.e. act secretly on my behalf to gain his confidence.
33 Give up my state.
34 i.e. convinced of his guilt or innocence.
35 Therewith.
36 Consequential.

Act 1, Scene 2: Edmund deceives Edgar (134–82)

The scene continues with another shrewd soliloquy by Edmund, who exploits the play's tension between fatalism (or Christian determinism) and free will, a common theme in Shakespeare's plays (see A. C. Bradley above, **pp. 55–6**). Edmund ridicules his father's belief that astrological forces such as eclipses, in opposition to the redemptive forces of Nature, are to blame for evil and corruption. Although the characters frequently call upon Greek and Roman gods and goddesses such as Nature, Edmund's vision of the world as cruel, cynical and unredemptive is contrasted with a Christian vision in the play, particularly in Lear's Christ-like suffering in the last three acts.

Edmund stresses that evil is created, not intrinsic, believing that humans are responsible for their own behaviour, whether they are villains, fools, or adulterers. His allusion to 'Bedlam' (the slang term for Bethlehem Hospital, a London insane asylum) ironically foreshadows his brother Edgar's disguise as Tom of Bedlam, a role in which Edgar freely chooses to play a fool and madman. In defending astrology, Edmund tells Edgar of the recent predictions of 'unnaturalness between the child and the parent, death, dearth, dissolutions of ancient amities, divisions in state, menaces and maledictions against king and nobles, needless diffidences, banishment of friends, dissipation of cohorts, nuptial breaches, and I know not what'. Ironically all of these tragic events will occur in the play, not as the result of astrological forces but of human free will. On recent critical re-interpretations of Shakespeare's use of free will, see R. A. Foakes above, **pp. 59–60**.

Enter EDGAR

EDMUND   [*Aside*] And out he comes, like the catastrophe[1] of the old comedy. Mine is villainous melancholy, with a sigh like them of Bedlam. [*To* EDGAR] O these eclipses do portend[2] these divisions. [*Sings*] Fa, sol, la, mi.

EDGAR   How now, brother Edmund, what serious contemplation are you in?

EDMUND   I am thinking, brother, of a prediction I read this other day, what should follow these eclipses.

EDGAR   Do you busy yourself about that?

EDMUND   I promise you, the effects he writ[3] of succeed unhappily, as of   10 unnaturalness between the child and the parent, death, dearth, dissolutions of ancient amities, divisions in state, menaces and maledictions against king and nobles, needless diffidences, banishment of

---

1   Denouement (or falling-off point after the climax).
2   Predict.
3   Wrote.

friends, dissipation of cohorts,[4] nuptial[5] breaches, and I know not what.

EDGAR   How long have you been a sectary astronomical?[6]

EDMUND   Come, come.[7] When saw you my father last?

EDGAR   Why, the night gone by.

EDMUND   Spake you with him?

EDGAR   Two hours together.   20

EDMUND   Parted you in good terms? Found you no displeasure in him by word nor countenance?

EDGAR   None at all.

EDMUND   Bethink yourself wherein you may have offended him, and at my entreaty[8] forbear his presence till some little time hath qualified[9] the heat of his displeasure, which at this instant so rageth in him that with the mischief of[10] your person it would scarce allay.[11]

EDGAR   Some villain hath done me wrong.

EDMUND   That's my fear, brother. I advise you to the best. Go armed. I bam no honest man, if there be any good meaning[12] towards you. I   30
have told you what I have seen and heard but faintly, nothing like the image and horror of it. Pray you, away!

EDGAR   Shall I hear from you anon?[13]

EDMUND   I do serve you[14] in this business.   [*Exit* EDGAR
A credulous[15] father and a brother noble,
Whose nature is so far from doing harms
That he suspects none; on whose foolish honesty
My practices[16] ride easy. I see the business.
Let me, if not by birth, have lands by wit.
All with me's meet[17] that I can fashion fit.[18]   [*Exit*   40

---

4   Allies.
5   Marital.
6   Zealous disciple of astrology.
7   Come on, come on.
8   Plea.
9   Modified.
10   i.e. harm to.
11   Subside.
12   Intent.
13   Soon (as throughout the text).
14   i.e. your interests.
15   Easily persuaded.
16   Plots.
17   Acceptable.
18   To fit, or to make work.

Act 1, Scene 4: Lear meets the disguised Kent (9–69)

In Act 1, Scene 3, Goneril and her steward Oswald discuss the unruly behaviour of Lear and his one-hundred-knight retinue, welcomed into her home as required by Lear's abdication demands in Act 1, Scene 1. Oswald has told Goneril that Lear struck one of her servants who had scolded Lear's Fool. She complains of Lear, 'he wrongs me; every hour/He flashes into one gross crime or other/That sets us all at odds. I'll not endure it'. She warns Oswald that, when Lear returns from hunting, 'I will not speak with him. Say I am sick', and instructs him and her other servants to be 'slack' (or negligent) in their usual obedience to the King.

Thus, in Act 1, Scene 3, we see Shakespeare establishing a motive for Goneril's later cruelty towards her father: his violent treatment of her staff, his constant verbal attacks on her, and the 'riotous' and uncontrolled behaviour of his attendant knights. Her complaints 'Idle old man,/That still would manage those authorities/That he hath given away!' and 'Old fools are babes again, and must be used/With checks as flatteries when they are seen abused' appear in the Quarto 1 text but not in the Folio. On Lear's scenes with his daughters, see A. C. Bradley above, **pp. 55–6**.

Goneril will also continue her conspiracy with her sister Regan by pitting their father against each of them: 'If he dislike it, let him to our sister,/Whose mind and mine I know in that are one,/Not to be overruled. [. . .] I'll write straight to my sister/To hold my very course.' In a play revolving around words, letters, whether fraudulent or truthful, will continue to figure prominently.

In the passage below from early in Act 1, Scene 4, Shakespeare juxtaposes Goneril's disloyal rejection of her father Lear at the end of Act 1, Scene 3 with the banished Kent's loyal acceptance of his king Lear. Kent's adoption of the disguise herein as Caius, never penetrated by others, emphasises, as will Edmund's disguise as Poor Tom, the fragility and mutability of identity. Lear and Caius-Kent's seemingly trivial introduction, 'What art thou?' 'A man, sir', ironically prefigures Lear's great discovery on the heath that furred gowns and other disguises hide the basic and common nature of us all.

Kent, ever the blunt servant, immediately responds in the terms of measurement that he knows Lear will understand: 'I do profess to be no less than I seem.' Lear certainly does not comprehend the irony of Kent's words, for his repetition of 'what art thou' after Kent's self-description demonstrates that Lear cannot yet fathom the concept of identity, nor can he separate the trappings of exterior form – 'what are you' – from basic, internal, nature – 'who are you'.

LEAR   How now, what art thou?

KENT   A man, sir.

LEAR   What dost thou profess? What wouldst thou with us?

KENT   I do profess to be no less than I seem, to serve him truly that will put me in trust, to love him that is honest, to converse with him that is wise and says little, to fear judgement, to fight when I cannot choose, and to eat no fish.

LEAR   What art thou?

KENT   A very honest-hearted fellow, and as poor as the king.

LEAR   If thou be as poor for a subject as he is for a king, th'art poor   10
enough. What wouldst thou?

KENT   Service.

LEAR   Who wouldst thou serve?

KENT   You.

LEAR   Dost thou know me, fellow?

KENT   No, sir, but you have that in your countenance which I would fain call master.

LEAR   What's that?

KENT   Authority.

LEAR   What services canst do?

KENT   I can keep honest counsel, ride, run, mar a curious tale in telling   20
it, and deliver a plain message bluntly. That which ordinary men are fit for, I am qualified in, and the best of me is diligence.

LEAR   How old art thou?

KENT   Not so young to love a woman for singing, nor so old to dote on her for anything. I have years on my back forty-eight.

LEAR   Follow me; thou shalt serve me if I like thee no worse after dinner. I will not part from thee yet. Dinner, ho, dinner! Where's my knave,[1] my fool? Go you and call my fool hither.   [*Exit First Knight*

Enter OSWALD

You, sirrah,[2] where's my daughter?

OSWALD   [*Contemptuously*] So please you—   [*Exit* 30

LEAR   What says the fellow there? Call the clotpoll[3] back.

[*Exeunt* SECOND KNIGHT *and* KENT

Where's my fool? Ho, I think the world's asleep.

Re-enter SECOND KNIGHT *and* KENT

---

1   Boy (or rogue).
2   Slave.
3   Blockhead.

How now? Where's that mongrel?

KENT   He says, my lord, your daughter is not well.

LEAR   Why came not the slave back to me when I called him?

SECOND KNIGHT   Sir, he answered me in the roundest[4] manner, he
would not.

LEAR   He would not?

SECOND KNIGHT   My lord, I know not what the matter is, but to my   40
judgement your highness is not entertained with that ceremonious
affection[5] as you were wont.[6] There's a great abatement[7] of kindness
appears as well in the general dependants as in the Duke himself also,
and your daughter.

LEAR   Ha? Say'st thou so?

KNIGHT   I beseech you pardon me, my lord, if I be mistaken, for my
duty cannot be silent when I think your highness wronged.

LEAR   Thou but remember'st me of mine own conception.[8] I have perceived a most faint neglect of late, which I have rather blamed as mine
own jealous curiosity than as a very pretence and purport of unkind-   50
ness. I will look further into't.

Act 1, Scene 4: Lear is reunited with the Fool (69–133)

If Lear does indeed have 'authority' in his countenance, Oswald refuses to
recognise it, nor does he see Lear as the country's patriarch and thus king but
as his employer Goneril's patriarch and thus simply as a father. As the scene
continues, we meet the Fool, Lear's court jester and surrogate son, but more
importantly his uninhibited alter ego and conscience.

The actor playing Cordelia would have doubled the role of the Fool (the two
characters never appear on stage at the same time). Thus, the Fool, 'who hath
much pined away' since Cordelia's departure, serves as a constant reminder,
directly or indirectly, of Cordelia to both Lear and the audience. That Lear
affectionately tolerates and encourages the Fool's freedom of speech (and fre-
quent rebuke of the increasingly foolish comments of Lear) stands in continual
contrast to Lear's rejection of Cordelia for her blunt words. This suggests that
Lear recognises that he has wronged Cordelia much earlier than he can admit it
in words in Act 4, Scene 4.

The Fool brings to the surface here several of the play's tensions, including

---

4   Bluntest, rudest.
5   Respect.
6   Accustomed.
7   Lessening.
8   Perception.

the trauma and guilt of father–child relationships and the whorish nature of women as wives, mothers and daughters. The speech he teaches Lear, on the wasted use of measurement to value invaluable things, to make more out of less (ending ultimately with 'more than two tens to a score', or nothing more than when he started) mocks Lear's actions in Act 1, Scene 1. When Lear complains 'This is nothing', the Fool responds, 'You gave me nothing for't. Can you make no use of nothing, uncle?' Lear's immediate response, 'Nothing can be made out of nothing', his words to Cordelia in Act 1, Scene 1, shows that he has fallen into his own trap of valuing foolish things. For a discussion of Alec Guinness's and Antony Sher's stage portrayals of the fool, see Ivor Brown and Sher above, **pp. 84–5** and **90–2**.

LEAR   But where's this Fool? I have not seen him this two days.

KNIGHT   Since my young lady's[1] going into France, sir, the Fool hath much pined away.

LEAR   No more of that, I have noted it. Go you and tell my daughter I would speak with her. [*Exit a Knight.*] Go you, call hither my fool.

[*Exit another Knight*

Enter OSWALD

O you, sir, you, sir, come you hither. Who am I, sir?

OSWALD   My lady's father.

LEAR   'My lady's father?' My lord's knave, you whoreson dog, you slave, you cur![2]

OSWALD   I am none of these, my lord, I beseech you, pardon me.   10

LEAR   Do you bandy looks with me,[3] you rascal? [*Strikes him*]

OSWALD   I'll not be struck, my lord.

KENT   Nor tripped neither, you base football player. [*Trips him*]

LEAR   [*To* KENT] I thank thee, fellow. Thou serv'st me, and I'll love thee.

KENT   [*To* OSWALD] Come, sir, I'll teach you differences.[4] Away, away! If you will measure your lubber's[5] length again, tarry; but away, you have wisdom. [*Kicks him out*]

LEAR   Now, friendly knave, I thank thee; there's earnest of thy service. [*Pays him*]

Enter FOOL

1   i.e. Cordelia's.
2   Worthless dog.
3   i.e. do you dare to look me straight in the eye.
4   Differences in rank.
5   Clumsy oaf's.

FOOL   Let me hire him, too; here's my coxcomb.[6] [*Offers* KENT *his fool's cap*]

LEAR   How now, my pretty knave, how dost thou?   20

FOOL   [*To* KENT] Sirrah, you were best take my coxcomb.

KENT   Why, fool?

FOOL   Why? For taking one's part that's out of favour. Nay, and thou canst not smile as the wind sits, thou'lt catch cold shortly. There, take my coxcomb. Why, this fellow [*pointing to* LEAR] hath banished two on's[7] daughters and done the third a blessing against his will. If thou follow him, thou must needs wear my coxcomb. [*To* LEAR] How now, nuncle,[8] would I had two coxcombs and two daughters.

LEAR   Why, my boy?

FOOL   If I gave them any living,[9] I'd keep my coxcombs myself. There's   30 mine; beg another of thy daughters.

LEAR   Take heed, sirrah, the whip.

FOOL   Truth is a dog that must to kennel. He must be whipped out, when the Lady brach[10] may stand by the fire and stink.

LEAR   A pestilent gall to me.

FOOL   Sirrah, I'll teach thee a speech.

LEAR   Do.

FOOL   Mark it, uncle:
Have more than thou showest,
Speak less than thou knowest,   40
Lend less than thou owest,[11]
Ride more than thou goest,[12]
Learn more than thou trowest,[13]
Set less than thou throwest,[14]
Leave thy drink and thy whore,
And keep in-a-door,
And thou shalt have more
Than two tens to a score.[15]

LEAR   This is nothing, fool.

FOOL   Then, like the breath of an unfeed[16] lawyer, you gave me nothing   50
for't. Can you make no use of nothing, uncle?

LEAR   Why, no, boy; nothing can be made out of nothing.

---

6   Clown's hat shaped like a rooster's comb.
7   Of his.
8   Contraction of 'mine uncle', used to mean here 'foolish man'.
9   Estates.
10 Bitch, female dog.
11 Own.
12 Walk.
13 Believe.
14 i.e. throw dice (as in gambling).
15 Two tens = a score.
16 Unpaid.

FOOL   [*To* KENT] Prithee, tell him so much the rent of his land comes to;
    he will not believe a fool.
LEAR   A bitter fool.

Act 1, Scene 4: Goneril confronts Lear (191–281)

As the scene continues, Lear asks, 'Who is it that can tell me who I am?' The response, 'Lear's shadow', is made by Lear in the Quarto text and by the Fool in the Folio (as presented below). Shakespeare plays with Renaissance Platonic images of the self as shadowy substance given form by reason and intellect, two human abilities Lear is fast losing as his madness sets in. Goneril proves here again to be the polished, persuasive speaker she was in Act 1, Scene 1, who has already learned to use her father's words to intimidate him. Whether this quarrel here justifies her further cruelty to her father, or is symptomatic of their long-strained relationship, Shakespeare leaves open. Clearly Lear cannot comprehend her hostility, the same type of hostility we saw him display to Cordelia in Act 1, Scene 1.

Here Lear extends the play's obsession with the male anxiety about children's true parentage, first voiced by Gloucester in the opening lines of Act 1, Scene 1. But in calling his daughter a bastard Lear calls himself a cuckold (the husband of an unfaithful wife), a term of ridicule and folly for Shakespeare's audience. In destroying his daughter's identity, he destroys his own, a fault we saw him commit earlier with Cordelia, as he slowly recognises when thinking of the ingratitude of which he accused her: 'O most small fault,/How ugly didst thou in Cordelia show.'

Goneril proves herself to be her father's daughter when she barters with him her love and support for the reduction of his retinue from one hundred to fifty knights; for her, as for him, agreeing to quantify an amount, in greater or lesser terms, substitutes for true love. Lear's answer is to condemn her femaleness, demanding of the goddess Nature, 'Into her womb convey sterility'. In denying her children, he strips himself of his own immortality through his descendants. Lear's emphasis here again reflects his contempt for female sexuality, which he equates to promiscuity and infidelity. See Kathleen McLuskie and Coppélia Kahn above, **pp. 60–2** and **62–4**.

GONERIL   Not only, sir, this, your all-licensed[1] Fool,
    But other of your insolent retinue
    Do hourly carp and quarrel, breaking forth
    In rank and not to be endurèd riots. Sir,
    I had thought by making this well known unto you
    To have found a safe redress,[2] but now grow fearful,

---

1   Given freedom (or licence) to say whatever he wants.
2   Remedy.

By what yourself too late have spoke and done,
That you protect this course, and put it on
By your allowance; which if you should, the fault
Would not 'scape[3] censure, nor the redress sleep,   10
Which in the tender[4] of a wholesome weal[5]
Might in their working do you that offence
That else were shame, that then necessity
Must call discreet[6] proceedings.

FOOL   For, you trow,[7] nuncle,
The hedge-sparrow fed the cuckoo so long,
That it had its head bit off by its young.
So out went the candle, and we were left darkling.[8]

LEAR   Are you our daughter?

GONERIL   Come, sir. I would you would make use of that good wisdom   20
Whereof I know you are fraught, and put away
These dispositions that of late transform you
From what you rightly are.

FOOL   May not an ass know when the cart draws the horse?
[Sings] Whoop, Jug,[9] I love thee!

LEAR   [Incredulous] Doth any here know me? Why, this is not Lear.
Doth Lear walk thus, speak thus? Where are his eyes?
Either his notion[10] weakens, or his discernings
Are lethargied. Sleeping or waking? Ha! Sure, 'tis not so.
Who is it that can tell me who I am?   30

FOOL   Lear's shadow.

LEAR   I would learn that, for by the marks
Of sovereignty, knowledge, and reason,
I should be false persuaded I had daughters.

FOOL   Which they will make an obedient father.

LEAR   Your name, fair gentlewoman?

GONERIL   Come, sir, this admiration is much of the savour
Of other your[11] new pranks. I do beseech you
Understand my purposes aright,
As you are old and reverend, should be wise.   40
Here do you keep a hundred knights and squires,
Men so disordered, so debauched and bold,
That this our court, infected with their manners,

3   Escape.
4   Care.
5   Commonwealth.
6   Appropriate.
7   Believe.
8   In the dark.
9   Disparaging word for a homely or troublesome woman.
10   Perception.
11   Of your.

Shows like a riotous inn; epicurism[12] and lust
Make it more like a tavern or brothel
Than a great palace. The shame itself doth speak[13]
For instant remedy. Be then desired
By her, that else will take the thing she begs,
A little to disquantity[14] your train,
And the remainder that shall still depend   50
To be such men as may besort[15] your age,
That know themselves and you.
LEAR   Darkness and devils!
    Saddle my horses, call my train together!
    Degenerate bastard, I'll not trouble thee.
    Yet have I left a daughter.
GONERIL   You strike my people, and your disordered rabble
    Make servants of their betters.

Enter ALBANY

LEAR   We that too late repents! O, sir, are you come?
    Is it your will that we prepare my horses?[16]
    Ingratitude! Thou marble-hearted fiend,   60
    More hideous when thou show'st thee in a child
    Than the sea-monster.
    [*To* GONERIL] Detested kite,[17] thou liest!
    My train are men of choice and rarest parts,
    That all particulars of duty know,
    And in the most exact regard support
    The worships of their name. O most small fault,
    How ugly didst thou in Cordelia show,
    That, like an engine, wrenched my frame of nature
    From the fixed place, drew from my heart all love,   70
    And added to the gall.[18] O Lear, Lear!
    [*Hitting his head*] Beat at this gate that let thy folly in
    And thy dear judgement out. Go, go, my people!
ALBANY   My lord, I am guiltless as I am ignorant
    Of what hath moved you.
LEAR   It may be so, my lord.
    Hark, Nature! Hear dear goddess!
    Suspend thy purpose if thou didst intend

12 Sensual indulgence.
13 Cry out.
14 Reduce.
15 Suit.
16 i.e. make ready to leave.
17 Bird of prey.
18 Bitterness.

To make this creature fruitful [*points at* GONERIL].
Into her womb convey sterility,
Dry up in her the organs of increase,   80
And from her derogate[19] body never spring
A babe to honour her. If she must teem,[20]
Create her child of spleen,[21] that it may live
And be a thwart[22] disnatured[23] torment to her.
Let it stamp wrinkles in her brow of youth,
With cadent[24] tears fret channels[25] in her cheeks,
Turn all her mother's pains and benefits
To laughter and contempt, that she may feel—
That she may feel—
How sharper than a serpent's tooth it is   90
To have a thankless child!

Act 2, Scene 2: Kent insults Oswald and is stocked (11–102)

At this point, Lear leaves but quickly returns to reject Goneril's offer to halve the amount of his retinue with the warning, 'Yet have I left a daughter,/Whom I am sure is kind and comfortable./When she shall hear this of thee, with her nails/She'll flay thy wolvish visage'. However, Goneril will ensure her sister Regan's support with a letter sent through Oswald. Lear's final threat to Goneril, 'Thou shalt find/That I'll resume the shape which thou dost think/I have cast off forever. Thou shalt, I warrant thee!', turns ironic when he resumes the shape he has just attempted to 'beat at' – that of a man made mad. As the scene concludes, we see the first breach between Goneril and Albany, whose attempt to stop his wife's mistreatment of her father she immediately dismisses as effeminate 'milky gentleness' and 'unharmful mildness'.

In Act 1, Scene 5, Lear sends Kent with a letter to Regan, who is shortly to arrive at Gloucester's house, stating his complaints about Goneril. The Fool warns Lear that his 'other daughter' Regan will act in the same way as Goneril. At this point Lear murmurs 'I did her wrong', perhaps a reference to Goneril, with whom he is still angry, but more probably to Cordelia, for whom he now has a proper measurement (Goneril) against which to judge and evaluate her.

Lear continues to see himself as the victim of one of his daughters (now

19 Debased.
20 Breed.
21 Violently tempered.
22 Interfering.
23 Unnatural.
24 Falling.
25 Ruts.

shifted to Goneril), complaining, 'I will forget my nature. So kind a father', forcing on to himself an identity we have not yet seen but to which he obstinately clings. The Fool consoles him by wishing, 'Thou shouldst not have been old before thou hadst been wise', to which Lear prays, 'O let me not be mad, sweet heaven! I would not be mad. Keep me in temper; I would not be mad'. At the end of this brief scene, he and his companions continue towards the home of Regan and Cornwall and the solace they expect to find there.

As Act 2 opens, Edmund meets his father's servant, Curan, who informs him that Regan and Cornwall are shortly to arrive at Gloucester's house. Curan also gossips about the 'likely wars toward 'twixt the two dukes of Cornwall and Albany'. Edmund will use both pieces of news to further incriminate his innocent brother Edgar in a plot to murder their father. Edmund stages a sword fight with Edgar; then, as Edgar flees at Edmund's urging, Edmund wounds himself and cries for help. Gloucester, who like Lear has 'but slenderly known himself' and the others around him, takes Edmund's lies for truth.

Thus Shakespeare continues to mirror the conflicts of Lear and his daughters with those of Gloucester and his sons. As the scene continues, Gloucester pledges to ask Cornwall's help in arresting Edgar, and thanks his 'loyal and natural boy' Edmund, offering him all his property. Cornwall and Regan enter, having heard the 'news' of Edgar's villainy and flight. They offer their sympathy first to Gloucester, who claims that his 'old' heart is 'cracked,' and then to Edmund, who has shown his father 'a child-like office'. As the scene concludes, Regan and Cornwall ask their 'good old friend' Gloucester for 'advice' on how to answer the letters they have received from Lear and from Goneril.

Act 2, Scene 2 begins with another encounter between the 'two messengers' Kent and Oswald; the latter does not recognise the man who tripped him in Act 1, Scene 4, instead addressing him as 'friend'. Oswald cannot understand Kent's abusive words which attempt to reduce him to 'nothing'. The farcical, one-sided duel between Kent and Oswald recalls the one immediately earlier between Edmund and Edgar. Whether Kent is justified in his abuse of Oswald, or overreacts through the passion of his own words, Shakespeare leaves his audience to decide.

Although Kent claims to be speaking plainly, that is, truthfully, Cornwall accuses him of manipulating his language so that, if his version of 'truth' does not suit the hearer, Kent will speak 'plain', that is, deceptively. In a sense, both Kent and Cornwall speak 'truthfully', for, as the Fool warns, 'truth and reason keep little company these days', especially since Lear abrogated the value of truth in Act 1, Scene 1.

OSWALD   Why dost thou use[1] me thus? I know thee not.
KENT   Fellow, I know thee.
OSWALD   What dost thou know me for?

1   Treat.

KENT   A knave, a rascal, an eater of broken meats,² a base, proud, shallow, beggarly, three-suited, hundred-pound, filthy, worsted-stocking knave;³ a lily-livered, action-taking⁴ knave; a whoreson, glass-gazing, superfinical⁵ rogue; one-trunk-inheriting slave; one that wouldst be a bawd⁶ in way of good service, and art nothing but the composition of a knave, beggar, coward, pander,⁷ and the son and heir of a mongrel bitch, whom I will beat into clamorous⁸ whining if thou   10
deny the least syllable of thy addition.⁹

OSWALD   What a monstrous fellow art thou, thus to rail on¹⁰ one that's neither known of thee nor knows thee!

KENT   What a brazen-faced varlet art thou to deny thou knowest me! Is it two days ago since I beat thee and tripped up thy heels before the king? Draw, you rogue! For though it be night, the moon shines.¹¹ I'll make a sop of the moonshine a'¹² you [drawing his sword]. Draw, you whoreson, cullionly barber-monger,¹³ draw!

OSWALD   Away, I have nothing to do with thee!

KENT   Draw, you rascal! You bring letters against the king and take   20
Vanity¹⁴ the puppet's part against the royalty of her father. Draw, you rogue, or I'll so carbonado your shanks¹⁵—draw, you rascal, come your ways!¹⁶

OSWALD   Help, ho, murder, help!

KENT   Strike, you slave! Stand, rogue! Stand, you neat¹⁷ slave, strike!

OSWALD   Help, ho, murder, help!

Enter EDMUND, *with his rapier drawn*, CORNWALL, REGAN, GLOUCESTER *and*
Servants

[. . .]

CORNWALL   Why art thou angry?

KENT   That such a slave as this should wear a sword
That wears no honesty. Such smiling rogues as these,
Like rats, oft bite those cords¹⁸ in twain   30

---

2   i.e. scraps.
3   i.e. dressed in one of the three typical suits of a servant, and wearing cheap wool socks.
4   Preferring to take legal action rather than fight.
5   Extra finicky.
6   Pimp.
7   Panderer.
8   Loud.
9   Titles.
10   Complain about.
11   i.e. there's enough light for a duel.
12   i.e. sop up the moonshine with.
13   Rascally effete (always at the barber's).
14   i.e. Goneril.
15   Cut and grill your legs.
16   Come on already.
17   Undiluted.
18   i.e. emotional bonds.

Which are too entrenched to unloose; smooth every passion
That in the natures of their lords rebel,
Bring oil to fire, snow to their colder moods,
Renege, affirm, and turn their halcyon beaks[19]
With every gale and vary of their masters,
Knowing naught, like dogs, but following.
[*To* OSWALD] A plague upon your epileptic visage!
Smile you[20] my speeches, as I were a fool?
Goose,[21] and[22] I had you upon Sarum Plain,[23]
I'd send you cackling home to Camelot.   40
CORNWALL   What, art thou mad, old fellow?
GLOUCESTER   How fell you out? Say that.
KENT   No contraries[24] hold more antipathy
Than I and such a knave.
CORNWALL   Why dost thou call him knave? What's his offence?
KENT   His countenance likes[25] me not.
CORNWALL   No more perchance does mine, or his, or hers.
KENT   Sir, 'tis my occupation to be plain.
I have seen better faces in my time
Than stands on any shoulder that I see   50
Before me at this instant.
CORNWALL   This is a fellow
Who, having been praised for bluntness, doth affect
A saucy roughness, and constrains the garb
Quite from his nature. He cannot flatter, he;
He must be plain; he must speak truth.
An[26] they will take't, so; if not, he's plain.[27]
These kind of knaves I know, which in this plainness
Harbour more craft and more corrupter ends
Than twenty silly-ducking observants[28]
That stretch their duties nicely.   60

---

19 i.e. changeable support.
20 You at.
21 i.e. despicable person.
22 If.
23 Salisbury, home of Camelot.
24 Enemies.
25 Pleases.
26 If.
27 i.e. equivocal.
28 Overly obsequious servants.

Act 2, Scene 2: Lear finds Kent in the stocks (196–252)

As the scene continues, Cornwall has Kent placed in 'the stocks', a wooden trap placed around his ankles as a form of public humiliation. Kent responds that, as he serves 'the king', the stocking of his messenger shows a 'too bold malice' against Lear. Regan supports her husband's decision, despite the pleading of Gloucester that Kent's 'master' Lear should discipline him, otherwise 'The king must take it ill/That he's so slightly valued in his messenger'. Regan and Cornwall leave Gloucester and Kent alone onstage; and, after some words of comfort to Kent, Gloucester leaves.

As Kent sits stocked, he reads a letter from Cordelia who has been apprised (by whom if not by Kent?) about his services in disguise to Lear. He then falls asleep, and Edgar enters to soliloquise on his devalued reputation and the intense hunt to capture him. He decides, as Kent had, to disguise his identity in order to survive. Edgar will adopt the persona of a 'poor Tom' (or inmate) of Bedlam (i.e. Bethlehem) Hospital for the insane in the 'basest and most poorest shape'. He smears himself with filth, knots his hair and trades all of his clothes for a rough blanket to wander the countryside as a 'roaring' madman, subject to the cruel forces of nature and of his abusive countrymen. He will re-evaluate his identity and the ways in which his society sees it, proclaiming in language unconsciously borrowed from his godfather Lear, 'Poor Tom!/That's something yet. Edgar I nothing am'. He then leaves.

As Lear, the Fool and his train continue their journey, they learn that Regan and Cornwall have left their house and have not sent his messenger Kent to inform them. Suddenly they encounter the stocked Kent, who, although serving as the play's apparent spokesman for truth, offers only a selection of the truth in recounting the reasons for his punishment. Here Shakespeare again reminds us that truth is relative and subjective, not fixed and indisputable, further emphasised by Lear's refusal to accept the truth of what he sees and hears, that his daughter and son-in-law have humiliated his servant. On Lear's 'hysterical passion' in this scene, see Coppélia Kahn above, **pp. 62–4**.

KENT   [*Waking*] Hail to thee, noble master.
LEAR   [*Incredulous*] How? Mak'st thou this shame thy pastime?
FOOL   Ha, ha. Look, he wears cruel garters.[1] Horses are tied by the
      heels, dogs and bears by th'neck, monkeys by th'loins, and men by
      th'legs. When a man's overlusty at legs,[2] then he wears wooden
      nether-stocks.[3]

---

1   i.e. wooden stocks on his legs, with a pun on 'crewel (or knitted) garters' (bands to hold up stockings).
2   i.e. eager to run away or to be lecherous.
3. Stockings for the lower part of the leg.

LEAR   What's he that has so much thy place⁴ mistook
    To set thee here?

KENT   It is both he and she,
    Your son and daughter.

LEAR   No.   10

KENT   Yes.

LEAR   No, I say.

KENT   I say, yea.

LEAR   No, no, they would not.

KENT   Yes, they have.

LEAR   By Jupiter,⁵ I swear no.

KENT   By Juno,⁶ I swear ay.

LEAR   They durst not do't:
    They would not, could not do't. 'Tis worse than murder
    To do upon respect such violent outrage.
    Resolve⁷ me with all modest haste which way   20
    Thou mayst deserve or they purpose⁸ this usage,
    Coming⁹ from us.

KENT   My lord, when at their home
    I did commend your highness' letters to them,
    Ere I was risen from the place that showed
    My duty kneeling, came there a reeking post,¹⁰
    Stewed¹¹ in his haste, half breathless, panting forth
    From Goneril, his mistress, salutations;
    Delivered letters spite of intermission,¹²
    Which presently they read, on whose contents
    They summoned up their men, straight took horse,   30
    Commanded me to follow and attend
    The leisure of their answer, gave me cold looks;
    And meeting here the other messenger,
    Whose welcome I perceived had poisoned mine—
    Being the very fellow that of late
    Displayed so saucily¹³ against your highness—
    Having more man than wit about me, drew.¹⁴
    He raised the house with loud and coward cries.

---

4   Rank (as servant to the King).
5   Highest of the Roman gods.
6   Wife of Jupiter and goddess of marriage and childbirth.
7   Inform.
8   Propose.
9   Having been sent.
10 Stinking messenger.
11 Sweating.
12 In the midst of my conversation with them.
13 Rudely.
14 i.e. drew my sword.

Your son and daughter found this trespass[15] worth
This shame[16] which here it suffers.   40
LEAR   O how this mother[17] swells up toward my heart!
Hysterica passio,[18] down thou climbing sorrow,
Thy element's[19] below. Where is this daughter?
KENT   With the earl, sir, within.
LEAR   Follow me not, stay there!   [Exit
KNIGHT   Made you no more offence than what you speak of?
KENT   No.

Act 2, Scene 2: Lear confronts Regan and Cornwall (316–71)

As the scene continues, Lear re-enters with his host Gloucester, furious at the
news that Regan and Cornwall 'deny' to speak with him. He repeatedly
demands they greet him, using as many forms of summons as he can: 'The king
would speak with Cornwall, the dear father/Would with his daughter speak,
commands her service.' The great psychological stress he is under reminds him
that 'We are not ourselves/When nature, being oppressed, commands the
mind/To suffer with the body'.

He commands again as he seemingly renounces his role as father to Regan:
'Tell the duke and's wife I'll speak with them,/Now, presently. Bid them come
forth and hear me.' In his anger, Lear again grapples with his fear that he is not
the true father of his children and that they offer nothing, or here 'naught'. His
angry curse to the gods about Goneril here, 'Dart your blinding flames/Into her
scornful eyes!', foreshadows the blinding of Gloucester.

Enter CORNWALL, REGAN, GLOUCESTER and Servants

LEAR   Good morrow to you both.
CORNWALL   Hail to your grace.   [KENT here set at liberty
REGAN   I am glad to see your highness.
LEAR   Regan, I think you are. I know what reason
   I have to think so. If thou shouldst not be glad,
   I would divorce me from thy mother's tomb,
   Sepulch'ring an adult'ress. [To KENT] Yea, are you free?
   Some other time for that.—Belovèd Regan,
   Thy sister is naught. O, Regan, she hath tied

15 i.e. my attempt to fight Oswald.
16 i.e. being stocked.
17 i.e. hysteria, a woman's disease.
18 i.e. hysterical passion, termed 'the suffocation of the mother' in this age.
19 Appropriate place.

Sharp-toothed unkindness like a vulture here [*points to his heart*].   10
I can scarce speak to thee, thou'lt not believe
Of how depraved a quality—O, Regan!
REGAN   I pray you, sir, take patience. I have hope
You less know how to value her desert[1]
Than she to slack her duty.
LEAR   Say? How is that?
REGAN   I cannot think my sister in the least
Would fail her obligation. If, sir, perchance
She have restrained the riots of your followers,
'Tis on such ground and to such wholesome end
As clears her from all blame.   20
LEAR   My curses on her!
REGAN   O, sir, you are old,
Nature in you stands on the very verge
Of her confine.[2] You should be ruled and led
By some discretion that discerns your state
Better than you yourself. Therefore I pray
That to our sister you do make return;
Say you have wronged her, sir.
LEAR   Ask her forgiveness?
Do you mark how this becomes[3] the house?
[*Kneels*] Dear daughter, I confess that I am old;
Age is unnecessary. On my knees I beg   30
That you'll vouchsafe[4] me raiment,[5] bed, and food.
REGAN   Good sir, no more. These are unsightly tricks.
Return you to my sister.
LEAR   [*Rising*] No, Regan.
She hath abated me of half my train,
Looked black upon me, struck me with her tongue
Most serpent-like, upon the very heart.
All the stored vengeances of heaven fall
On her ingrateful top! Strike her young bones,
You taking airs,[6] with lameness!
CORNWALL   Fie,[7] fie, sir!
LEAR   You nimble lightnings, dart your blinding flames   40
Into her scornful eyes! Infect her beauty,
You fen-sucked fogs, drawn by the powerful sun
To fall and blast her pride.

---

1   Worth.
2   Edge of her limit, i.e. he's at the end of his lifespan.
3   Cheapens.
4   Grant.
5   Clothing.
6   Malignant spirits.
7   For shame (a rebuke).

REGAN   O the blest gods! So will you wish on me
 When the rash mood—
LEAR   No, Regan, thou shalt never have my curse.
 Thy tender-hafted[8] nature shall not give
 Thee o'er to harshness. Her eyes are fierce, but thine
 Do comfort and not burn. 'Tis not in thee
 To grudge my pleasures, to cut off my train,   50
 To bandy hasty words, to scant my sizes,[9]
 And in conclusion, to oppose the bolt[10]
 Against my coming in. Thou better know'st
 The offices of nature, bond of childhood,
 Effects of courtesy, dues of gratitude.
 Thy half of the kingdom hast thou not forgot
 Wherein I thee endowed.
REGAN   Good sir, to th'purpose.   [*Tucket*[11] *within*
LEAR   Who put my man i'th'stocks?

Act 2, Scene 2: Goneril and Regan reject Lear (377–482)

The scene continues with the entrance of Goneril, and Lear will once more find himself in the positioning of bargaining with his daughters. However, this time he will not dictate the terms of the bargain but be forced to acquiesce to the terms imposed on him. Goneril and Regan's negotiations to reduce the size of Lear's train from one hundred knights to fifty to twenty-five to, ironically, nothing mock the love-test of Act 1, Scene 1 in which Lear negotiated to increase the size of the kingdom, according to the amount of love measured out by his three daughters. Far from eschewing 'nothing' as he did in Act 1, Scene 1, Lear must now accept it.

Lear's magnificent speech beginning 'O reason not the need' expresses all that the audience has felt since the imposition of the love-test in Act 1, Scene 1, that love or any other human emotion or need cannot be measured or reasoned. That Lear does not understand the meaning of his own words here is confirmed by his daughters' refusal to indulge his wishes, as they had done in Act 1, Scene 1.

LEAR   Who stocked my servant? Regan, I have good hope
 Thou didst not know on't. Who comes here? O heavens!

8 Gentle.
9 Reduce my allowances.
10 i.e. bolt the doors.
11 Trumpet flourish.

If you do love old men, if your sweet sway
Allow obedience, if yourselves are old,
Make it your cause, send down and take my part!
[*To* GONERIL] Art not ashamed to look upon this beard?
O Regan, wilt thou take her by the hand?

GONERIL   Why not by the hand, sir? How have I offended?
All's not offence that indiscretion finds,
And dotage terms so.

LEAR   O sides,[1] you are too tough!   10
Will you yet hold? How came my man i'th'stocks?

CORNWALL   I set him there, sir, but his own disorders
Deserved much less advancement.

LEAR   You? Did you?

REGAN   I pray you, father, being weak, seem so.
If till the expiration of your month
You will return and sojourn with my sister,
Dismissing half your train, come then to me.
I am now from home and out of that provision
Which shall be needful for your entertainment.

LEAR   Return to her, and fifty men dismissed?   20
No, rather I abjure all roofs and choose
To wage against the enmity of the air,
To be a comrade with the wolf and owl—
Necessity's sharp pinch! Return with her?
Why, the hot-blood in France, that dowerless took
Our youngest born, I could as well be brought
To knee his throne and, squire-like, pension beg,[2]
To keep base life afoot. Return with her?
Persuade me rather to be slave and sumpter[3]
[*pointing at* OSWALD] To this detested groom.[4]

GONERIL   At your choice, sir.   30

LEAR   Now I prithee, daughter, do not make me mad.
I will not trouble thee, my child. Farewell.
We'll no more meet, no more see one another.
But yet thou art my flesh, my blood, my daughter,
Or rather a disease that lies within my flesh,
Which I must needs call mine. Thou art a boil,
A plague-sore, an embossèd[5] carbuncle
In my corrupted blood. But I'll not chide thee.

---

1   i.e. body.
2   i.e. beg sustenance.
3   Beast of burden.
4   Servant.
5   Bulging.

Let shame come when it will, I do not call it.
I do not bid the thunder-bearer shoot,   40
Nor tell tales of thee to high-judging Jove.[6]
Mend when thou canst, be better at thy leisure.
I can be patient, I can stay with Regan,
I and my hundred knights.

REGAN   Not altogether so, sir.
I looked not for you yet, nor am provided
For your fit welcome. Give ear, sir, to my sister,
For those that mingle reason with your passion
Must be content to think you are old, and so—
But she knows what she does.

LEAR   Is this well spoken now?

REGAN   I dare avouch[7] it, sir. What, fifty followers?   50
Is it not well? What should you need of more?
Yea, or so many, sith[8] that both charge and danger
Speaks 'gainst so great a number? How in a house
Should many people under two commands
Hold amity? 'Tis hard, almost impossible.

GONERIL   Why might not you, my lord, receive attendance
From those that she calls servants, or from mine?

REGAN   Why not, my lord? If then they chanced to slack you,
We could control them. If you will come to me—
For now I spy a danger—I entreat you   60
To bring but five and twenty; to no more
Will I give place or notice.

LEAR   I gave you all—

REGAN   [Contemptuously] And in good time you gave it.

LEAR   —Made you my guardians, my depositaries,[9]
But kept a reservation[10] to be followed
With such a number. What, must I come to you
With five and twenty, Regan, said you so?

REGAN   And speak't again, my lord. No more with me.

LEAR   Those wicked creatures yet do seem well-favoured   70
When others are more wicked. Not being the worst
Stands in some rank of praise. [To GONERIL] I'll go with thee.
Thy fifty yet doth double five and twenty,
And thou art twice her love.

GONERIL   Hear me, my lord.
What need you five and twenty? Ten? Or five?

6   Another name for Jupiter, highest of the gods, who shoots thunder-bolts.
7   Confirm.
8   Since.
9   i.e. I deposited my power in you.
10 Condition.

To follow in a house, where twice so many
Have a command to tend you?
REGAN   What need one?
LEAR   O reason not the need! Our basest beggars
Are in the poorest thing superfluous.
Allow not nature more than nature needs,   80
Man's life's as cheap as beast's. Thou art a lady;
If only to go warm were gorgeous,[11]
Why needs not what thou gorgeous wearest,
Which scarcely keeps thee warm. But for true need—
You heavens, give me that patience, patience I need!
You see me here, you gods, a poor old fellow,
As full of grief as age, wretched in both.
If it be you that stirs these daughters' hearts
Against their father, fool me not so much
To bear it tamely.[12] Touch me with noble anger,   90
O, let not women's weapons, water-drops,
Stain my man's cheeks. No, you unnatural hags,
I will have such revenges on you both
That all the world shall—I will do such things—
What they are, yet I know not, but they shall be
The terrors of the earth! You think I'll weep;
No, I'll not weep,   [Storm and tempest
I have full cause of weeping, but this heart
Shall break in a hundred thousand flaws
Or e'er I'll weep. O Fool, I shall go mad!   100

[Exeunt LEAR, GLOUCESTER, KENT, FOOL and Knight

CORNWALL   Let us withdraw; 'twill be a storm.
REGAN   This house is little. The old man and his people
Cannot be well bestowed.
GONERIL   'Tis his own blame hath put himself from rest,
And must needs taste his folly.
REGAN   For his particular,[13] I'll receive him gladly,
But not one follower.
CORNWALL   So am I purposed.

---

11 i.e. if only clothing was valued for its warmth rather than for its gorgeous appearance.
12 Accept it without fighting back.
13 i.e. as for him alone.

Act 3, Scene 2: Lear goes mad on the heath (1–69)

At this point, Gloucester re-enters alone to warn Lear's daughters and son-in-law that Lear will not be able to survive on the heath in the storm. The others are unmoved, particularly Goneril, who orders her host 'Shut up your doors' against Lear and his train. Cornwall repeats the order and Gloucester obliges them only reluctantly as Act 2 ends.

In Act 3, Scene 1, Kent and a Gentleman sympathetic to Lear discuss Lear's wanderings in the storm, accompanied only by the Fool, who 'labours to out-jest/His heart-struck injuries'. Kent warns the Gentleman that there is 'div-ision,/Although as yet the face of it be covered/With mutual cunning, 'twixt Albany and Cornwall' and that the powers of France are making ready to invade. Thus Lear's 'division of the kingdoms' resulted not in unity but in further division and civil war between his two sons-in-law. Kent sends the Gentleman to Dover to report Lear's 'unnatural and bemadding sorrow' to the newly arrived Cordelia, now Queen of France and head of its army, sending as a token of his identity his ring. After seeing it, Cordelia will inform the Gentleman of Kent's true identity.

Act 3, Scene 2 begins with Lear and the Fool braving the storm. Each of them will see women's promiscuity and vanity as the source of evil, but Lear seems to have learned 'nothing' since the beginning of the play, claiming 'I will be the pattern of all patience./I will say nothing'. Lear will also rationalise his madness by portraying himself as a victim: 'I am a man more sinned against than sinning.' Yet a sign of the love and care he should have displayed to his daughters, particularly to Cordelia, comes in his question to the Fool (a surrogate for Cordelia): 'How dost my boy? Art cold?' Here Shakespeare offers us the first, brief glimpse of an unselfish and sympathetic Lear.

On Lear's behaviour in this scene, see Charles Lamb and William Hazlitt above, **pp. 50–1** and **51–2**.

Storm still. Enter LEAR *and the* FOOL

LEAR   Blow, wind, and crack your cheeks! Rage, blow,
You cataracts and hurricanoes,[1] spout
Till you have drenched the steeples, drowned the cocks![2]
You sulphurous and thought-executing[3] fires,
Vaunt-couriers[4] to oak-cleaving thunderbolts,
Singe my white head. And thou all-shaking thunder,
Smite flat the thick rotundity of the world,

1   Deluges and hurricanes.
2   Weathercocks or weather-vanes.
3   Capable of executing thought.
4   Forerunners.

Crack nature's mould, all germens[5] spill at once
That make ingrateful man.

FOOL   O nuncle, court holy water[6] in a dry house is better than this   10
rain-water out a'door. Good nuncle, in,[7] and ask thy daughters'
blessing. Here's a night pities neither wise man nor fool.

LEAR   Rumble thy bellyful; spit, fire; spout, rain!
Nor rain, wind, thunder, fire are my daughters.
I task not you, you elements, with unkindness.
I never gave you kingdom, called you children.
You owe me no subscription.[8] Why then, let fall
Your horrible pleasure. Here I stand your slave,
A poor, infirm, weak, and despised old man.
But yet I call you servile ministers,[9]   20
That have with two pernicious daughters joined
Your high engendered[10] battle 'gainst a head
So old and white as this. O, 'tis foul!

FOOL   He that has a house to put his head in has a good head-piece.[11]
[Sings] The codpiece[12] that will house
Before the head has any,
The head and he shall louse;[13]
So beggars marry many.
The man that makes his toe
What he his heart should make,   30
Shall have a corn cry woe,
And turn his sleep to wake.[14]
For there was never yet fair woman but she made mouths in a glass.[15]

LEAR   No, I will be the pattern of all patience. [He sits]

Enter KENT *as Caius*

I will say nothing.

KENT   Who's there?

FOOL   Marry, here's grace, and a codpiece; that's a wise man and a
fool.

---

5   Seeds.
6   i.e. flattery.
7   i.e. go in.
8   Loyalty.
9   Agents required to serve.
10   Heavenly.
11   Brain.
12   Covering for male genitals worn over breeches.
13   i.e. the man who fornicates ('houses' his codpiece) before he has a roof over his head will become a
     lice-covered beggar.
14   i.e. the man who kicks out ('toes') what he really desires in his heart will suffer pain and
     sleeplessness.
15   Vainly regards herself in a mirror.

KENT   Alas, sir, sit you here? Things that love night
Love not such nights as these. The wrathful skies   40
Gallow[16] the very wanderers of the dark
And makes them keep[17] their caves. Since I was man,[18]
Such sheets of fire, such bursts of horrid thunder,
Such groans of roaring wind and rain I ne'er
Remember to have heard. Man's nature cannot carry
The affliction nor the force.
LEAR   Let the great gods,
That keep this dreadful pother[19] o'er our heads,
Find out their enemies now. Tremble, thou wretch,
That hast within thee undivulgèd crimes
Unwhipped of justice. Hide thee, thou bloody hand,[20]   50
Thou perjured and thou simular man[21] of virtue
That art incestuous. Caitiff,[22] in pieces shake,
That under covert and convenient seeming[23]
Hast practised on man's life.
Close pent-up guilts,[24] rive[25] your concealèd centres
And cry these dreadful summoners grace.[26]
I am a man more sinned against than sinning.
KENT   Alack, bare-headed?
Gracious my lord, hard by here is a hovel.
Some friendship will it lend you 'gainst the tempest.   60
Repose you there, whilst I to this hard house—[27]
More hard than is the stone whereof 'tis raised,
Which even but now, demanding[28] after you,
Denied me to come in—return and force
Their scanted[29] courtesy.
LEAR   My wit begins to turn.[30]
[To the FOOL] Come on, my boy. How dost, my boy? Art cold?
I am cold myself.

16 Frighten.
17 Keep inside.
18 i.e. an adult.
19 Uproar.
20 i.e. the bloody hand of a murderer.
21 Pretender.
22 Wretch.
23 Deception.
24 i.e. expose your guilt.
25 Split.
26 Ask for mercy.
27 i.e. Gloucester's house.
28 Asking.
29 Withheld.
30 i.e. I'm beginning to lose my mind.

Act 3, Scene 4: Lear meets Tom of Bedlam (19-109)

As Act 3, Scene 2 ends, Kent leads Lear to the hovel where he can take shelter from the storm. In the Folio text only, the Fool recites a future prophecy of the magician Merlin about the 'great confusion' in Lear's (and probably King James I's) kingdom that will come to England due to hypocrites, villains and others who are corrupt or intemperate.

In Act 3, Scene 3, Gloucester complains to a seemingly sympathetic Edmund of Goneril, Regan and Cornwall's usurpation of his own house and their demand that he neither speak, entreat or 'any way' sustain Lear. Of this private confession, Gloucester begs Edmund, 'Say you nothing'. Gloucester speaks of the 'division betwixt the dukes' and reveals that he has received a letter too 'dangerous' to be spoken of, which suggests that Lear's sufferings will be 'revenged home' by the forces (presumably French) already landed in the kingdom.

Gloucester again asks that Edmund keep secret from Cornwall all of Gloucester's attempts to aid Lear and to say that he is ill if sent for. Gloucester pledges that he will relieve Lear 'though I die for't'. After Gloucester goes in search of Lear, Edmund glories in his chance to betray his treacherous father to Cornwall, claiming that this 'fair deserving' will draw for him 'that which my father loses: no less than all'. Edmund recognises, as did Goneril and Regan, that 'the younger rises when the old do fall'. Any sympathy we felt earlier for Edmund has now been transferred to his father.

As Act 3, Scene 4 begins, Kent attempts to coerce Lear and the Fool into the hovel. Lear tells the worried Kent that it is not the external, natural storm that causes his suffering but the internal, unnatural 'tempest' in his mind, which 'doth from my senses take all feeling else,/Save what beats there: filial ingratitude'. Lear again obsessively recalls the injustices done to him by his two eldest daughters but slowly begins to accept blame for beginning the chain of events that has caused such political and personal corruption and chaos, saying 'O I have ta'en/Too little care of this'. On Ian Holm's portrayal of Lear in this scene, see Alexander Macaulay above, **p. 92**.

The entrance of Edgar disguised and acting like a madman (compare Samuel Harsnett above, **p. 40**) ironically both illuminates Lear's new understanding of the bare 'unaccommodated' nature of man (released from the clothing which hides all) and supports his disgust for the lasciviousness of women. We have not seen Edgar mistreated by any women in the play but have heard instead in Act I, Scene I of his father's contempt for his mistress, Edmund's mother. Immediately afterwards, we watched Lear's mistreatment of Cordelia. Yet Edgar, like Lear, blames women for his corruption, warning Lear not to let their seductive appearance 'betray thy poor heart to women'. Shakespeare may simply have been relying on common Renaissance beliefs that lust caused madness, but he also appears to be trying to ridicule the notion that all evil resides in women (on this point, see Coppélia Kahn above, **pp. 62–4**).

LEAR   O Regan, Goneril,
    Your old kind father, whose frank heart gave you all—
    O that way madness lies! Let me shun that,
    No more of that.
KENT   Good my lord, enter.
LEAR   Prithee, go in thyself, seek thy own ease.
    This tempest will not give me leave to ponder
    On things would hurt me more, but I'll go in.   [*Exit* FOOL
    Poor naked wretches, wheresoe'er you are,
    That bide¹ the pelting of this pitiless night,
    How shall your houseless heads and unfed sides,²   10
    Your looped and windowed raggedness defend you
    From seasons such as these? O I have ta'en
    Too little care of this. Take physic, pomp,
    Expose thyself to feel what wretches feel,
    That thou mayst shake the superflux³ to them
    And show the heavens more just.

Enter FOOL *from the hovel*

FOOL   Come not in here, nuncle! Here's a spirit! Help me, help me!
KENT   Give me thy hand. Who's there?
FOOL   A spirit. He says his name's Poor Tom.
KENT   What art thou that dost grumble there in the straw? Come forth!   20

Enter EDGAR *as Poor Tom, dirty and dressed only in a blanket*

EDGAR   Away, the foul fiend follows me. Through the sharp hawthorn
    blows the cold wind. Go to thy cold bed and warm thee.
LEAR   Hast thou given all to thy two daughters, and art thou come to
    this?
EDGAR   Who gives anything to Poor Tom, whom the foul fiend hath led
    through fire and through ford and whirlpool, o'er bog and quagmire;
    that has laid knives under his pillow and halters in his pew;⁴ set rats-
    bane by his pottage;⁵ made him proud of heart to ride on a bay
    trotting-horse over four-inched bridges, to course⁶ his own shadow
    for a traitor. Bless thy five wits, Tom's a-cold! Bless thee from whirl-   30
    winds, star-blasting and taking.⁷ Do Poor Tom some charity, whom

1   Abide.
2   i.e. body.
3   Surplus.
4   i.e. in a church pew.
5   Poison by his soup.
6   Hunt.
7   Injury from the astrological elements and disease.

the foul fiend vexes. There could I have him now, and there, and there, and there again! [*Storm still*

LEAR   What, has his daughters brought him to this pass? Couldst thou save nothing? Didst thou give them all?

FOOL   Nay, he reserved[8] a blanket, else we had been all shamed.

LEAR   Now all the plagues, that in the pendulous air Hang fated o'er men's faults, fall on thy daughters!

KENT   He hath no daughters, sir.

LEAR   Death, traitor! Nothing could have subdued nature   40 To such a lowness but his unkind daughters. Is it the fashion that discarded fathers Should have thus little mercy on their flesh? Judicious punishment, 'twas this flesh Begot those pelican[9] daughters.

EDGAR   Pillicock[10] sat on Pillicock's hill;[11] allo, lo, lo.

FOOL   This cold night will turn us all to fools and madmen.

EDGAR   Take heed a'th'foul fiend, obey thy parents, keep thy words justly, swear not, commit not with man's sworn spouse,[12] set not thy sweet heart on proud array.[13] Tom's a-cold.   50

LEAR   What hast thou been?

EDGAR   A servingman, proud in heart and mind, that curled my hair, wore gloves in my cap, served the lust of my mistress' heart, and did the act of darkness[14] with her. Swore as many oaths as I spake words, and broke them in the sweet face of heaven. One that slept in the contriving of lust and waked to do it. Wine loved I deeply, dice dearly, and in woman out-paramoured the Turk.[15] False of heart, light of ear, bloody of hand; hog in sloth, fox in stealth, wolf in greediness, dog in madness,[16] lion in prey. Let not the creaking of shoes nor the rustlings of silks betray thy poor heart to women. Keep thy foot out of brothel, thy   60 hand out of placket,[17] thy pen from lender's book,[18] and defy the foul fiend. Still through the hawthorn blows the cold wind. Heigh no nonny. Dauphin,[19] my boy, my boy! *Cessez*,[20] let him trot by.   [*Storm still*

LEAR   Why, thou wert better in thy grave than to answer with thy uncovered body this extremity of the skies. Is man no more but this?

---

8   Kept.
9   i.e. a pun on the notion that pelican mothers feed their young on their own blood; here they are feeding on the blood of their young.
10   Slang for penis.
11   Slang for vagina.
12   i.e. commit adultery with another man's wife.
13   i.e. covet material goods.
14   i.e. fornicated.
15   i.e. had more lovers than the Turkish Sultan.
16   Rabid condition.
17   i.e. ladies' skirts.
18   Money-lender's account book.
19   i.e. his horse, named for a French prince.
20   'Stop' in French.

Consider him well. Thou owest the worm no silk, the beast no hide, the sheep no wool, the cat no perfume. Here's three on's[21] are sophisticated, thou art the thing itself. Unaccommodated man is no more but such a poor, bare, forked[22] animal as thou art. Off, off, you lendings![23] Come unbutton—[*tries to strip off his clothes*].   70

FOOL   Prithee, nuncle, be content. This is a naughty night to swim in.

Act 3, Scene 6: Lear's mock-trial of Goneril and Regan (20–60)

As the scene continues, Gloucester enters, and, like Lear, he does not recognise Edgar. He complains to Lear, 'Hath your grace no better company?' In violation of Regan's command that he 'shut up' his doors to Lear, Gloucester attempts to coax Lear into shelter, but the king continues to question the 'philosopher' Edgar. Gloucester blames Lear's madness on the attempts of Goneril and Regan to seek their father's death, and tells the disguised Kent that 'poor banished' Kent had predicted this would come to pass. Gloucester complains of his own impending madness, caused by the plot against his life by Edgar, yet his realisation 'I loved him, friend,/No father his son dearer' either has come too late or is as hypocritical as Lear's outbursts about Cordelia in Act 1, Scene 1. At the end of the scene, Lear finally enters the hovel, ordering in all his companions.

In Act 3, Scene 5, Cornwall plots 'revenge' against Gloucester for aiding Lear and abetting Cordelia's return to England, revealed by the secret letter Edmund has stolen from his father. Cornwall offers Gloucester's earldom to Edmund and orders him to seek and waylay Gloucester so that Cornwall can apprehend him. Cornwall concludes the scene by making Edmund another bargain in a type of love-test: if Edmund helps to secure the traitor Gloucester, Cornwall claims, 'I will lay trust upon thee, and thou shalt find a dearer father in my love'.

In Act 3, Scene 6, Gloucester shows Lear, Kent, the Fool and Edgar into the shelter. As Lear goes increasingly mad, and Edgar continues to feign madness, the Fool questions Lear about the nature of madness. Prompted by the Fool's comment that a man's mad if he trusts in 'a whore's oath', Lear decides to place Goneril and Regan on trial for their mistreatment of him, with himself, Edgar and the Fool as their judges. In this 'mock-trial', which does not appear in the Folio (and was probably cut by Shakespeare), Lear uses pieces of furniture as stand-ins for his absent daughters, and is humoured in his madness by his companions.

On the staging of the mock-trial, see Harley Granville-Barker above, **pp. 81–2**; for Edward Bond's adaptation of it, see Bond above, **pp. 89–90**.

21 Of us.
22 Two-legged.
23 Clothes.

LEAR   It shall be done. I will arraign them straight. [*To* EDGAR] Come,
sit thou here, most learnèd justice.
[*To the* FOOL] Thou, sapient[1] sir, sit here. No, you she-foxes—[2]
EDGAR   Look where she stands and glares! Want'st[3] thou eyes at trial,
madam?
[*Sings*] Come o'er the bourn,[4] Bessy, to me.[5]
FOOL   [*Sings*] Her boat hath a leak
And she must not speak
Why she dares not come over to thee.
EDGAR   The foul fiend haunts poor Tom in the voice of a nightingale.   10
Hoppedance[6] cries in Tom's belly for two white herring. Croak not,
black angel! I have no food for thee.
KENT   How do you, sir? Stand you not so amazed.
Will you lie down and rest upon the cushions?
LEAR   I'll see their trial first. Bring in their evidence.
[*To* EDGAR] Thou robèd man of justice, take thy place.
[*To the* FOOL] And thou, his yoke-fellow[7] of equity,
Bench by his side. [*To* KENT] You are o'th'commission;[8]
Sit you too.
EDGAR   Let us deal justly.   20
Sleepest or wakest, jolly shepherd?
Thy sheep be in the corn,
And for one blast of thy minikin[9] mouth
Thy sheep shall take no harm.
Purr, the cat, is grey.
LEAR   Arraign her first; 'tis Goneril. I here take my oath before this
honourable assembly, she kicked the poor king her father.
FOOL   Come hither, mistress. Is your name Goneril?
LEAR   She cannot deny it.
FOOL   Cry you mercy, I took you for a joint-stool.[10]   30
LEAR   And here's another whose warped looks proclaim
What store her heart is made on—Stop her there!
Arms, arms, sword, fire! Corruption in the place!
False justicer, why hast thou let her 'scape?[11]

---

1   Wise.
2   i.e. predators.
3   Lack.
4   Brook.
5   Edgar is singing a contemporary song which is continued by the Fool.
6   The name of a devil.
7   Partner.
8   i.e. also on the panel of judges.
9   Nonsense word (Edgar is reciting foolish verses here and elsewhere).
10   A professionally made stool.
11   Escape.

EDGAR   Bless thy five wits.
KENT   O pity! Sir, where is the patience now
That you so oft have boasted to retain?
EDGAR   [*Aside*] My tears begin to take his part so much
They'll mar my counterfeiting.[12]

Act 3, Scene 7: Gloucester's blinding (1–106)

As Act 3, Scene 6 continues, Lear descends completely into madness, mumbling the same type of incoherent speeches that Edgar has as Poor Tom; but, as Edgar and the audience have just learned, Lear's decline moves us to tears. He is still preoccupied with his daughters, but his madness has liberated his conscious mind, so that he can ask with the clarity of a moral philosopher or psychologist, 'Let them anatomise Regan; see what breeds about her heart. Is there any cause in nature that makes these hard hearts?' (ironically answered in Act 4, Scene 7 by Cordelia as 'no cause, no cause'). We can consider Act 3, Scene 6 the climax, or turning-point, of the play.

Gloucester returns to warn Kent that there is a plot against Lear's life and that he must be taken to Dover for his own safety. Edgar is then left alone onstage to soliloquise briefly on Lear's suffering. In a play dependent on constant contrast and comparison to determine true value, and the reversal of parent–child roles, Edgar measures his miseries against Lear's, concluding 'How light and portable my pain seems now,/When that which makes me bend makes the king bow./He childed as I fathered'.

Act 3, Scene 7 has been described by numerous critics over the centuries as the 'cruellest' scene in English literature (on its staging by Peter Brook, see Dennis Kennedy above, **pp. 85–8**). The conspiracy of Goneril, Regan and Cornwall, abetted by Edmund, to punish Gloucester's treachery in aiding Lear's escape by plucking out his eyes is truly shocking. Here we see the pent-up frustration of Lear's elder daughters and his son-in-law in not being able to punish their own patriarch Lear, and they project their anger on to his substitute and surrogate, Gloucester. Whether Gloucester deserves punishment for assisting Lear, or even for his callous treatment of both his sons in the play's earliest scenes, is for the audience to decide. However, this form of punishment is as excessive as the other immoderate behaviour we have seen throughout the first three acts.

Shakespeare has now made such an unsympathetic figure entirely sympathetic, so that, as with Lear's suffering finally moving us to tears (and empathy) in Act 3, Scene 6, we are prepared to be moved by Gloucester's suffering. Not ironically, Goneril and Regan, with whom we might have sympathised early in the play, we have now come to despise. This alteration (or slow exchange) of

12 Disguise as a madman.

sympathy towards the characters makes us question whom we value at any given point, so that none of the characters has a fixed value throughout the play but a constantly shifting one, relative to each situation and each other (on the 'construction' of the play by the audience, see Terence Hawkes above, **pp. 65–6**).

Shakespeare could have chosen not to stage Act 3, Scene 7 and instead had a set of characters come onstage to discuss the blinding of Gloucester after it had occurred offstage. Thus Shakespeare could have used the same method as in *Hamlet* (a play written some years before *King Lear*) in which he did not stage the murder of old Hamlet but had the Ghost of Hamlet narrate the events afterwards to his astonished son. That Shakespeare did stage this blinding scene in *King Lear* tells us that by the peak of his career (1606) and the composition of this play he seemed to want to insist that the audience directly witness and be complicit in the cruelty inherent in tragedy.

Goneril determines Gloucester's exact punishment, 'Pluck out his eyes!', but leaves the stage without participating in the act, as her sister does, yet she is not innocent or less guilty than Regan in such 'monstrous' cruelty. While Lear demonstrates that 'bare, unaccommodated man' will go mad when on the heath and beyond the reach of human society or its laws, Goneril and Regan enact such madness when similarly relieved of the moral restrictions of others. It is only those in the lower ranks of this society, the servants, who attempt to force moral law on to the Duke of Cornwall and Regan by trying to stop Gloucester's blinding and by healing him afterwards.

In this scene, the emotional and spiritual blindness of which Kent warned Lear in Act 1, Scene 1 ('See better, Lear') is transformed into physical blindness. Although Cornwall plucks out Gloucester's eyes, women create this evil, according to the men in this scene. As one of the servants warns at the scene's conclusion, 'Women will all turn monsters' (on 'monstrous' children, see James I, Charles Gildon, Samuel Taylor Coleridge and Kathleen McLuskie above, **pp. 40–2, 48, 53** and **60–2**). Because of its importance, and in order to maintain its shocking pace and rhythm, this scene is presented whole here without further headnotes.

Enter CORNWALL, REGAN, GONERIL, EDMUND *and Servants*

CORNWALL [*To* GONERIL]   Post speedily to my lord your husband; show him this letter. The army of France is landed. [*To Servants*] Seek out the villain Gloucester.

[*Exeunt some Servants*

REGAN   Hang him instantly!

GONERIL   Pluck out his eyes!

CORNWALL   Leave him to my displeasure. Edmund, keep you our sister company. The revenges we are bound to take upon your traitorous father are not fit for your beholding. Advise the duke, where you are going, to a most festinate preparation.[1] We are bound to the like. Our post shall be swift and intelligent betwixt us. Farewell, dear sister; 10 farewell, my lord of Gloucester.

Enter OSWALD

How now, where's the king?
OSWALD   My lord of Gloucester hath conveyed him hence.
  Some five or six and thirty of his knights,
  Hot questrists[2] after him, met him at gate,
  Who, with some other of the lord's dependants,
  Are gone with him towards Dover, where they boast
  To have well-armèd friends.
CORNWALL   Get horses for your mistress.   [*Exit* OSWALD
GONERIL   Farewell, sweet lord, and sister.   20
CORNWALL   Edmund, farewell.   [*Exeunt* GONERIL *and* EDMUND
                    [*To Servants*] Go seek the traitor Gloucester.
  Pinion[3] him like a thief; bring him before us.   [*Exeunt other Servants*
  Though we may not pass upon his life
  Without the form of justice, yet our power
  Shall do a courtesy to our wrath, which men
  May blame but not control.

Enter GLOUCESTER *brought in by two or three Servants*

                    Who's there—the traitor?
REGAN   Ingrateful fox! 'Tis he.
CORNWALL   Bind fast his corky[4] arms.
GLOUCESTER   What means your graces? Good my friends, consider
  You are my guests. Do me no foul play, friends.   30
CORNWALL   Bind him, I say.
REGAN   Hard, hard! O filthy traitor!
GLOUCESTER   Unmerciful lady as you are, I am true.
CORNWALL   To this chair bind him. Villain, thou shalt find—
                    [REGAN *plucks* GLOUCESTER's *beard*
GLOUCESTER   By the kind gods, 'tis most ignobly[5] done,
  To pluck me by the beard.
REGAN   So white, and such a traitor?
GLOUCESTER   Naughty lady,

1 Speedy preparation, for the coming battle.
2 Followers.
3 Bind.
4 Withered.
5 Dishonourably.

These hairs which thou dost ravish[6] from my chin
Will quicken and accuse thee. I am your host.
With robbers' hands my hospitable favours[7]
You should not ruffle[8] thus. What will you do?   40
CORNWALL   Come, sir, what letters had you late from France?
REGAN   Be simple answered,[9] for we know the truth.
CORNWALL   And what confederacy[10] have you with the traitors
    Late footed in the kingdom?
REGAN   To whose hands
    You have sent the lunatic king? Speak.
GLOUCESTER   I have a letter guessingly[11] set down,
    Which came from one that's of a neutral heart,
    And not from one opposed.
CORNWALL   Cunning!
REGAN   And false!
CORNWALL   Where hast thou sent the king?
GLOUCESTER   To Dover.
REGAN   Wherefore to Dover? Wast thou not charged at peril—   50
CORNWALL   Wherefore to Dover? Let him first answer that.
GLOUCESTER   I am tied to th'stake, and I must stand the course.
REGAN   Wherefore to Dover, sir?
GLOUCESTER   Because I would not see thy cruel nails
    Pluck out his poor old eyes, nor thy fierce sister
    In his anointed flesh stick boarish[12] fangs.
    The sea, with such a storm as his bowed head
    In hell-black night endured, would have buoyed up
    And quenched the stellèd[13] fires.
    Yet, poor old heart, he holpt[14] the heavens to rage.   60
    If wolves had at thy gate howled that stern time,
    Thou shouldst have said, 'Good porter, turn the key:
    All cruels else subscribe'.[15] But I shall see
    The wingèd vengeance overtake such children.
CORNWALL   See't shalt thou never. Fellows, hold the chair.
    Upon those eyes of thine I'll set my foot.
GLOUCESTER   He that will think to live till he be old,
    Give me some help!   [CORNWALL puts out one of GLOUCESTER's eyes
                    O cruel! O ye gods!

---

6   Force.
7   i.e. hospitality.
8   Treat roughly.
9   Answer truthfully.
10   Alliance.
11   Imprecisely.
12   i.e. sharp.
13   Starry.
14   Helped.
15   i.e. you would have housed him to protect him from the cruelty of wolves.

REGAN   One side will mock another: t'other, too.

CORNWALL   If you see vengeance—

FIRST SERVANT   Hold your hand, my lord!   70
   I have served you ever since I was a child,
   But better service have I never done you
   Than now to bid you hold!

REGAN   How now, you dog?

FIRST SERVANT   If you did wear a beard upon your chin,
   I'd shake it on this quarrel. What do you mean?

CORNWALL   My villain![16]   [*They draw and fight*

FIRST SERVANT   Why then, come on, and take the chance of anger
      [*wounds* CORNWALL]

REGAN   [*To another Servant*] Give me thy sword. A peasant stand up
   thus!

[*She takes a sword and runs at the First Servant from behind and kills him*

FIRST SERVANT   [*To* GLOUCESTER] Oh, I am slain, my lord, yet have you
      one eye left
   To see some mischief on him. O!   [*He dies*   80

CORNWALL   Lest it see more, prevent it. Out vile jelly!
                    [*He puts out* GLOUCESTER's *other eye*
   Where is thy lustre now?

GLOUCESTER   All dark and comfortless! Where's my son Edmund?
   Edmund, enkindle[17] all the sparks of nature[18]
   To quit this horrid act.

REGAN   Out, villain!
   Thou call'st on him that hates thee. It was he
   That made the overture of thy treasons to us,
   Who is too good to pity thee.

GLOUCESTER   O my follies! Then Edgar was abused.[19]
   Kind gods, forgive me that, and prosper him.   90

REGAN   Go thrust him out at gates, and let him smell
   His way to Dover. How is't, my lord? How look you?

CORNWALL   I have received a hurt. Follow me, lady.
   [*To Servants*] Turn out that eyeless villain. Throw this slave
   Upon the dunghill.
                    [*Exit a Servant with* GLOUCESTER *and First Servant's body*
                    Regan, I bleed apace.[20]

16 Servant.
17 Flame up.
18 i.e. filial love.
19 Wronged.
20 Greatly.

Untimely comes this hurt. Give me your arm.
[*Exeunt* CORNWALL *and* REGAN

SECOND SERVANT   I'll never care what wickedness I do,
    If this man come to good.
THIRD SERVANT   If she live long
    And in the end meet the old course of death,   100
    Women will all turn monsters.
SECOND SERVANT   Let's follow the old earl and get the Bedlam[21]
    To lead him where he would. His roguish madness
    Allows itself to anything.
THIRD SERVANT   Go thou. I'll fetch some flax and whites of eggs
    To apply to his bleeding face. Now, heaven help him.   [*Exeunt*

Act 4, Scene 1: Edgar finds his father (10–82)

As Act 4 opens, Edgar appears in the dual guises in which he has been recalled in the last scene, as Gloucester's 'abused' son and as 'the Bedlam', Poor Tom. Gloucester's heartbreaking reunion with the loving son whom he has exiled is an act we witness with Edgar alone, as Gloucester does not recognise him. This reunion is a precursor of another in Act 4, in which the mad Lear cannot immediately recognise his loving, exiled daughter Cordelia. In Act 3, Scene 6 Edgar compared his suffering to his godfather Lear's; in Act 4, Scene 1 he compares it to his father's.

The central question here is why Edgar does not reveal himself to his father earlier (in contrast to the source material; see Philip Sidney above, **pp. 38–40**). He claims later in Act 4, Scene 6 that he can only cure his father of 'despair' if he remains in disguise. But perhaps Shakespeare decided that Gloucester is too old and defeated ever to be truly reconciled to his son, or that it would have be too heartbreaking to watch such a reconciliation staged, at least before Lear's and Cordelia's reunion. Shakespeare apparently wanted Edgar to continue to act as our guide – his shock reflects that of the audience, like him, 'scared' out of our 'good wits' by the extreme cruelty we have witnessed. Or perhaps Shakespeare relied on all of these reasons for keeping Edgar incapable of offering Gloucester the solace of a loving son. Gloucester has not yet accepted his share of responsibility for his fate and blames the gods, not himself, for his blinding: 'As flies to wanton boys are we to th'gods;/They kill us for their sport.'

Enter GLOUCESTER *led by an* OLD MAN

EDGAR   [. . .] Who's here?

---

21 i.e. Poor Tom.

My father, parti-eyed?[1] World, world, O world!
But that thy strange mutations make us hate thee,
Life would not yield to age.

OLD MAN   O my good lord,
I have been your tenant and your father's tenant
This fourscore—

GLOUCESTER   Away, get thee away! Good friend, be gone.
Thy comforts can do me no good at all;
Thee they may hurt.

OLD MAN   Alack, sir, you cannot see your way.   10

GLOUCESTER   I have no way, and therefore want no eyes.
I stumbled when I saw. Full oft 'tis seen
Our means[2] secure us, and our mere defects
Prove our commodities.[3] Ah, dear son Edgar,
The food of thy abusèd[4] father's wrath,
Might I but live to see thee in my touch,
I'd say I had eyes again.

OLD MAN   How now? Who's there?

EDGAR   [Aside] O gods! Who is't can say 'I am at the worst'?
I am worse than e'er I was.

OLD MAN   'Tis poor mad Tom.   20

EDGAR   [Aside] And worse I may be yet. The worst is not
As long as we can say 'This is the worst.'

OLD MAN   Fellow, where goest?

GLOUCESTER   Is it a beggarman?

OLD MAN   Madman and beggar too.

GLOUCESTER   He has some reason, else he could not beg.
In the last night's storm I such a fellow saw,
Which made me think a man a worm. My son
Came then into my mind, and yet my mind
Was then scarce friends with him. I have heard more since.
As flies to wanton[5] boys are we to th'gods;   30
They kill us for their sport.

EDGAR   [Aside] How should this be?
Bad is the trade that must play the fool to sorrow,
Ang'ring itself and others.—[To GLOUCESTER] Bless thee, master.

GLOUCESTER   Is that the naked fellow?

OLD MAN   Ay, my lord.

GLOUCESTER   [To OLD MAN] Then prithee get thee gone. If for my sake
Thou wilt o'ertake us hence a mile or twain

1   Partly eyed.
2   Wealth.
3   Suitability.
4   Wronged.
5   Naughty.

I'th'way toward Dover, do it for ancient love,
And bring some covering for this naked soul,
Who I'll entreat to lead me.

OLD MAN   Alack, sir, he is mad.   40

GLOUCESTER   'Tis the time's plague when madmen lead the blind.
Do as I bid thee; or rather do thy pleasure.
Above the rest,[6] be gone.

OLD MAN   I'll bring him the best 'parel[7] that I have,
Come on't[8] what will.   [*Exit*

GLOUCESTER   Sirrah,[9] naked fellow.

EDGAR   Poor Tom's a-cold. I cannot dance it farther.

GLOUCESTER   Come hither, fellow.

EDGAR   Bless thy sweet eyes, they bleed.

GLOUCESTER   Know'st thou the way to Dover?

EDGAR   Both stile and gate, horseway and footpath. Poor Tom hath   50
been scared out of his good wits. Bless thee, good man, from the foul
fiend. Five fiends have been in poor Tom at once: of lust, as Obidicut;
Hobbididence, prince of dumbness; Mahu, of stealing; Modo, of
murder; Flibbertigibbet,[10] of mopping and mowing,[11] who since possesses chambermaids and waiting-women. So, bless thee, master.

GLOUCESTER   Here, take this purse, thou whom the heavens' plagues
Have humbled to all strokes. That I am wretched
Makes thee the happier. Heavens deal so still.
Let the superfluous and lust-dieted[12] man
That stands your ordinance,[13] that will not see   60
Because he does not feel, feel your power quickly.
So distribution[14] should undo excess,
And each man have enough. Dost thou know Dover?

EDGAR   Ay, master.

GLOUCESTER   There is a cliff whose high and bending head
Looks sternly in the confinèd deep.
Bring me but to the very brim of it,
And I'll repair the misery thou dost bear
With something rich about me. From that place
I shall no leading need.

EDGAR   Give me thy arm.   70
Poor Tom shall lead thee.   [*Exeunt*

---

6   Above all.
7   Apparel.
8   Of it.
9   Servant.
10   i.e. Tom has named five devils.
11   i.e. making fun of their employers (as female servants were thought to do).
12   i.e. gluttonous and lustful in appetite.
13   Puts up with your injunction.
14   i.e. of wealth.

Act 4, Scene 2: Albany confronts Goneril (30–69)

As Act 4, Scene 2 opens, Goneril and Edmund learn from Oswald that Goneril's husband Albany has welcomed news of the French army's arrival and been disgusted at the news of Edmund's treachery against his father. Goneril sends Edmund back to Cornwall to prepare their army against the French, offering him her favour to wear in battle as well as her sexual favours, claiming of Albany, 'a fool usurps my bed'. After Edmund's exit, Albany enters to confront his wife. For the first time in the play since Cordelia's chastisement of her at the end of Act 1, Scene 1, Goneril faces moral judgement.

We have had little opportunity to examine Albany's character before this scene; his name recalls 'Albion', the Roman name for Britain, suggesting his link to the country's glorious civilisation. Here, perhaps surprisingly, he becomes the play's moral spokesperson, reminding his wife, 'Proper deformity shows not in the fiend/So horrid as in woman'. Her response is to call him 'a moral fool' (ironically symbolised earlier by Poor Tom who has spoken nothing but the truth).

The audience's allegiance to (and sympathy for) various characters continues to shift until this point in the play, so that Albany's moral authority may still be questionable here, especially as his words are an ironic echo of Lear's angry words not just to Goneril and Regan in Act 2 but to Cordelia in Act 1, Scene 1. Albany's words are easily dismissed by his wife, who accuses him of effeminacy as she attempts to usurp his masculinity. His contempt of his wife later when a messenger enters to bring the news of Gloucester's blinding and Cornwall's death strengthens his moral resolve.

> GONERIL I have been worth the whistling.[1]
> ALBANY   O Goneril,
>   You are not worth the dust which the rude wind
>   Blows in your face. I fear your disposition;
>   That nature which condemns its origin
>   Cannot be bordered certain in itself.
>   She that herself will sliver and disbranch
>   From her material sap, perforce[2] must wither
>   And come to deadly use.
> GONERIL   No more, the text is foolish.
> ALBANY Wisdom and goodness to the vile seem vile;   10
>   Filths[3] savour but themselves. What have you done?
>   Tigers, not daughters, what have you performed?
>   A father and a gracious, aged man,[4]

1 Watching out for.
2 Necessarily.
3 i.e. filthy creatures.
4 i.e. Lear.

Whose reverence even the head-lugged[5] bear would lick,
Most barbarous, most degenerate, have you madded.
Could my good brother[6] suffer you to do it?
A man, a prince, by him so benefited?
If that the heavens do not their visible spirits
Send quickly down to tame these vile offences,
It will come.
Humanity must perforce prey on itself   20
Like monsters of the deep.
GONERIL   Milk-livered[7] man,
That bear'st a cheek for blows, a head for wrongs,
Who hast not in thy brows an eye discerning
Thine honour from thy suffering, that not know'st
Fools do those villains pity who are punished
Ere they have done their mischief. Where's thy drum?[8]
France spreads his banners in our noiseless[9] land,
With plumèd helm thy state begins thereat,[10]
Whilst thou, a moral fool, sits still and cries
'Alack, why does he so?'
ALBANY   See thyself, devil: 30
Proper deformity shows not in the fiend
So horrid as in woman.
GONERIL   O vain fool!
ALBANY   Thou changèd and self-covered[11] thing, for shame
Be-monster not thy feature! Were't my fitness
To let these hands obey my blood,
They are apt enough to dislocate and tear
Thy flesh and bones. Howe'er thou art a fiend,
A woman's shape doth shield thee.
GONERIL   Marry, your manhood, mew![12]

Act 4, Scene 6: Gloucester and Edgar reach Dover (1–80)

In Act 4, Scene 3, which appears only in the Quarto and was probably cut during
the play's later performances, Kent and a Gentleman discuss the return of

---

5   i.e. dragged by the head.
6   i.e. Cornwall.
7   Cowardly.
8   i.e. the drum of battle.
9   i.e. unprepared.
10 i.e. with war (symbolised by the enemy's 'plumèd helm') your state is being met ('thereat').
11 Disguised.
12 i.e. she ridicules his masculinity by saying 'By Mary [a mild epithet], your manhood, miaow!'.

Cordelia, now very much a queen, but of France, not England. Her husband has returned home but has left behind as general of his army the Marshal of France, Monsieur La Far. Although absent from this scene, as she has been since Act 1, Scene 1, Cordelia is portrayed as sharing Lear's suffering in nearly Christ-like terms with 'holy water' in her eyes, making her Lear's if not the play's redeemer and, eventually, sacrificial victim. The tenderness she offers in this scene in the words ascribed to her is nearly heartbreaking: 'Faith, once or twice she heaved the name of father/Pantingly forth, as if it pressed her heart;/ Cried "Sisters, sisters! Shame of ladies! Sisters!/Kent! Father! Sisters! What, i'th'storm? i'th'night?"'

Shakespeare may have decided to offer her in Act 4, Scene 3 in narrative rather than onstage to prepare us slowly for her return after an absence of three acts; that is, he wants us to get to know her again before we see her. However, the Cordelia described here is not the stubborn, blunt, confrontational daughter of Act 1, Scene 1, sorely impatient with her impatient father. Either she misrepresented herself to us early in the play or she has acquired, by absorbing her father's suffering, the patience, sorrow and compassion that he has come to possess during the storm. Kent also reports that Lear is so ashamed at his 'unkindness' towards his youngest daughter and his kindness to his 'dog-hearted daughters' Goneril and Regan that he now refuses to see Cordelia.

In the next scene (Act 4, Scene 4 in the Quarto text; Act 4, Scene 3 in the Folio) Cordelia enters with the Doctor attending on Lear. In her final pledge, 'O dear father,/It is thy business that I go about', she recalls the pledge of Jesus, who as a child left his parents' home to debate with elders in the temple. To his parents' worried reproaches, he replied, 'I must be about my Father's business' (Luke 2:49). Thus her return as a Christian saviour seems complete.

Cordelia's determination to enforce her father's right to the throne in Act 4, Scene 4 (Act 4, Scene 3 Folio) is immediately juxtaposed with Regan's to deny it in Act 4, Scene 5 (Act 4, Scene 4 Folio), in which Oswald informs Regan of Albany's preparation to battle France's forces. Regan's primary concern is her jealousy over the developing love affair between her sister Goneril and Edmund. Regan tries to persuade Oswald to show her letters from Goneril to Edmund, promising, 'I'll love thee much/Let me unseal the letter', but he refuses this bargain (or love-test). Regan asks Oswald to carry a letter from her to Edmund, and her only regret is 'It was great ignorance, Gloucester's eyes being out,/To let him live'. The scene ends as she promises a reward to whoever 'cuts him off'.

This scene of filial (and sibling) contempt, juxtaposed earlier to that with Cordelia's filial love, is immediately juxtaposed again with another scene of filial love. In Act 4, Scene 6 (Act 4, Scene 5 Folio) we see the blind and suicidal Gloucester being compassionately led by Edgar (now disguised as a peasant so that he can later rescue Gloucester in that guise). Edgar tries to convince him that they have climbed to the top of the Dover cliffs, when, in fact, they are still on flat ground. The doubting Gloucester then questions the change in his companion, who no longer uses the words or accent of Poor Tom. Edgar responds, 'In nothing am I changed/But in my garments', reinforcing the play's concern with relative versus fixed concepts of identity, disguise, self-knowledge and truth.

Dover's cliffs serve as the symbolic centre of England here, and Edgar's celebration of the stunning view offered from the top is drawn from memory, not from sight, ironically suggesting that eyesight is the least trustworthy way to discern value. After his suicide attempt, Gloucester's new companion, Edgar in the guise of a peasant, convinces him that he has indeed fallen from the top of the cliffs to the beach below and that his survival is miraculous. Edgar describes Gloucester's previous companion (Poor Tom) as a deformed 'fiend', but Gloucester remarks, 'That thing you speak of,/I took it for a man', ironically echoing Lear's comment in Act 3, Scene 4 on Poor Tom, 'Is man no more than this [. . .] a poor, bare, forked animal'.

Enter GLOUCESTER *and* EDGAR *dressed like a peasant*

GLOUCESTER   When shall we come to th'top of that same hill?
EDGAR   You do climb up it now. Look how we labour!
GLOUCESTER   Methinks the ground is even.
EDGAR   Horrible steep.
   Hark, do you hear the sea?
GLOUCESTER   No, truly.
EDGAR   Why, then your other senses grow imperfect
   By your eyes' anguish.
GLOUCESTER   So may it be indeed.
   Methinks thy voice is altered, and thou speakest
   With better phrase and matter than thou didst.
EDGAR   You're much deceived. In nothing am I changed
   But in my garments.
GLOUCESTER   Methinks you're better spoken.   10
EDGAR   Come on, sir, here's the place. Stand still. How fearful
   And dizzy 'tis to cast one's eyes so low!
   The crows and choughs[1] that wing the midway air
   Show scarce so gross as beetles. Halfway down
   Hangs one that gathers samphire,[2] dreadful trade!
   Methinks he seems no bigger than his head.
   The fishermen that walk upon the beach
   Appear like mice, and yon tall anchoring barque[3]

---

1   Jackdaws.
2   A herb.
3   Ship.

Diminished to her cock,[4] her cock a buoy
Almost too small for sight. The murmuring surge   20
That on the unnumbered idle pebble chafes
Cannot be heard. It's so high I'll look no more,
Lest my brain turn and the deficient sight
Topple down headlong.
GLOUCESTER   Set me where you stand.
EDGAR   Give me your hand. You are now within a foot
Of th'extreme verge. For all beneath the moon
Would I not leap upright.
GLOUCESTER   Let go my hand.
Here friend 's[5] another purse; in it a jewel
Well worth a poor man's taking. Fairies and gods
Prosper it with thee. Go thou farther off.   30
Bid me farewell, and let me hear thee going.
EDGAR   Now fare you well, good sir.
GLOUCESTER   With all my heart.
EDGAR   [Aside] Why I do trifle thus with his despair
Is done to cure it.
GLOUCESTER   [He kneels] O you mighty gods!
This world I do renounce, and in your sights
Shake patiently my great affliction off.
If I could bear it longer and not fall
To quarrel with your great opposeless[6] wills,
My snuff[7] and loathèd part of nature should
Burn itself out. If Edgar live, O bless him.—   40
Now, fellow, fare thee well.
EDGAR   [Walking away] Gone, sir; farewell.
                              [GLOUCESTER falls forward
[Aside] And yet I know not how conceit may rob
The treasury of life when life itself
Yields to the theft. Had he been where he thought,
By this had thought been past.—[To GLOUCESTER] Alive or dead?
Ho, you, sir! Hear you, sir? Speak!—
[Aside] Thus might he pass[8] indeed. Yet he revives.—
What[9] are you, sir?
GLOUCESTER   Away, and let me die.
EDGAR   Hadst thou been aught but gossamer,[10] feathers, air,
So many fathom down precipitating,   50
Thou hadst shivered like an egg. But thou dost breathe,

4   Cock-boat, rowing-boat.
5   Is.
6   Impossible to oppose.
7   i.e. snuffed-out.
8   Pass away.
9   Who.
10 i.e. a filmy substance.

Hast heavy substance, bleed'st not, speak'st, art sound.
Ten masts[11] at each make not the altitude
Which thou hast perpendicularly fell.
Thy life's a miracle. Speak yet again.

GLOUCESTER   But have I fallen or no?

EDGAR   From the dread summit of this chalky bourn.[12]
Look up a-height:[13] the shrill-gorged[14] lark so far
Cannot be seen or heard; do but look up.

GLOUCESTER   Alack, I have no eyes.   60
Is wretchedness deprived that benefit
To end itself by death? 'Twas yet some comfort
When misery could beguile the tyrant's rage
And frustrate his proud will.

EDGAR   Give me your arm.
Up; so. How is't? Feel you your legs? You stand.

GLOUCESTER   Too well, too well.

EDGAR   This is above all strangeness.
Upon the crown of the cliff what thing was that
Which parted from you?

GLOUCESTER   A poor unfortunate beggar.

EDGAR   As I stood here below, methought his eyes
Were two full moons. He had a thousand noses,   70
Horns whelked[15] and waved like the enridgèd sea.
It was some fiend. Therefore, thou happy father,
Think that the clearest gods, who make them honours
Of men's impossibilities, have preserved thee.

GLOUCESTER   I do remember now. Henceforth I'll bear
Affliction till it do cry out itself
'Enough, enough,' and die. That thing you speak of,
I took it for a man. Often would it say
'The fiend, the fiend!' He led me to that place.

EDGAR   Bear free and patient thoughts.   80

Act 4, Scene 6: Gloucester and Edgar find Lear (80–183)

At this point of reconciliation and rescue between Edgar and the man who still does not recognise him, Lear enters 'mad' and crowned with a garland of

---

11 Ship-masts.
12 Boundary.
13 On high.
14 Shrill-throated.
15 Twisted.

flowers. The awesome natural world that has restored Gloucester has Lear as its monarch. Although clearly out of his wits, Lear is 'every inch a king' and speaks with authority and shrewdness.

Enter LEAR, *mad*

EDGAR   But who comes here?
    The safer sense will ne'er accommodate
    His master thus.
LEAR   No, they cannot touch me for coining.[1] I am the king himself.
EDGAR   O thou side-piercing sight!
LEAR   Nature is above art in that respect. There's your press-money.[2] That fellow handles his bow like a crow-keeper.[3] Draw me[4] a clothier's yard.[5] Look, look, a mouse! Peace, peace, this toasted cheese will do[6] it. There's my gauntlet.[7] I'll prove it on a giant. Bring up the brown bills.[8] O well flown, bird,[9] in the air. Hagh! Give the word!   10
EDGAR   Sweet marjoram.[10]
LEAR   Pass.
GLOUCESTER   I know that voice.
LEAR   Ha, Goneril! Ha, Regan! They flattered me like a dog and told me I had white hairs in my beard ere the black ones were there. To say 'ay' and 'no' to everything that I said 'ay' and 'no' to was no good divinity.[11] When the rain came to wet me once and the wind to make me chatter, when the thunder would not peace at my bidding, there I found them, there I smelt them out. Go to, they are not men of their words. They told me I was everything. 'Tis a lie; I am not ague-   20 proof.[12]
GLOUCESTER   The trick of that voice I do well remember.
    Is't not the king?
LEAR   Ay, every inch a king.
    When I do stare, see how the subject quakes.
    I pardon that man's life. What was thy cause?[13]
    Adultery?

---

1   Condemn me for minting coins (a king's prerogative).
2   i.e. money given to new soldiers.
3   i.e. without skill.
4   i.e. draw the archer's bow for me.
5   i.e. thirty-seven inches.
6   Catch.
7   Glove (in promise of a challenge or duel).
8   i.e. soldiers.
9   i.e. arrow.
10 i.e. a herbal remedy for mental illness.
11 Theology.
12 Immune to sickness.
13 Legal charge against you.

Thou shalt not die for adultery. No,
The wren goes to't, and the small gilded fly
Does lecher[14] in my sight.
Let copulation thrive, for Gloucester's bastard son   30
Was kinder to his father than my daughters
Got[15] 'tween the lawful sheets.
To't, luxury,[16] pell-mell,[17] for I lack soldiers.
Behold yon simp'ring dame,
Whose face between her forks[18] presageth snow,
That minces virtue, and does shake the head
To hear of pleasure's name—
The fitchew[19] nor the soilèd horse goes to't[20] with a more riotous
appetite. Down from the waist they're centaurs,[21] though women all
above. But to the girdle[22] do the gods inherit; beneath is all the fiend's.   40
There's hell, there's darkness, there's the sulphury pit, burning, scald-
ing, stench, consummation. Fie, fie, fie! Pah, pah! Give me an ounce of
civet,[23] good apothecary, to sweeten my imagination. There's money
for thee.

GLOUCESTER   O, let me kiss that hand!

LEAR   Here, wipe it first; it smells of mortality.

GLOUCESTER   O ruined piece of nature! This great world
Should so wear out to naught. Do you know me?

LEAR   I remember thy eyes well enough. Dost thou squiny[24] on me?
No, do thy worst, blind Cupid, I'll not love.   50
Read thou that challenge, mark the penning[25] of't.

GLOUCESTER   Were all the letters suns, I could not see one.

EDGAR   [Aside] I would not take this from report;[26] it is,
And my heart breaks at it.

LEAR   Read.

GLOUCESTER   What? With the case[27] of eyes?

LEAR   O ho, are you there with me? No eyes in your head, nor no
money in your purse? Your eyes are in a heavy case, your purse in a
light; yet you see how this world goes.

GLOUCESTER   I see it feelingly.   60

---

14 Commit lechery.
15 Begot.
16 Lechery.
17 Promiscuously.
18 Legs.
19 Polecat.
20 Copulates.
21 Mythical lecherous creature with the body of a human above the waist and a horse below it.
22 Waist.
23 i.e. perfume.
24 Squint.
25 Penmanship.
26 i.e. I could not believe this if it were reported to me.
27 Sockets.

LEAR   What, art mad? A man may see how the world goes with no eyes.
Look with thy ears. See how yon justice[28] rails upon yon simple thief.
Hark in thy ear: handy-dandy,[29] which is the thief, which is the just-
ice? Thou hast seen a farmer's dog bark at a beggar?

GLOUCESTER   Ay, sir.

LEAR   And the creature run from the cur? There thou mightst behold
the great image of authority. A dog's obeyed in office.
Thou rascal beadle,[30] hold thy bloody hand.
Why dost thou lash that whore? Strip thine own back.
Thy blood hotly lusts to use her in that kind   70
For which thou whip'st her. The usurer[31] hangs the cozener.[32]
Through tattered clothes great vices do appear:
Robes and furred gowns hide all. Get thee glass eyes,
And, like a scurvy politician, seem
To see the things thou dost not. Now, now,
Pull off my boots. Harder, harder! So.

EDGAR   [Aside] O matter and impertinency[33] mixed,
Reason in madness.

LEAR   If thou wilt weep my fortune, take my eyes.
I know thee well enough. Thy name is Gloucester.   80
Thou must be patient. We came crying hither.
Thou know'st the first time that we smell the air
We wail and cry. I will preach to thee. Mark me.

GLOUCESTER   Alack, alack the day!

LEAR   When we are born, we cry that we are come
To this great stage of fools. This a good block.[34]
It were a delicate stratagem to shoe
A troop of horse with felt,
And when I have stole upon these son-in-laws,
Then kill, kill, kill, kill, kill, kill!   90

Act 4, Scene 7: Lear is reunited with Cordelia (14–84)

As the scene continues, Lear flees, pursued by the Gentlemen sent by Cordelia.
Left alone together on stage, Gloucester and Edgar attempt to come to terms

28 Yonder judge.
29 i.e. take your choice.
30 Constable.
31 Money-lender.
32 Swindler.
33 i.e. rational matter and nonsense.
34 i.e. block of wood or felt.

with each other, although Edgar still hesitates to reveal his true identity. They encounter Oswald, who attempts to kill the 'traitor' Gloucester. Edgar kills Oswald and discovers that he is carrying letters from Goneril to Edmund recommending that he kill Albany. As Act 4, Scene 7 (Act 4, Scene 6 Folio) opens, Cordelia and Kent have been reunited and discuss with the Doctor the condition of Lear, who has been brought to Cordelia's camp. Kent tells her he will maintain his disguise as Caius. Cordelia is still absolute about the value of measurement, announcing that she can never repay Kent's kindness to her father, for 'My life will be too short,/And every measure fail me'. Kent is as blunt as ever.

When he awakes, Lear is convinced that he is in hell: 'I am bound/Upon a wheel of fire, that mine own tears/Do scald like molten lead', suffering for the sins of his life. He comes to realise that he has been responsible for his own suffering and that of others, acknowledging that Cordelia has 'some cause' not to love him. Her response is 'No cause, no cause' (an ironic echo of 'nothing' or 'no thing'). At the moment when she can be most forthright, she chooses not to be, but the sparseness of her words is appropriate here. Lear can only describe himself now as 'a very foolish, fond old man' (compare their reunion in the source play *King Leir* above, **pp. 30–1**). As heart-breaking as the scene is, its juxtaposition here with Edgar's second rescue of his father reminds us that whilst Shakespeare reunites father and daughter here, with each recognising and accepting the other, Gloucester cannot recognise his own son, although he immediately recognised the voice and presence of Lear.

CORDELIA   O you kind gods,
  Cure this great breach in his abusèd nature;
  The untuned and hurrying senses, O, wind up
  Of this child-changèd[1] father!
DOCTOR   So please your majesty,
  That we may wake the king? He hath slept long.
CORDELIA   Be governed by your knowledge and proceed
  I'th'sway of your own will.[2] Is he arrayed?
DOCTOR   Ay, madam: in the heaviness of his sleep
  We put fresh garments on him.

  Enter LEAR, *asleep, in a chair carried in by Servants. Music plays*

GENTLEMAN   Good madam, be by when we do awake him;   10
  I doubt not of his temperance.[3]
CORDELIA   Very well.

---

1   Changed by his children into a child.
2   i.e. as you see fit.
3   i.e. I'm worried about his behaviour.

DOCTOR   Please you, draw near. Louder the music there!
CORDELIA   [*Kisses him*] O my dear father, restoration hang
    Thy medicine on my lips, and let this kiss
    Repair those violent harms that my two sisters
    Have in[4] thy reverence made.
KENT   Kind and dear princess!
CORDELIA   Had you not been their father, these white flakes[5]
    Had challenged pity of them. Was this a face
    To be exposed against the warring winds?
    To stand against the deep dread-bolted thunder,   20
    In the most terrible and nimble stroke
    Of quick cross lightning? To watch,[6] poor perdu,[7]
    With this thin helm?[8] Mine injurious dog,
    Though he had bit me, should have stood that night
    Against my fire. And wast thou fain,[9] poor father,
    To hovel thee with swine and rogues forlorn
    In short and musty straw? Alack, alack,
    'Tis wonder that thy life and wits at once
    Had not concluded all. [*To the Doctor*] He wakes. Speak to him.
DOCTOR   Madam, do you; 'tis fittest.   30
CORDELIA   How does my royal lord? How fares your majesty?
LEAR   You do me wrong to take me out o'the grave.
    Thou art a soul in bliss,[10] but I am bound
    Upon a wheel of fire, that mine own tears
    Do scald like molten lead.
CORDELIA   Sir, know me.
LEAR   You're a spirit, I know. Where did you die?
CORDELIA   Still, still far wide.[11]
DOCTOR   He's scarce awake. Let him alone a while.
LEAR   Where have I been? Where am I? Fair daylight?
    I am mightily abused. I should e'en die with pity   40
    To see another thus. I know not what to say.
    I will not swear these are my hands. Let's see:
    I feel this pin prick. Would I were assured
    Of my condition.
CORDELIA   O look upon me, sir,
    And hold your hands in benediction[12] o'er me.
    No, sir, you must not kneel.

4   i.e. to.
5   i.e. of hair.
6   Keep watch.
7   Lost watchman.
8   i.e. poor protection for his head.
9   Grateful.
10 Heaven.
11 Confused.
12 Blessing.

LEAR   Pray do not mock.
 I am a very foolish, fond old man,
 Fourscore and upward, and to deal plainly,
 I fear I am not in my perfect mind.
 Methinks I should know you and know this man;   50
 Yet I am doubtful, for I am mainly ignorant
 What place this is, and all the skill I have
 Remembers not these garments, nor I know not
 Where I did lodge last night. Do not laugh at me,
 For, as I am a man, I think this lady
 To be my child Cordelia.
CORDELIA   And so I am.
LEAR   Be your tears wet? Yes, faith. I pray, weep not.
 If you have poison for me, I will drink it.
 I know you do not love me, for your sisters
 Have, as I do remember, done me wrong.   60
 You have some cause; they have not.
CORDELIA   No cause, no cause.
LEAR   Am I in France?
KENT   In your own kingdom, sir.
LEAR   Do not abuse[13] me.
DOCTOR   Be comforted, good madam. The great rage
 You see is cured in him, and yet it is danger
 To make him even o'er the time he has lost.
 Desire him to go in. Trouble him no more
 Till further settling.
CORDELIA   Will't please your highness walk?
LEAR   You must bear with me. Pray now, forget
 And forgive. I am old and foolish.   70
                    [*Exeunt all except* KENT *and Gentleman*

Act 5, Scene 3: Lear and Cordelia are imprisoned (1–106)

After Lear and Cordelia leave, Kent and the Gentleman discuss Edmund taking
his place as the head of the late Cornwall's army. As Act 5 begins, Edmund and
Regan enter with some of their soldiers and fear that Albany, who is 'full of
alteration/And self-reproving', will not join them. Regan jealously asks Edmund if
he loves Goneril and has already slept with her. Edmund assures her that he
loves Goneril only in the 'honoured' way and claims not to have found his way

---

13 i.e. lie to.

to her 'forefended' (or forbidden) bed. Regan vows, 'I never shall endure her'. Albany and Goneril enter with their soldiers and prepare for battle. The disguised Edgar enters and hands Goneril's letters to Edmund, taken from Oswald, to her husband Albany. As Edgar leaves, he offers to return after the battle as truth's 'champion'. Left alone on stage at the end of Act 5, Scene 1, Edmund decides to pit the two sisters against each other.

Act 5, Scene 2 begins with Cordelia's French army passing over the stage followed by her entrance, in the Quarto 1 text 'with her father in [i.e. being led by] her hand' (the Folio alters the direction to '[Enter] Lear, Cordelia, and soldiers') and a quick exit. Edgar, still disguised as a peasant, immediately enters with Gloucester, whom he also leads. Instead of witnessing the battle here (as Shakespeare makes us do in many of his other plays), we hear a shocked Edgar narrate the result of it to his father, perhaps because we as audience have already witnessed enough cruelty and violence. Shakespeare may thus have wished to emphasise the suffering of domestic, personal battle rather than of civil or foreign war. Edgar tells his father that Cordelia's army has been defeated and she and her father have been taken captive by Cornwall's army, led by Edmund. Gloucester gives up all hope and refuses to move to safety, but Edgar warns him 'Men must endure/Their going hence even as their coming hither: Ripeness is all'; that is, a man cannot choose his own time of death but only adhere to his destiny.

In the first part of the final scene of Act 5, Scene 3, Edmund mocks his brother's comment that 'ripeness is all' by advising his Captain that 'men/Are as the time' in commanding him to execute Lear and Cordelia in secret. Edmund, like Edgar, knows that time and chance must be manipulated and that freedom is a state of mind. Lear and Cordelia have learned the same, vowing to consider their time in prison a gift rather than a penance, in which they can 'live,/And pray, and sing, and tell old tales, and laugh/At gilded butterflies' as if they were 'God's spies'. Lear will ask of the now-saintly Cordelia her 'forgiveness', and in doing so reveal the result of his 'pilgrimage' in the play from sinner to penitent.

As the scene continues, the competition of the two sisters is mirrored in the duel pledged between Albany and Edmund as they throw down their gauntlets as a challenge to each other. 'Truth and honour' are now commodities with relative rather than fixed meanings. The scene borrows heavily from the language established at the beginning of the play: words of measurement and comparison such as 'more', 'most', 'equally', 'best' and 'worst' are used so indiscriminately that they have no meaning.

Enter EDMUND *with* LEAR *and* CORDELIA *prisoners and* CAPTAIN *and Soldiers*

> EDMUND   Some officers take them away: good guard,[1]
> Until their greater pleasures best be known
> That are to censure them.

---

1   i.e. place them under close guard.

CORDELIA   We are not the first
Who with best meaning have incurred the worst.
For thee, oppressèd king, am I cast down,
Myself could else outfrown² false fortune's frown.
Shall we not see these daughters and these sisters?
LEAR   No, no. Come, let's away to prison.
We two alone will sing like birds i'th'cage.
When thou dost ask me blessing, I'll kneel down   10
And ask of thee forgiveness: so we'll live,
And pray, and sing, and tell old tales, and laugh
At gilded butterflies, and hear poor rogues
Talk of court news, and we'll talk with them too—
Who loses and who wins; who's in, who's out—
And take upon 's³ the mystery of things,
As if we were God's spies; and we'll wear out
In a walled prison packs and sects⁴ of great ones
That ebb and flow by th'moon.
EDMUND   Take them away.
LEAR   Upon such sacrifices, my Cordelia,   20
The gods themselves throw incense. [*Embracing her*] Have I caught
    thee?
He that parts us shall bring a brand from heaven
And fire us hence like foxes. Wipe thine eyes.
The good years shall devour 'em, flesh and fell.⁵
Ere they shall make us weep, we'll see 'em starve first.
Come.   [*Exeunt* LEAR *and* CORDELIA, *guarded*
EDMUND   Come hither, Captain. Hark.
Take thou this note. Go follow them to prison.
One step I have advanced thee; if thou dost
As this instructs thee, thou dost make thy way   30
To noble fortunes. Know thou this: that men
Are as the time is; to be tender-minded
Does not become a sword. Thy great employment
Will not bear question: either say thou'lt do't,
Or thrive by other means.
CAPTAIN   I'll do't, my lord.
EDMUND   About it, and write 'happy'⁶ when thou hast done.
Mark, I say, instantly, and carry it so
As I have set it down.
CAPTAIN   I cannot draw a cart nor eat dried oats;
If it be man's work, I'll do it.   [*Exit* 40

2   i.e. stand up to.
3   Us.
4   i.e. factions.
5   i.e. entirely.
6   i.e. successful.

Flourish. Enter ALBANY, GONERIL, REGAN *and Soldiers*

ALBANY   Sir, you have showed today your valiant strain,
And fortune led you well. You have the captives
That were the opposites[7] of this day's strife.
We do require them of you, so to use[8] them
As we shall find their merits and our safety
May equally determine.

EDMUND   Sir, I thought it fit
To send the old and miserable king
To some retention and appointed guard,
Whose age has charms in it, whose title more,
To pluck the common bosom on his side   50
And turn our impressed lances in our eyes
Which do command them. With him I sent the queen—
My reason all the same—and they are ready
Tomorrow, or at further space, to appear
Where you shall hold your session.[9] At this time
We sweat and bleed. The friend hath lost his friend,
And the best quarrels in the heat are cursed
By those that feel their sharpness.
The question of Cordelia and her father
Requires a fitter place.

ALBANY   Sir, by your patience,   60
I hold you but a subject of this war,
Not as a brother.

REGAN   That's as we list[10] to grace him.
Methinks our pleasure should have been demanded
Ere you had spoke so far. He led our powers,
Bore the commission of my place and person,
The which immediate may well stand up
And call itself your brother.

GONERIL   Not so hot![11]
In his own grace he doth exalt himself
More than in your advancement.

REGAN   In my right,
By me invested, he compeers[12] the best.   70

GONERIL   That were the most if he should husband you.

REGAN   Jesters do oft prove prophets.

---

7   Opponents.
8   i.e. make use of.
9   Trial.
10 Choose.
11 Rashly.
12 Is the equal of.

GONERIL   Holla,[13] holla!
  That eye that told you so looked but asquint.[14]
REGAN   Lady, I am not well, else I should answer
  From a full-flowing[15] stomach. [*To* EDMUND] General,
  Take thou my soldiers, prisoners, patrimony.[16]
  Witness the world that I create thee here
  My lord and master.
GONERIL   Mean you[17] to enjoy him then?
ALBANY   The let-alone[18] lies not in your good will.
EDMUND   Nor in thine, lord.
ALBANY   Half-blooded[19] fellow, yes.   80
EDMUND   Let the drum strike, and prove my title good.
ALBANY   Stay yet, hear reason. Edmund, I arrest thee
  On capital treason, and in thine attaint[20]
  This gilded serpent [*pointing to* GONERIL]. [*To* REGAN] For your
     claim, fair sister,
  I bar it in the interest of my wife.
  'Tis she is subcontracted to this lord,
  And I, her husband, contradict the banns.[21]
  If you will marry, make your love to me,
  My lady is bespoke.[22]
GONERIL   An interlude![23]
ALBANY   Thou art armed, Gloucester.   90
  If none appear to prove upon thy head
  Thy heinous, manifest, and many treasons,
  There is my pledge. [*Throws down his gauntlet*]
                        I'll prove it on thy heart,
  Ere I taste bread, thou art in nothing less
  Than I have here proclaimed thee.
REGAN   Sick, O sick!
GONERIL   [*Aside*] If not, I'll ne'er trust poison.
EDMUND   There's my exchange! [*Throws down his gauntlet*]
                        What[24] in the world he is
  That names me traitor, villain-like he lies.
  Call by thy trumpet: he that dares, approach;

---

13 Hello.
14 Distortedly.
15 i.e. with a great deal of fury.
16 Property.
17 Do you intend.
18 i.e. the power to stop us.
19 Illegimate.
20 i.e. as your accomplice.
21 i.e. wedding announcement.
22 Spoken for.
23 Play.
24 Whoever.

On him, on you—who not?—I will maintain $\qquad$ 100
My truth and honour firmly.
ALBANY   A herald, ho!
EDMUND   A herald, ho! A herald!

Enter a Herald and a trumpeter

ALBANY   Trust to thy single virtue,[25] for thy soldiers,
All levied in my name, have in my name
Took their discharge.
REGAN   This sickness grows upon me.
ALBANY   She is not well. Convey her to my tent.

[*Exit* REGAN, *led by servants*

Act 5, Scene 3: The death of Edmund, Goneril, Regan, Cordelia and Lear (160–325)

As the scene continues, Edmund's challenges multiply as Edgar enters in disguise to force his own love-test and competition. The rituals of his formal challenge, including the three sounds of the trumpet, bring a majesty and depth as well as a religious doom to the proceedings. When confronted with her letters to Edmund, Goneril commands, 'Ask me not what I know', by which she declines to speak further, reminding us that from the beginning of Act I, Scene I she has possessed the ability to use, or not use, words to her full advantage. Although she refuses to confess, Edmund does not refuse, and he, unlike Goneril, will ask for forgiveness and repentance before dying. Edgar will remove his disguise and reveal his true identity.

Edgar's reconciliation with his dying brother is as brief as his reconciliation with his dying father, to whom, he tells us, he revealed himself a 'half-hour' earlier (compare the source material by Philip Sidney above, **pp. 38–40**). Shakespeare may imply here that in this very public play, in which family relationships are continually held up to humiliating public scrutiny and trial (as in the love-test in Act I, Scene I and the mock-trial in Act 3, Scene 6), that he has finally given Edgar and Gloucester the privacy they have earned. Similarly, Cordelia's hanging is not staged but narrated by Lear; we must take on faith that his version of the truth of her death is the correct one. Gloucester dies of a 'burst' heart; Lear will die in the same way, both in the company of their most beloved child (on the unbearable 'cruelty' of Cordelia's death, see Samuel Johnson above, **pp. 49–50**).

In Quarto I, Lear dies believing that Cordelia is dead, and the Duke of Albany speaks the play's final, reconciliatory lines. In the Folio, with the addition of the

---

25 i.e. own strength.

lines 'Do you see this? Look on her, look, her lips,/Look there, look there!', Lear
dies believing that Cordelia is still breathing, and thus alive, and Edgar offers the
play's final lines (the Folio ending is presented here). While Edgar, Kent, Albany
and the others who survive at the play's conclusion can proclaim that Lear's and
Gloucester's suffering teach us to 'speak what we feel, not what we ought to
say', Shakespeare finally presents the play's moral issues as ambiguous, or at
least unresolved.

Shakespeare may be conceding here that the platitude offered by Edgar in the
final lines is an appropriate and tidy way to tie up the story of so much emotional suffering but is as deceptive and untrustworthy as any other formal
words spoken in the play. As audience, we have no guarantee that the play
represents what the author feels, although it certainly offers what he ought to
say at its conclusion (on this point, see Peter Brook above, **pp. 58–9**). In this
way, the play remains circular, bringing us back to the central questions raised at
the beginning, questions that can be continually asked but never definitively
answered. This circularity may offer more redemption, and less bleakness, than
the definitive, fixed and unredemptive conclusion offered in so many recent
theatre and film productions of the play.

EDMUND   What you have charged me with, that have I done,
   And more, much more; the time will bring it out.
   'Tis past, and so am I. [*To* EDGAR] But what art thou
   That hast this fortune[1] on me? If thou beest noble,
   I do forgive thee.
EDGAR   Let's exchange charity.
   I am no less in blood than thou art, Edmund.
   If more, the more thou hast wronged me.
   My name is Edgar, and thy father's son.
   The gods are just, and of our pleasant vices
   Make instruments to scourge us.   10
   The dark and vicious place where thee he got[2]
   Cost him his eyes.
EDMUND   Thou hast spoken truth.
   The wheel is come full circle; I am here.
ALBANY   Methought thy very gait[3] did prophesy
   A royal nobleness. I must embrace thee.
   Let sorrow split my heart if I did ever
   Hate thee or thy father.
EDGAR   Worthy prince, I know't.
ALBANY   Where have you hid yourself?

1   i.e. fortunate victory.
2   Begot.
3   i.e. physical demeanour.

How have you known the miseries of your father?   20
EDGAR   By nursing them, my lord. List[4] a brief tale,
And when 'tis told, O that my heart would burst!
The bloody proclamation to escape
That followed me so near—O, our lives' sweetness,
That with the pain of death would hourly die
Rather than die at once!—taught me to shift
Into a madman's rags, to assume a semblance
That very dogs disdained, and in this habit
Met I my father with his bleeding rings,
The precious stones new-lost; became his guide,   30
Led him, begged for him, saved him from despair,
Never—O father!—revealed myself unto him
Until some half-hour past, when I was armed.
Not sure, though hoping of this good success,
I asked his blessing, and from first to last
Told him my pilgrimage, but his flawed heart—
Alack, too weak the conflict to support—
'Twixt two extremes of passion, joy and grief,
Burst smilingly.
EDMUND   This speech of yours hath moved me,
And shall perchance do good. But speak you on,   40
You look as you had something more to say.
ALBANY   If there be more, more woeful, hold it in,
For I am almost ready to dissolve
Hearing of this.
EDGAR   This would have seemed a period
To such as love not sorrow; but another
To amplify too much would make much more
And top extremity.
Whilst I was big in clamour,[5] came there in a man
Who, having seen me in my worst estate,
Shunned my abhorred society. But then, finding   50
Who 'twas that so endured, with his strong arms
He fastened on my neck and bellowed out
As he'd burst heaven; threw him on my father;
Told the most piteous tale of Lear and him
That ever ear received; which in recounting
His grief grew puissant and the strings of life
Began to crack. Twice then the trumpets sounded,
And there I left him tranced.[6]
     ALBANY   But who was this?

4   Listen to.
5   Loudly decrying.
6   Entranced with grief.

EDGAR   Kent, sir, the banished Kent, who in disguise
Followed his enemy king and did him service   60
Improper for a slave.

Enter a GENTLEMAN, *with a bloody knife*

GENTLEMAN   Help, help!
ALBANY   What kind of help? What means that bloody knife?
GENTLEMAN   It's hot, it smokes, it came even from the heart
of — O, she's dead!
ALBANY   Who, man? Speak!
GENTLEMAN   Your lady, sir, your lady; and her sister
By her is poisoned: she hath confessed it.
EDMUND   I was contracted⁷ to them both; all three
Now marry in an instant.   70
ALBANY   Produce⁸ their bodies, be they alive or dead.
This justice of the heavens that makes us tremble,
Touches us not with pity.

Enter KENT *as himself*

EDGAR   Here comes Kent, sir.
O, 'tis he. [*To* KENT] The time will not allow the compliment
That very manners urges.
KENT   I am come
To bid my king and master aye⁹ good night.
Is he not here?
ALBANY   Great thing of us forgot!
Speak, Edmund; where's the king, and where's Cordelia?

The bodies of GONERIL *and* REGAN *are brought in*

Seest thou this object, Kent?
KENT   Alack, why thus?
EDMUND   Yet Edmund was beloved.   80
The one the other poisoned for my sake,
And after slew herself.
ALBANY   Even so.—Cover their faces.
EDMUND   I pant for life. Some good I mean to do,
Despite of my own nature. Quickly send—
Be brief in't—to th'castle, for my writ¹⁰

7   Engaged.
8   Bring out.
9   Forever.
10   Written order.

Is on the life of Lear and on Cordelia.
Nay, send in time.

ALBANY   Run, run, O run!

EDGAR   To who, my lord?—Who hath the office? [*To* EDMUND] Send
Thy token of reprieve.

EDMUND   Well thought on. Take my sword. The captain,   90
Give it the captain!

EDGAR   [*To* CAPTAIN] Haste thee for thy life.   [*Exit* CAPTAIN

EDMUND   He hath commission from thy wife and me
To hang Cordelia in the prison and
To lay the blame upon her own despair,
That she fordid[11] herself.

ALBANY   The gods defend her. Bear him hence a while.

                                        [EDMUND *is carried off*

Enter LEAR *with* CORDELIA *in his arms, and the* CAPTAIN.

LEAR   Howl, howl, howl, howl! O, you are men of stones!
Had I your tongues and eyes, I would use them so
That heaven's vault should crack. She's gone for ever.
I know when one is dead and when one lives.   100
She's dead as earth. [*He lays her down*]
                    Lend me a looking-glass,[12]
If that her breath will mist or stain the stone,
Why then she lives.

KENT   Is this the promised end?

EDGAR   Or image of that horror?

ALBANY   Fall,[13] and cease.

LEAR   This feather stirs, she lives: if it be so,
It is a chance which does redeem all sorrows
That ever I have felt.

KENT   Ah, my good master!

LEAR   Prithee away!

EDGAR   'Tis noble Kent, your friend.

LEAR   A plague upon you, murderous traitors all.
I might have saved her; now she's gone for ever.   110
Cordelia, Cordelia, stay a little. Ha?
What is't thou sayst?—Her voice was ever soft,
Gentle, and low, an excellent thing in women.—
I killed the slave that was a-hanging thee.

CAPTAIN   'Tis true, my lords, he did.

LEAR   Did I not, fellow?

11 Killed.
12 Mirror.
13 i.e. let go.

I have seen the day with my good biting falchion[14]
I would have made them skip. I am old now,
And these same crosses[15] spoil me. [*To* KENT] Who are you?
Mine eyes are not o'the best, I'll tell you straight.
KENT   If fortune bragged of two she loved or hated,   120
One of them we behold.
LEAR   This is a dull sight. Are you not Kent?
KENT   The same,
Your servant Kent. Where is your servant Caius?
LEAR   He's a good fellow, I can tell you that.
He'll strike, and quickly too. He's dead and rotten.
KENT   No, my good lord, I am the very man—
LEAR   I'll see that straight.
KENT   —That from your first of difference and decay
Have followed your sad steps.
LEAR   You're welcome hither.
KENT   Nor no man else. All's cheerless, dark, and deadly.   130
Your eldest daughters have fordone[16] themselves
And desperately[17] are dead.
LEAR   So think I, too.
ALBANY   He knows not what he sees, and vain it is
That we present us to him.
EDGAR   Very bootless.[18]

Enter a MESSENGER

MESSENGER   Edmund is dead, my lord.
ALBANY   That's but a trifle here.
You lords and noble friends, know our intent.
What comfort to this great decay may come
Shall be applied. For us, we will resign
During the life of this old majesty
To him our absolute power; [*to* EDGAR *and* KENT] you, to your rights, 140
With boot[19] and such addition as your honours
Have more than merited. All friends shall taste
The wages of their virtue, and all foes
The cup of their deservings. O see, see!
LEAR   And my poor fool is hanged. No, no life?
Why should a dog, a horse, a rat have life,
And thou no breath at all? O, thou wilt come no more,

---

14 Sword.
15 Burdens.
16 Killed.
17 In desperation.
18 Useless.
19 Advantage.

Never, never, never, never, never.
[*To* EDGAR] Pray you, undo this button. Thank you, sir.
O, O, O, O.   150
Do you see this? Look on her, look, her lips,
Look there, look there!   [*He dies.*
EDGAR   He faints! My lord, my lord!
KENT   Break, heart, I prithee break.
EDGAR   Look up, my lord!
KENT   Vex not his ghost. O, let him pass. He hates him
   That would upon the rack[20] of this tough world
   Stretch him out longer.
EDGAR   O, he is gone indeed.
KENT   The wonder is he hath endured so long.
   He but usurped his life.
ALBANY   Bear them from hence. Our present business
   Is general woe. [*To* EDGAR *and* KENT] Friends of my soul, you twain   160
   Rule in this kingdom and the gored[21] state sustain.
KENT   I have a journey,[22] sir, shortly to go;
   My master calls, and I must not say no.
EDGAR   The weight of this sad time we must obey,
   Speak what we feel, not what we ought to say.
   The oldest have borne most; we that are young
   Shall never see so much, nor live so long.
                                        [*Exeunt with a dead march*[23]

20 Torture rack.
21 Pierced.
22 i.e. towards death.
23 i.e. funeral music.

4

Further Reading

Further Reading

Introduction

As one of Shakespeare's most influential and most discussed plays, *King Lear* has been the focus of critics, editors, directors, actors, and reading and theatrical audiences since the seventeenth century. As a result, there is a vast body of scholarly and mass-market books and articles available on virtually every possible aspect of the play. Also, as noted at various points above, the play exists in one unauthorised (Quarto 2) and two authorised (Quarto 1 and Folio) early texts which vary considerably from each other. Thus editors have continually struggled to decide whether to set their editions entirely from one text or from portions of two or more texts, with the result that no two editors since 1709 have produced exactly the same text of *King Lear*.

Below is an annotated list of some recommended recent editions of the play currently available in print or electronic form. All date from after the 'textual revolution' of the 1980s and 1990s, which centred on the possibility of revision in *King Lear* and fundamentally changed the editing of the play (see Michael Warren above, **pp. 64–5**). It is certainly worth looking at older editions (most notably Edmond Malone's in his 1790 collected edition of Shakespeare or those in the first Arden and Cambridge series in the early twentieth century), but students may not find these editions readily available outside a library. The recommended editions are followed by an annotated list of selected recent books on the various aspects of the play on which this Sourcebook has focused, including critical reception, performance history and textual studies. Finally, there appears a longer, unannotated list of selected further references that can help students pursue the literary and historical issues raised in the Sourcebook's extracts and recommended editions and books.

Recommended Editions of *King Lear*

The Oxford Shakespeare: The Complete Works. Gen. eds Stanley Wells and Gary Taylor. Oxford: Clarendon Press, 1999, pp. 909–74. Presents separate, edited texts of the Quarto 1 text, entitled *The History of King Lear*, and the Folio text, entitled *The Tragedy of King Lear*.

The Norton Shakespeare. Eds Stephen Greenblatt, Walter Cohen, Jean E. Howard, and Katharine Eisaman Maus. New York, NY: W. W. Norton & Company, 1997, pp. 2307–553. Reprints the edited texts of Quarto 1 and the Folio from *The Oxford Shakespeare* as parallel, facing-page texts and also includes a 'Conflated Text' of the play.

The First Quarto of King Lear. Ed. Jay Halio. Cambridge: Cambridge University Press, 1994. An edition based on Quarto 1. Very useful in itself and in comparison with Halio's Folio-based edition (see below).

King Lear. Ed. Jay Halio. Cambridge: Cambridge University Press, 1992. An edition based on the Folio. Very useful introduction and textual analyses of the Quarto 1, Quarto 2 and Folio texts; very thorough discussion of performance history. Inexpensive and good value.

King Lear. Ed. R. A. Foakes. Walton-on-Thames: Thomas Nelson & Sons Ltd, 1997. A conflated edition using the Folio as copy-text and presenting Quarto variants marked by superscript letters, with a very full and very useful introduction as well as appendices on textual matters. Inexpensive and good value.

William Shakespeare. *The Complete King Lear 1608–1623*. Prepared by Michael Warren. Berkeley, Calif.: University of California Press, 1989. Extremely useful set of booklets presenting parallel, facing-page texts of the Quarto 1 and Folio texts, and photographic, unedited facsimiles of Quarto 1, Quarto 2 and Folio texts. Difficult to find in print, but usually available in university libraries.

Recommended Book-length Studies of *King Lear*

General studies of the play

Adelman, Janet. *Suffocating Mothers: Fantasies of Maternal Origin in Shakespeare's Plays, 'Hamlet' to 'The Tempest'*. London: Routledge, 1992. Includes a very useful discussion of gender issues in *King Lear* from a psychoanalytic perspective.

Carson, Christie and Jacky Bratton (eds). *The Cambridge 'King Lear' CD-Rom: Text and Performance Archive*. Cambridge: Cambridge University Press, 2000. Extremely useful presentation of the various texts, including Jay Halio's editions of the Quarto 1 and Folio texts and his conflated edition of the play, as well as the full text of Tate's adaptation. Also includes superb discussions of textual and performance issues and history, including an unsurpassed archive of illustrations from eighteenth- to ninteenth-century productions and photographs from twentieth-century productions.

Bullough, Geoffrey (ed.). *The Narrative and Dramatic Sources of Shakespeare's Plays*, Volume 7. London: Routledge & Kegan Paul, 1973. Essential guide presenting full-length reprints of all of Shakespeare's direct and indirect sources for *King Lear*, including the *King Leir* source play.

Elton, William. *King Lear and the Gods*, 2nd edn. Lexington, Ky.: University

Press of Kentucky, 1988. First published in 1966 and still influential, it offers a discussion of the play's main issues.

Knight, G. Wilson. *The Wheel of Fire*, 5th edn. Cleveland, Ohio: World Publishing, 1962. Still influential and powerful discussion of the nature of Shakespearean tragedy, first published in 1930.

Mack, Maynard. *'King Lear' in Our Time*. Berkeley, Calif.: University of California Press, 1965. Brief but very interesting set of essays on symbolism and performance issues in the play.

Ogden, James and Arthur H. Scouten (eds). *Lear from Study to Stage: Essays in Criticism*. London: Associated University Presses, 1997. Useful essays on a variety of thematic, textual and performance issues.

Vickers, Brian (ed.). *Shakespeare: The Critical Heritage*, 6 vols. London: Routledge & Kegan Paul, 1974–82. Essential and thorough guide to early critical reception of Shakespeare's plays with extremely useful extracts.

On the play in performance

Bratton, J. S. *Plays in Performance: King Lear, William Shakespeare*. Bristol: Bristol Classical Press, 1987. Not as complete as her discussion of the same topic in *The Cambridge 'King Lear' CD-Rom: Text and Performance Archive* but still very useful.

Cox, Brian. *The Lear Diaries: The Story of the Royal National Theatre's Productions of Shakespeare's 'Richard III' and 'King Lear'*. London: Methuen, 1992. Very engaging diary of Cox's experiences rehearsing and performing the role of Lear in a production that toured the world.

Leggatt, Alexander. *Shakespeare in Performance: 'King Lear'*. Manchester: Manchester University Press, 1991. Impressive discussion of various productions of the play.

Marowitz, Charles. 'Lear Log', *The Drama Review*, 8 (1963), pp. 103–21. Diary chronicling Peter Brook's rehearsal process for the 1962 stage production.

Rosenberg, Marvin. *The Masks of 'King Lear'*. London: Associated University Presses, 1972. Scene-by-scene, extremely detailed discussions of numerous international stage productions and films of the play.

On textual matters, including authorial revision and printing history

Blayney, Peter W. M. *The Texts of 'King Lear' and Their Origins*. Cambridge: Cambridge University Press, 1982. Extremely thorough and detailed study of the printing of the Quarto 1 text.

Greg, W. W. *The Shakespeare First Folio: Its Bibliographical and Textual History*. Oxford: Clarendon Press, 1955. Still standard and influential study of the printing history of the Quarto and First Folio texts of all of Shakespeare's plays.

Honigmann, E. A. J. *The Stability of Shakespeare's Text*. London: Edward

Arnold, Ltd, 1965. First modern book to reintroduce the theory of authorial revision in Shakespeare's plays; very persuasive and still influential.

Ioppolo, Grace. *Revising Shakespeare*. Cambridge, Mass.: Harvard University Press, 1991. Presents an overview of the practice of authorial revision with case studies of several plays by Shakespeare, including *King Lear*, as well as selected plays by his contemporaries.

Taylor, Gary and Michael Warren (eds). *The Division of the Kingdoms: Shakespeare's Two Versions of 'King Lear'*. Oxford: Clarendon Press, 1983. A collection of very influential essays with case studies of authorial revision between Quarto 1 and Folio texts of the play.

Urkowitz, Steven. *Shakespeare's Revision of 'King Lear'*. Princeton, NJ: Princeton University Press, 1980. Influential and very useful overview of the case for authorial revision in *King Lear*.

Further References

Adelman, Janet. *Twentieth-Century Interpretations of 'King Lear'*. London: Prentice-Hall, 1978.

Ashton, Robert. *James I by His Contemporaries: An account of his career and character as seen by some of his contemporaries*. London: Hutchinson, 1969.

Barroll, Leeds. *Politics, Plague and Shakespeare's Theater: The Stuart Years*. Ithaca, NY: Cornell University Press, 1991.

Booth, Stephen. *'King Lear', 'Macbeth': Indefinition and Tragedy*. New Haven, Conn.: Yale University Press, 1983.

Cressy, David. *Birth, Marriage and Death, Ritual, Religion and the Life Cycle in Tudor and Stuart England*. Oxford: Oxford University Press, 1997.

Dollimore, Jonathan. *Radical Tragedy*, 2nd edn. Brighton: Harvester Press, 1989.

Doran, Madeline. *The Text of 'King Lear'*. Stanford, Calif.: Stanford University Press, 1931.

Fraser, Antonia. *The Weaker Vessel: Woman's lot in seventeenth century England*. London: Weidenfeld & Nicolson, 1984.

Goldberg, Jonathan. *James I and the Politics of Literature*. Stanford, Calif.: Stanford University Press, 1989.

Gurr, Andrew. *The Shakespearean Stage, 1574–1642*, 3rd edn. Cambridge: Cambridge University Press, 1992.

Halio, Jay. *Critical Essays on 'King Lear'*. New York, NY: G. K. Hall, 1996.

Howard, Tony. 'When Peter Met Orson: The 1953 CBS *King Lear*', in *Shakespeare, the Movie: Popularising the plays on film, TV, and video*, ed. Lynda E. Boose and Richard Burt. London and New York: Routledge, 1997, pp. 121–34.

Kermode, Frank. *King Lear: A Casebook*. London: Macmillan; rev. edn 1992.

Kinney, Arthur. 'Speculating Shakespeare, 1605–1606'. In *Elizabethan Theater: Essays in Honor of S. Schoenbaum*, ed. R. B. Parker, S. P. Zitner. Newark, Del.: University of Delaware Press, 1996, pp. 252–70.

Leggatt, Alexander. *Harvester New Critical Introductions to Shakespeare: 'King Lear'*. New York, NY: Harvester Wheatsheaf, 1988.

Loomba, Ania. *Gender, Race, Renaissance Drama*. Manchester: Manchester University Press, 1989.

Maguire, Nancy Klein. 'Nahum Tate's *King Lear*: "the King's Blest Restoration"'. In *The Appropriation of Shakespeare: Post Renaissance Reconstructions of the Works and the Myth*, ed. Jean Marsden. New York, NY: Harvester Wheatsheaf, 1991, pp. 29–43.

Patterson, Anabel. *Censorship and Interpretation*. Madison, Wisc.: University of Wisconsin Press, 1984.

Richman, David. 'The *King Lear* Quarto in rehearsal and performance'. *Shakespeare Quarterly*, 37 (1986), 374–82.

Sharpe, Kevin. *Politics and Ideas in Early Stuart England*. London: Pinter, 1989.

Stone, Lawrence. *The Family, Sex and Marriage in England 1500–1800*. London: Weidenfeld & Nicolson, 1977.

Snyder, Susan. *The Comic Matrix of Shakespeare's Tragedies*. Princeton, NJ: Princeton University Press, 1979.

Spurgeon, Caroline. *Shakespeare's Imagery and What It Tells Us*. Cambridge: Cambridge University Press, 1935.

Stríbrný, Zdenek, *Shakespeare in Eastern Europe*. Oxford: Oxford University Press, 2000.

Taylor, Gary. 'The War in *King Lear*'. *Shakespeare Survey*, 33 (1980), 27–34.

Warren, Michael J. 'Quarto and Folio King Lear and the Interpretation of Albany and Edgar.' In *Shakespeare, Pattern of Excelling Nature*, ed. David Bevington and Jay L. Halio. Newark, Del.: University of Delaware Press, 1978, pp. 95–107.

Wortham, Christopher. 'James I and the Matter of Britain'. *English: The Journal of the English Association*, 45 (1996), 97–122.

Index